THE EROTIC W

The
Erotic
Word

SEXUALITY, SPIRITUALITY, AND THE BIBLE

David M. Carr

OXFORD

UNIVERSITY PRESS

OXFORD
UNIVERSITY PRESS

Oxford University Press, Inc., publishes works that further
Oxford University's objective of excellence
in research, scholarship, and education.

Oxford   New York
Auckland   Cape Town   Dar es Salaam   Hong Kong   Karachi
Kuala Lumpur   Madrid   Melbourne   Mexico City   Nairobi
New Delhi   Shanghai   Taipei   Toronto

With offices in
Argentina   Austria   Brazil   Chile   Czech Republic   France   Greece
Guatemala   Hungary   Italy   Japan   Poland   Portugal   Singapore
South Korea   Switzerland   Thailand   Turkey   Ukraine   Vietnam

Copyright © 2003 by Oxford University Press, Inc.

First published in 2003 by Oxford University Press, Inc.
198 Madison Avenue, New York, New York 10016

First issued as an Oxford University Press paperback, 2005

www.oup.com

Oxford is a registered trademark of Oxford University Press

All rights reserved. No part of this publication may be reproduced,
stored in a retrieval system, or transmitted, in any form or by any means,
electronic, mechanical, photocopying, recording, or otherwise,
without the prior permission of Oxford University Press.

Library of Congress Cataloging-in-Publication Data
Carr, David McLain, 1961–
The erotic Word : sexuality, spirituality, and the Bible / David Carr.
    p. cm.
Includes bibliographical references and index.
ISBN-13 978-0-19-515652-2; 978-0-19-518162-3 (pbk.)

1. Sex in the Bible.   2. Gardens in the Bible.   3. Sex—Religious aspects—Christianity
Gardens—Religious aspects—Christianity.   I. Title.
BS680.S5 C37 2002
220.8'3067—dc21   2002074851

9 8 7 6 5

Printed in the United States of America
on acid-free paper

To Colleen, my love

Acknowledgments

I wrote this book with the goal of making my Biblical scholarship available to a broad circle of people. I hope that my scholarly colleagues will find something of interest here too. Note: In the process of revision I followed editorial suggestions to spell out the name of the God of Israel (Yahweh) rather than give only consonants (as is my usual practice in publications). The concern was that a spelling of the divine name with just consonants (YHWH) would have confused many readers. My apologies go to those Jewish readers for whom this presents a significant problem.

As I have tried to make this book ever clearer, I received expert guidance from my editor at Oxford, Cynthia Read. I also owe many thanks to more colleagues than I can number, who added to my research through their written works, conference presentations, and conversations. In particular, I want to thank the following for reading drafts of part or all of the book: Clinton McCann, Marcus Borg, Othmar Keel, Michael Fox, Mark Smith, emilie townes, Martti Nissenen, Steven McKenzie, Linda Day, Debra Haffner, and Judith Plaskow. A number of friends and family read portions of the book and provided helpful ideas on how to make it more accessible. I am deeply grateful that they took time from their extremely busy lives to enrich my work with their input. They include Stuart Lishan, Kim Raderstorf, Kyoko Mori, Mark Carr, and Michael Kanieki. The quotes from students in this book reflect only a small sliver of what I have learned over the course of several seminars on the Song of Songs, first at Methodist Theological School in Ohio and later at Union Theological Seminary in New York. Of course, none of these people bear responsibility for errors or gaps that remain. All helped me make this book much better than it would have been without their aid.

I have also been helped by several institutions over the course of my work. The Wabash Center on Teaching and Learning Theology and Religion provided help at the outset through funding a teaching project focused on the Song of Songs and giving me a follow-up research grant. I also wish to thank the library staff at the two institutions where I have worked over the course of my research for this book. Kevin Smith and Emily Badertscher at Methodist Theological School and Betty Bolden, Seth Kasten, and Michael Boddy at Union Theological Seminary were particularly involved in helping me. Two faculty secretaries, Datha Myers at Methodist Theological School and Millie Erhlich at Union Theological Seminary, did much to make this project easier. Finally, both institutions provided substantial support over the course of my work, including Union's grant of a sabbatical over the last year while I completed the book.

Some of the ideas in this book appeared in another form in the following publications: "The Song of Songs as a Microcosm of the Canonization and Decanonization Process," in *Canonization and Decanonization,* ed. A. van der Kooij and Karel van der Toorn (Leiden: Brill, 1998), 173–89; "The Song of Songs and Falling in Love with God," *Bible Today* 36 (1998): 153–58; "Rethinking Sex and Spirituality: The Song of Songs and Its Readings," *Soundings: An Interdisciplinary Journal* 81 (1999): 418–35; "Gender and the Shaping of Desire in the Song of Songs and Its Interpretations," *Journal of Biblical Literature* 119 (2000): 233–48; "Ancient Sexuality and Divine Eros: Rereading the Bible through the Lens of the Song of Songs," *Union Seminary Quarterly Review* 54 (2001): 1–18; and "Passion for God: A Center in Biblical Theology," *Horizons in Biblical Theology* 23 (2001): 1–24.

Special thanks go to my wife, Colleen Conway, a New Testament professor at Seton Hall University. Not only did our love provide much inspiration for this book, but she read multiple drafts of every section and joined in countless conversations about the Bible, gender, sex, and love. She has taught me the connection between eros and intellect.

Contents

THE EROTIC WORD

1

Introduction

THE BIBLE AND EROS

The Bible. Sexuality. What word next comes to mind? Few people I know would say "spirituality." Yet, in this book I will be arguing that the Bible, particularly the Old Testament, can help us bring our sexual and spiritual lives together. Biblical garden texts will be our orientation points. Starting with the paradise garden in Eden and continuing to the New Testament, we will examine often overlooked sensual aspects of the Biblical tradition. Many Biblical texts testify to how love can go wrong. Yet I will be arguing that we can read the broader Bible as a call to a life of erotic passion: passion for others, passion for God, passion for the earth.

This book focuses throughout on the connection between sexuality and spirituality. So often the Bible has been used to separate the two. The garden of Eden story has been seen as an account of sexual sin. Laws in Leviticus are used to stigmatize gay and lesbian people. Many have used the New Testament to condemn "the flesh" in general. When the Bible is used in these and other ways to shut down sexuality (or certain sexualities), spirituality is shut down as well. Meanwhile, there are other forms of passion that are spiritually important too: love for beauty, for friends, for good work, and so on. Advertising, media, peers, family, and work make multiple claims on our hearts. The Bible can help us attend to the spiritual dimensions of such multiple claims and passions. Read as a whole, it can bring many aspects of our erotic life together. That is what this book aims to do.

The Origins of This Book in a Puzzle *Intense enthusiasm* about the Song of Songs

I did not set out to write this book on the Bible as a whole. Instead, I started with a puzzle having to do with the Song of Songs (also called the

Song of Solomon or Canticles), a tiny group of love poems tucked away in the Old Testament. In these poems, a man and a woman sing their love for one another. Occasionally a chorus adds its voice to the poetic drama. These poems take up only about ten and a half pages of the standard Hebrew Bible, ministers rarely preach on them, and the standard Biblical introductions rarely devote more than a page or two to their discussion.

This tiny, ignored book was once among the most often copied, commented on, and preached on portions of the Bible. Rabbi Akiba, one of the founding figures in rabbinic Judaism, is reported to have said: "The whole of time is not worth the day on which the Song of Songs was given to Israel. All the writings are holy; the Song of Songs is the holy of holies." Within the Christian tradition, the Song of Songs (hereafter often just "the Song" in this book) was one of the most often read and commented on parts of the entire Christian Biblical canon. There are more Latin manuscripts of the Song than any other Biblical book, and there are more medieval sermons on the Song than all other Biblical books except the Psalms and John. For these ancient men and women, the Song of Songs was their fifth gospel. It was read more often in some contexts than the Gospels of Matthew, Mark, and Luke.

What is interesting to me as a Biblical scholar is that people cherished the Song of Songs only as long as they could read it as a song of love between God and God's people. Some saw the poems as about God and the individual believer. Others saw them as about Christ and the church. Most Jews read the Song as about Yahweh (the God of Israel) and the people of Israel.

Then, in the 1800s, an increasing number of Biblical scholars began arguing that the Song was not about the love between God and God's people. Instead, it was meant to evoke the love between a woman and a man. This reading did not take hold at first. As it did, however, Christians and Jews started to turn away from the Song. It might be used for marriage counseling occasionally, but few used it to depict God's relationship with God's people. Biblical scholarship had, in effect, killed the influence of the Song of Songs on communities of faith. Though the Song was still in the Bible, it was "merely" sexual.

I became interested in trying to put these two readings together. Might it be possible, I wondered, to read the Song on multiple levels, *both* as a song of passion between humans *and* as something more? Typically, the ancients read the Song as a song of love between God and humans, *not* about actual sexual passion. They rejected and even persecuted those who said otherwise. Recently, Biblical scholars had done the reverse: argued that the Song was sexual and not spiritual. But might there be some truth in both approaches? I was naturally allied with those who read the Song as a book about human love. Still, I felt something was lost when communities stopped reading this book as something more. Furthermore, what did this have to say about Biblical scholarship as a whole? In at least this instance, the historical method at the heart of much of what I do appeared to have killed the use of a Biblical book by communities of faith. Was this an exception? Or might this just be an extreme instance of a broader pattern?[1]

The Church and the Separation
of Sexuality from Spirituality

One key issue at the heart of all this is the assumption that sexuality and spirituality are opposites. So far I have been talking about opposing interpretations of the Song: the Song was perceived as either sexual *or* spiritual. Yet these opposing readings reflect a much deeper separation of sexuality and spirituality, mind and body, which runs through the heart of Western culture, particularly Western Christian culture.

From the outset, Christianity has depicted sex as a dangerous, chaotic, antispiritual force. In this, the early Christians were influenced by antisexual elements of the Greek tradition. Already in the sixth century, the Greek Pythagorean philosophic movement had praised keeping the body pure from sex. Perhaps influenced by that, some of Plato's most important works (for example, the *Republic*) argue that the only way a soul can gain freedom from the chaos of temporary pleasures like sex is to redirect its desire to higher goods, like beauty and truth. The Stoic movement also encouraged the cultivation of *apatheia*, the freedom from being moved by any passion. There were other, more eros-affirming strains of Hellenistic culture, but the early Christians built on and extended the more antisexual elements.[2]

The belief of early Christians in the end of the world may have influenced them in this antisexual direction. If everything were ending soon, why be distracted by sex and family? The Gospels depict Jesus as single. His single life anticipated a coming kingdom of God where people "neither marry nor [are] given in marriage" but instead are "like angels in heaven" (Mark 12:25).[3] This Jesus rejects the traditional family in favor of those who "do God's will" (Mark 3:31–35),[4] and in one gospel he even praises those who "made themselves eunuchs for the sake of the kingdom of heaven" (Matt. 19:10–12).

Anticipating just such an end to the world, the apostle Paul likewise criticized the institution of family. When one of his communities, the Corinthians, wrote to inquire if "it is well for a man not to touch a woman" (1 Cor. 7:1), Paul urged unmarried believers not to marry unless marriage was the only way to keep from being "aflame with passion" (1 Cor. 7:8–

9). Though Paul cites Jesus in telling people to stay in already existing marriages (1 Cor. 7:10–11), his own discussions focus on how married life is only for those who cannot maintain self-control without sex (1 Cor. 7: 1–9). Later on, he argues that "those who marry will experience distress in the flesh" (1 Cor. 7:28) and that their "interests are divided" (7:32–34). Given how soon the world would end, Paul thought it best for singles to remain single, for married couples to remain married, and for even those who are married to avoid sex if they could do so without losing self-control (1 Cor. 7:25–40).[5]

Other types of sex had no place in Paul's world. Like many of his time, he was intensely hostile to all forms of nonmarital sexuality: adultery, sex between men, and sex between women.[6] For him, these were all works of the flesh, which opposed the spirit and freedom. His opposition to sex is well summed up in his words to the community in Galatia:

> Live by the Spirit, I say, and do not gratify the desires of the flesh.
> . . . For what the flesh desires is opposed to the Spirit, and what the
> Spirit desires is opposed to the flesh; for these are opposed to each
> other, to prevent you from doing what you want. . . . Now the
> works of the flesh are obvious: fornication, impurity, licentiousness.
> . . . Those who belong to Christ Jesus have crucified the flesh with
> its passions and desires. If we live by the Spirit, let us also be guided
> by the Spirit. (Gal. 5:16–25)[7]

Most of the rest of Christian history is dominated by this hostility toward sex, including marital sex. Often this hostility is articulated through interpretation of Biblical texts like the garden of Eden story in Genesis 2–3. The great Eastern theologian Gregory Nazianzen blamed Eve for "beguiling [Adam] by means of pleasure."[8] Augustine, who set the foundation for Western Christian theology, argued that unruly sexual desire was God's punishment for Adam and Eve's disobedience.[9] Theologians like these see sex as a sadly necessary evil to have children, but otherwise praise the celibate life as humanity's highest calling.[10] Eventually, large sections of the church developed a "culture of celibacy," where priests, leaders, and authoritative thinkers were required to abstain from sex and were marked as spiritually superior for doing so.[11]

Though there are certainly exceptions to this antisexual attitude, most of Christianity has been more hostile toward sex than is almost any other world religion.[12] Many non-Christian cultures allow for birth control, masturbation, or premarital sex. In contrast, the early church prescribed strict punishments for all of these and for other forms of nonreproductive sex.[13] Judaism celebrates marital love and sex between spouses. Some Jewish laws stipulate that a Jewish man must be willing to have sex with his wife on Sabbath eve, even if he refrains on other days of the week.[14] In contrast, early Christian writers forbade even marital sex across huge parts of the church year, including church seasons, holidays, and fast days.[15] Such rulings reinforced the impression that bodily pleasure and spirituality do not mix.

To be sure, in more recent times, large portions of the church have affirmed marriage and a slightly more positive place for sex in life. Starting about four hundred years ago, Protestant reformers like Martin Luther argued that sex is medicine for the soul, as important to life as eating and drinking.[16] Such churchmen endorsed marital sex even when it did not lead to having children. Yet this was not an emergent affirmation of sex per se. One of the main reasons Luther and others endorsed marital sex was because they saw it as an antidote to sex outside the family. Moreover, he, Calvin, Wesley, and other founders of Protestant denominations still argued strongly that the celibate single life was spiritually preferable to marriage.[17]

American culture has been deeply shaped by the family focus of Protestants like these. From the Puritans onward, Americans have long associated the church with the "family." During the Victorian period of the 1800s, this evolved into a celebration of the nuclear family and the marital love between a husband and his wife.[18] Increasingly, women—at least white, middle-class women—were depicted as naturally passionless, while men had to work to tame their lawless desires. African slaves, American Indians, and others were depicted as sexual savages. In this context, the churches, particularly groups of Christian women within them, fought to protect the nuclear family and purge society of sexual "deviance" through outlawing contraception, eliminating red-light districts, and ending the sexual double standard by requiring men to be faithful to their wives.[19]

Even now, at the beginning of the twenty-first century, major sections of the church are defined by their opposition to various forms of sexuality. Roman Catholics and evangelical Protestant Christians are at the forefront of fights against homosexuality, sex between teenagers, and other forms of nonmarital sex. Moreover, Biblical texts about homosexuality and other aspects of sexuality often figure prominently in such debates. In light of this, it is little wonder that many people do not associate spirituality with the Bible and sex.

Meanwhile, in recent years, sex has been separated from spirituality by a completely different way of viewing it: as a commodity to be exchanged between consenting adults. In the past, sex had been viewed mostly as an affair of power (males over women or younger boys), payment (prostitution), or love. But especially during the sexual revolution of the 1960s and 1970s, more people began to see sex as something that could be freely given between two adults who were not necessarily "in love" with one another.[20]

At a time when religious authorities had largely lost their hold on the enforcement of specific sexual mores, much sexual behavior was modeled on the trade of economic goods, which increasingly dominated the rest of society.[21] Industrial capitalism was ever more dominant. More women and men were laborers, having to sell their services on the wage market. As employers and employees increasingly saw people as commodities, it was easier to view sex as a commodity too.[22] And though this model has diminished some with the onset of AIDS and other diseases, it remains a powerful force for good or ill. Often, more openness has been good, particularly for those poorly served by traditional marriage structures. At other points, exchange of sex has become a new way for people's spirits to be separated from their bodies.

In sum, the battle lines shift, but many still find their sexuality disconnected from their spirituality. While some move toward sex as a good to be exchanged, much of the church continues to define itself by wars against various forms of sexuality. Previously, the church emphasized celibacy as humanity's true calling. Any bodily pleasure was implicitly antispiritual. Now, in many contexts, married sex is OK, but other forms of sexual desire or behavior are not. Generally, men are depicted as sexual animals, while women are seen as "naturally" passionless, except insofar as they desire their men. Few live up to the contradictory ideas about sex in circulation in contemporary culture: sex (or sexual attraction) as bad, romance as heavenly, family as good, women as pure, sex as a good to be exchanged, and so on. This is not an issue of having one ideal that does not correspond to our natural desires. It is an issue of having multiple cultural-religious ideals that are not reconciled with each other or our bodies. We are alienated from our erotic selves. As a result, our sexuality and spirituality are sharply separated. Both are harmed.

So much for general history. What about personal experience? Perhaps you have your own story to share about this: a gay friend who could never forgive the church for its role in encouraging young men like him to hate their sexual desires, a female friend for whom sex was so associated with religiously based shame that she was incapable of enjoying it, a lesbian couple who sought out non-Christian forms of spirituality more affirming of their love. Sometimes it is a question of a person feeling permanently judged by Christians and Christian traditions for a sexual misdeed that he or she would never want to repeat. Take, for example, a man who left an unhappy marriage to be with another woman and now feels torn between joy in his new marriage and a sense that he is continuing his sin by loving his new wife.

Redefining Eros

Out of exactly such conflicts, some have attempted to rethink Christian theology in an eros-affirming way. In particular, women, gay and lesbian people, and others whose sexuality is most judged by traditional Christianity are exploring what it might mean to speak of a broader eros that encompasses the myriad of ways people live out their deepest selves. One part of the past repression of sex has been restriction of it to a small part of life—closeted, heterosexual, exclusive. In contrast, some thinkers are urging a wider concept of eros that would embrace not only sexual passion, but work, play, deep friendship, art, and many other sorts of profound pleasure. Such an eros would include the passion of lovers' desire, and also the sensual joy of a shared meal or an abiding thirst for justice.

In a now classic essay, Audre Lorde, a member of a number of these marginalized groups, defines "the erotic" as

> those physical, emotional, and psychic expressions of what is deepest and strongest and richest within each of us, being shared: the passions of love, in its deepest meanings.[23]

This is a vision of eros as flavoring all of life. Many people experience such passion most in sexual longing and fulfillment. But others know similarly intense passion when playing music, windsurfing on a sunlit bay, or discussing a new and exciting idea with a friend. So often, the word *erotic* is taken as equivalent to "sexual." Yet the word *eros* originates in Greek culture, where it included all sorts of core desires: certainly the sexual, but also intellectual, artistic, and spiritual yearnings.

Lorde is not a theologian. Nevertheless, she provides tools to Jewish and Christian writers who want to counter the ancient Christian animosity toward sexuality and eros in general. Writing in the wake of the sexual revolution in the 1970s and early 1980s, Christian feminists like Carter Heyward and Rita Nakashima Brock rejected a reduction of sex to pornography and affirmed the power of eros—broadly defined—as a central aspect of the Christian life.[24] Judith Plaskow, a Jewish feminist, showed how the category of eros could be a resource for reenvisioning Jewish theology and practice.[25] And gay men such as Daniel Spencer and Michael Clark added their experiences to the discussion, with a particular emphasis on the implications of erotic theology for the care of creation.[26]

One exercise that I have found helpful in conveying the interplay of sexuality and spirituality comes from the psychotherapist and writer Terry Kellogg. At a workshop on intimacy, he asked, "What kinds of words would

transcendence   truth
Spotlight

you say for spirituality? Give me one-word concepts of spirituality. What would you say?" He and the audience arrived at a list including:

wholeness	love
reverence	oneness
relationship	communion
meaning	letting go
safety	spontaneity
faith	gratitude
transcendence	warmth
trust	connectedness
serenity	

Kellogg went on to say, "Think back to the words we just used. How many of those words would not apply to sexuality as well?" Much of the rest of his lecture then explored how spirituality and sexuality are interwoven, and how problems in one often translate into problems in the other.[27]

I work here on that premise—that sexuality and spirituality are intricately interwoven, that when one is impoverished, the other is warped, and that there is some kind of crucially important connection between the journey toward God and the journey toward coming to terms with our own sexual embodiment. Both sexuality and spirituality require space in one's life to grow. Neither flourish amidst constant busy-ness and exhaustion. Both require an openness to being deeply affected by someone outside oneself, whether one's lover or God. Both involve the whole self. Finally, at their most intense, both spirituality and sexuality involve an interplay between closeness and distance. Neither sexuality nor spirituality work if one is seeking a constant "high." Just as it is a mistake to expect everyone to feel a constant mystical connection to God, so also many people harm themselves and others through seeking consistently superlative sexual ecstasy.

Just such considerations led me to rethink the sexual-spiritual split in past readings of the Song of Songs and in Christianity in general. I do not mean to sexualize anyone's relationship with God. Nevertheless, I wonder about how narrowly people define sex and then separate it from their spirituality. Many assume that real sex is a genital thing that men do with women, mainly out of an ancient drive to reproduce. Yet Freud argued persuasively that the channeling of sexual drive into heterosexual behavior was something society did in order to encourage reproduction. He argued that humans are born polysexual beings, attaching sexlike erotic desire to almost anything. Boys and girls learn to focus this energy in societally approved ways through a complex process of attachments and disattachments to parents and others.

Our resulting belief in the "naturalness" of certain forms of sex is as arbitrary as any ancient sexual superstitions. To be sure, reproductive sex plays an essential role in the continuation of the human species. Yet whatever its origins, human eros has long been about far, far more than this. Humans are distinguished from most of the mammalian world by the fact that even bodily sex is not specifically connected to female fertility cycles.[28] Add to this the fact that human cultures have shown an almost infinite variety in the structuring of sexual activities. Although cultures almost always include some provision for reproduction (groups like the Shakers being an important exception), otherwise human groups show an amazing flexibility in the kinds of arrangements and behaviors that are endorsed or condemned.[29]

In light of this, the Western confinement of "real" sex to orgasmic or heterosexual sex appears increasingly restrictive. Why is it that we so sharply separate sex from the rest of our lives? Why are we surprised when our words for spirituality resemble our words for sexuality? Why is it that the theological readings of the Song of Songs are so rare now that we find it curious that the ancients would have read such erotic poetry as being about God?

Once we start asking such questions, we are prepared to reread Biblical texts like the Song of Songs without the opposition between sex and spirituality that has so often preoccupied those before us. The original author may have meant just to create some beautiful, erotic love poems. Later readers of the Song often aimed to use it to replace human erotic love with an erotic love of God. But we, in our sex-saturated and yet often spiritually empty culture, somehow need both. Rather than enshrining sexuality by itself or pursuing a sex-denying spirituality, perhaps Biblical texts can be used to do something more—to cultivate a human passion less divided by categories like sexuality and spirituality. Perhaps texts like the Song can help us cultivate eros or, more specifically, erotic love.

The Erotic Word and Biblical Gardens

This book is about far more than the Song of Songs. The more I have become clear about the way the Bible has been used to repress sexuality, the more I have moved toward a rereading of the Bible as a whole. I do this out of a conviction that real change requires an engagement with the cultural resources we already have. Only thus can our solutions connect with where we are and take us forward. To be sure, there are some who would prefer simply to disregard the Bible, but it is too deeply embedded in many of us and in our culture. We ignore it at our peril. Just when we think we are free of it, old interpretations of the Bible come back and misguide us again.

That is where my rereading of the Bible comes in. It is aimed at bridging the sexual-spiritual divide that continues to characterize much of Western culture. Where past interpretations of the Bible have repressed human long-ing, we will see how the Bible can be read to celebrate human eros, in-cluding sexual eros. For too long the Bible has been used to shut down eros and alienate human beings from our bodies. This book will show how the Bible might be used to cultivate a rich life of passion—for God, for the earth, for others. Of course, not all eros is good. The Bible reflects this too. Nevertheless, this book will show how the Bible also affirms a link between spirituality and a broad range of erotic dimensions of human life.

This eros-positive reading of the Bible must be selective, just as all read-ings of the Bible are. But this reading can be more faithful to the Bible itself because it does not pretend to present the one Biblical perspective on sexuality or law. Past readings have often been distorted by their authors' desires to make the Bible fit a particular program. Early Christians used the Bible to repress sexuality, ignoring ways the Bible did not fit such a program. Victorian reformers thought the Bible promoted an ideal of the family, and they downplayed the antifamily portions of the New Testament. Recent promotion of the family among conservative Christians is a variant of this approach. At no period have religious interpreters presented an objective picture of a single Biblical norm regarding sexuality. That is because there is no such single Biblical norm. Instead, any such group promoting one picture of sexuality as "Biblical truth" only reveals the failure of that group to be honest about its own selectivity and larger aims.

Before moving on, it is important to note that sex is not and will not be a positive category for many people, at least as long as "sex" is limited to erotic bodily contact. Many have been so wounded by sexual violation that sex is irredeemably distressing for them. Others cannot or do not want to be sexual because of physical limitations or because they are not with some-one with whom they want that kind of relationship. In a society where bodily sex is sometimes presented as the be-all and end-all of human ex-istence, it is important to recognize that sexual eros is not everything.[30] And it is important to recognize that there are forms of sex that are violent, painful, and harmful. This will come up again later.

Such "no's" to sexual eros should be articulated, but the main point of *this* book is to say a Biblical "yes" to erotic love. This erotic love encom-passes bodily contact, but is not confined to such desire. Instead, it is a category embracing all forms of core longing, including our sexually erotic love for others.[31]

In saying that this vision is "Biblical," I speak out of years of research that I and others have done on sexuality, eros, and gender in the Bible. The focus here is on how the Bible can help us interpret the world and navigate our way through it. From ancient times this has required selectivity in the choice of Biblical viewpoints and creativity in combining them. Rabbis combined and reformulated ancient Torah laws. Christians found pointers to Christ in the Old Testament. Devout African-American Christians refused to read the letters of Paul because slavemasters had used Paul to enforce obedience.[32] Anyone who has been influenced by the Bible has had to choose which parts to be influenced by and how. In the past, this selectivity often has been biased toward repressing sexuality and separating eros from other forms of love. This reading aims for a responsible alternative.

Journey through Biblical Gardens

The main part of the book is organized around three "garden" texts: the garden of Eden text in the Torah, Isaiah's vineyard garden in the Prophets, and the sensual and sexual garden of the Song of Songs in the Writings. These three gardens will be textual orientation points along our way to look at sexuality and spirituality in these major parts of the Hebrew Bible.[33] Moreover, this garden motif will be a thread that then guides us through several key texts in the New Testament.

In the world of the Bible, gardens (and vineyards) are places where lovers meet to make love. At the same time, gardens and vineyards often symbolize women and female sexuality. Because of women's childbearing and nursing roles, Biblical texts often use female imagery to evoke sexuality and reproduction. Thus, gardens (and vineyards) symbolize both the female lover and the place of lovemaking. The two shade into one another. Finally, gardens, unlike fields, require careful tending. Some ancient Near Eastern myths praise gods or humans who "plow a field," sowing their seed to have offspring. The focus is only on reproduction, and the sex is only perfunctory. But tending a garden is a much more sustained process, just like lovemaking. This may be one reason why ancient erotic literature uses the image of garden more often than that of field.[34] As we will see, the erotic associations of such gardens continue even into the New Testament. Some of the most eros-affirming parts of early Christian tradition are New Testament texts that allude to Old Testament gardens.

Overall, we will see how the Bible includes multiple pictures of the erotic in human life. Yes, there are narratives and laws that enshrine the often brutal, male-centered structures that governed public life in ancient Israel.

Yet the Bible also includes dreams of alternatives, like the garden of Eden story and the Song of Songs.

These Biblical texts were formed in a culture dominated by models alien to us, but they still evoke a picture of sexuality and spirituality that goes beyond their immediate situation. Borrowing a term from Sheila Briggs, we can recognize that Biblical texts include a "surplus of experience" that is not contained within the limits of the harsh reality in which they were written.[35] All ancient authors were inevitably shaped by their culture and preconceptions, as we are. Nevertheless, the best world literature contains visions of human life that transcend the authors' limitations. This book looks for that surplus of experience, that is, how Biblical texts present glimpses of love that are relevant today.

Is it really possible for the Bible to help us? Perhaps the Bible is inextricably connected to the forces of reaction, self-righteousness, and judgment. Are erotic love and Biblical spirituality irreconcilable? This book is written in the belief that another reading is possible, that the Bible can be used to cultivate a responsible, rich, and sensual love toward God, other humans, and creation. Let the reader decide.

text trans cards writers perspective

I

The Eden Garden and the Law

2
Before the Garden

MADE IN GOD'S BODILY IMAGE

> And God said, "Let us make humanity in our image
>   and in accordance with our likeness,
> so that they may rule over the fish of the sea,
>   the birds of the heavens, the farm animals,
>   and all the earth, and all the animals that creep on the earth."
>
> And God created humanity in his image,
>   in the image of God, God created it,
>   male and female God created them.
>
> —Genesis 1:26–27

The Bodily Image of God

We start with a prelude to the garden of Eden text: the description of the creation of humanity in Genesis 1. This text has often puzzled interpreters: "God created humanity in his image . . . male and female he created them." What might this mean? Most assume that it means almost anything other than a physical resemblance to God. They insist that the "image" of God in humans is rationality, a moral will, original righteousness, human dominion over the earth, a spiritual nature, the capacity for a special relationship with God, and so on. Many distinguish between the "image," which is human nature that cannot be lost, and the "likeness," which is the relation to God that can be lost. Virtually all agree that the Bible surely could not be asserting that God has a humanlike body.[1]

A closer look reveals that Genesis 1 does mean that: humans were made in the bodily image of God. There were numerous ancient precedents to this idea. Ancient kings in particular often asserted that they were the image of the head deity. But Genesis 1 is unique in applying this concept to humanity in general, all men and women. It depicts a kinglike deity creating the cosmos through royal decrees ("let there be light") and then making humans as godlike replicas to rule the earth. Thus, if we take Genesis 1 seriously, our bodies mark our status as divinely appointed rulers of the earth. Our sexualities reflect God's creative power. Our bodies are not spiritual obstacles. Instead, the Bible begins with an affirmation of male and female sexual bodies as signs of the divine.

Such an approach to Genesis 1 contrasts with early Christian critiques of the flesh and much subsequent theology. Let us look now at reasons why early interpreters did not pursue this reading of Genesis 1 and why such an interpretation makes sense.

Does God Have an Image?

Past interpreters were often too influenced by Greek philosophical ideas about God to take Genesis 1 literally. Major philosophers in the Greek tradition had argued that the true God (as opposed to the gods of mythology) had no body at all. Instead, he/she was an incorporeal principle or force. Building on this tradition, early Christian interpreters and their heirs assumed that Genesis 1 must be talking about something else—anything else—than actual physical resemblance between God and humans. As in the case of the Song of Songs, these interpreters went beyond the surface of Genesis 1 to read it as testimony to a spiritual or conceptual resemblance between God and humanity, not a bodily resemblance.

Yet ancient Israelites had no trouble imagining God having a humanlike body. To be sure, they believed you could die if you saw God, and they came to believe that it was forbidden to depict God in art. But many Biblical texts assume that God has a humanlike bodily form with hands, feet, eyes, and even "loins." The Sinai story in Exodus describes Moses and a small group of Israelites seeing "the God of Israel" enthroned at the top of the mountain; his "feet" were on a pavement of sapphire (Exod. 24:10). Isaiah 6 describes the prophet Isaiah seeing "the Lord seated on a high and lofty throne; and the edges of his robe filled the temple" (Isa. 6:1). Ezekiel 1 describes how the prophet Ezekiel saw a sapphire throne, with God as an "appearance of a human" sitting on it, with some kind of gleam above his loins and fire below (Ezek. 1:26–27). And these are just some of the textual images that stand alongside many ancient artistic depictions of a male God, which have been found in Israel in recent years.[2]

Fig. 2.1. Hadadyisi. Cover photograph of *Biblical Archaeologist* 45, no. 3 (1982). Reproduced by permission of the American Schools of Oriental Research.

Yes, the ancient Israelites used all kinds of metaphors for the devine, describing their God as a rock, eagle, and so on. But both archaeological and Biblical evidence suggest that Israel was exactly in accord with its neighbors in imagining its God primarily in human form.

The 3,000-year-old statue in figure 2.1 brings together a divine image with language like that found in Genesis 1. It is a representation of Hadad-yisi, king of Sikan, an ancient city in the upper reaches of Mesopotamia (ancient Iraq). Hadadyisi probably had this statue constructed to stand in the sanctuary before his god, Hadad, when Hadadyisi could not be around. The version relevant for us (in Aramaic, a language close to Hebrew) identifies the statue as "the *likeness* of [the governor/king] Hadadyisi which he set up before [the god] Hadad of [the city] Sikan." Later he had the statue improved, and he added to the inscription: "The *image* of Hadadyisi . . . this *likeness* he made better than before. . . . Before [the God] Hadad who dwells in Sikan, lord of the Khabur, he [King Hadadyisi] set up his *image*." Throughout, King Hadadyisi uses Aramaic words for *image* and *likeness* that occur in Hebrew form in Genesis 1.

This statue is an important clue for understanding what *image* and *likeness* mean in Genesis 1.[3] When Hadadyisi speaks of the *likeness* he set up, he is speaking of his statue. He means the same when he uses the term *image*. So also, the wording of Genesis 1 seems to make the point clear, almost as if to guard against misunderstanding. Four times, it uses these terms for material image to claim a bodily resemblance between humans and God:

> Let us make humanity in our *image*
>   and in accordance with our *likeness*. . . .

> And God created humanity in his *image*,
>   in the *image* of God, God created it,
>   Male and female God created them. (emphases added)

However strange it may seem to us, this text presupposes that God has a body and that humans were made to resemble it.[4]

The main point of the text, however, is not that God has a body. That was assumed. Instead, the main idea here, the new element, is that embodied human beings, men and women, are made in the divine image. Moreover, God appears especially happy with this work. The text ends by saying, "And God saw all that God had made, and it was indeed *very* good" (Gen. 1:28; emphasis added).

The Purpose of the Divine Image in Humans

This idea of creation in the divine image(s) is a powerful inversion of human imagery for God. If you ask most people what they picture when they think of God, they will usually come up with (at least initially) some kind of humanlike image: a white-haired old man, a goddess figure, a picture of Jesus, and so on. Many modern thinkers see this as an imperfect human way of imagining the unimaginable. Genesis 1, however, turns that around. It suggests that God had the human bodily form *first*. Humans did not project it onto God. God made humans—men and women—in the image and likeness that God already had.

One may ask, "What is so important about God's creation of humanity in God's image?" The text is clear. Often overlooked aspects of the Hebrew indicate that the image and likeness are for a particular purpose:

> And God said, "Let us make humanity in our image
>   and in accordance with our likeness,
> so *that* they may rule over the fish of the sea,
>   the birds of the heavens, the farm animals,
>   and all the earth, and all the animals that creep on the earth."
>   (Gen. 1:26; emphasis added)[5]

Humans, in other words, were made in godlike form so they could rule over creation. Genesis 1 suggests that God made humans as miniature godlike replicas to roam over the earth. Other creatures—fish, birds, farm animals—could look at us and recognize in our godlike form the mark of our divine authority.

Israelites would have encountered this idea of a ruler made in the image of God from neighboring cultures. In ancient Egypt and Mesopotamia, kings would praise themselves as made in the image of the head god of the pantheon. Subjects of such kings were to see their god reflected in their king and bow down. For example, one Mesopotamian citizen wrote in a letter to the king:

> The father of the king, my lord,
> was the (very) image of [the god] Bel,
> and the king my lord,
> is likewise the (very) image of Bel.[6]

Such language was even more common in Israel's neighbor Egypt, especially during the time of the New Kingdom, when Egypt dominated the land of Israel. One royal inscription from that time describes the head god, Amun, telling the king of creating him in his image:

> I [the god Amun] created this land in its length and breadth, in order
> to execute what my divine Ka wishes, . . . You rule the land as king,
> just as I was once king of upper and lower Egypt. You tend the land
> with a loving heart, You are my beloved son, who came forth out of
> my love, my *image* that I set on earth. I let you rule the land in

peace, where you destroy the rulers of all the foreign lands. (emphasis added)[7]

Like Genesis 1, this text talks of creating a human in God's image in order to rule. But this and other Egyptian and Mesopotamian texts speak of only the king as being the image of God.

In contrast, Genesis 1:26–27 democratizes this idea, applying it to everybody. Where ancient Israel's neighbors saw the king and only the king as bearing the divine image,[8] ancient Israel saw all humans, both male and female, as made in God's image. Where ancient Israel's neighbors saw the image of God in the king as a stamp of authority over human subjects, ancient Israel saw God's image in humans as a stamp of their godlike authority over the rest of creation.

God's climactic creative act is to stamp humans with divine form so that they may exercise a royal authority over what God has created. Every bit of Genesis 1 up to the creation of humans has underlined God's own king-like ability to order creation. Repeatedly, God issues decrees ("let there be light"), which are instantly executed ("and there was light"; Gen. 1:3). By the time we get to humans, God has ordered the entire cosmos through just a few days of such decrees. Then God makes humans, male and female, in God's image to "rule" over creation. Indeed, the Hebrew verb used here to describe human rule over creation, *radah*, is used elsewhere in the Bible to describe the king's rule over his subjects.[9] When this kinglike God tells humans to "fill the earth and subdue it," the word for *subdue* (*kavash*) is the same one used elsewhere for rape (for example, Esther 7:8) and oppression (Jer. 34:16).

The Divine Image and Us

Already this idea of creation in God's bodily image is quite a contrast with the way the Bible is usually read. For hundreds of years, Biblical interpreters, particularly Christians, have used the Bible to deny the body and have seen the body as a sign of human limitation. Recall, for example, the quotes in the previous chapter of Paul's influential condemnation of the flesh and its desires (Gal. 5:16–19). Yet Genesis 1 suggests something different: that the human body, rather than being a sign of human limitation, is actually a mark of our connection to God. Contrary to ancient Western presuppositions, the human body is *not* a mark of slavery to the earth. Instead, Genesis 1 asserts that the human body, male or female, is a mark of an awesome, free authority over creation for which we humans were created. We are not slaves to our flesh. Our flesh is the mark of our royal dominion over earth and its creatures.

Still, I would not be talking about Genesis 1 here if its only focus were the human destiny to subdue/rape the earth. Though it may be true that humans have increasingly succeeded in "subduing" or even "raping" the earth, would we agree with Genesis 1 in seeing this as divinely intended? I think not. In the midst of deepening ecological crises, we need images of care for the earth, not images of subduing it.

But there is another side to this text that is often missed: its suggestion that human sexuality is also a reflection of divinity. After all, the text stresses the gendered character of humans made in God's image: "male and female he created them" (Gen. 1:27). This assertion that God made males and females in God's image strains against the logic of monotheism. How could it be that only one God could create both men and women in God's image? The text does not go so far as to describe multiple gods—male and female— creating both sexes of humans. It does not say, "male and female, *they* created them." Nevertheless, it is striking that this account starts with God talking to a group in proposing to make humanity in "our" image: "Let us make humanity in *our* image and in accordance with *our* likeness."

When the text uses such plural language, the author probably had in mind the idea of a divine council, where God is the head of a broader group of divine beings, with whom God consults.[10] This idea is an ancient one. It comes up elsewhere in the Bible, in the book of Job, for example, where God consults with God's advisors about virtuous Job.[11] But why bring up the idea of the divine council here? Could it be that this divine council in Israel, like the divine councils in neighboring cultures, could include both male and female divine beings? That way, one God could speak of creating humanity in "our" image and still end up creating both male and female humans.[12] It is hard to know for sure. What is clear is that this text goes far in describing the one God's creation of both male and female sexual beings in the divine image(s). At the point of the creation of male and female humans, and only at this point, Genesis 1 diverges from God in the singular to talk of God in the plural.

We may not share the text's assumption that God has a human form nor its ideas about a divine council, but we can still learn from its affirmation of the divine character of the human body. Even now, many people work with the assumption that they are divided between their souls/spirits and the bodies that contain them. For many, there is nothing further from the spirit than bodily urgings toward erotic connection to other people. But the Bible's first description of human beings asserts that we were created, male and female, in the bodily image of God. We bear God's form, not first in our brains, spirits, or souls, but in our entire male and female embodied selves.

Sex is included in this. This is already implicit in how Genesis goes out of its way to affirm that both men and women were made in God's image. But the focus on sexuality becomes explicit when the text goes on to describe God blessing those men and women by calling on them to "be fruitful and multiply" (Gen. 1:28). Here, male and female bodies are both godlike and sexual, and there is no contradiction between the two.

Indeed, if we were to broaden our idea of the erotic to include nonsexual forms of connection and creativity, then we could say that the sexual humans of Genesis 1 are made in the image of an erotic God. To be sure, the God of Genesis 1 is not sexually erotic like the gods of Egypt, Mesopotamia, or other cultures near Israel. For example, Genesis 1 does not describe life being created through the sky god's impregnation of the earth goddess with rain.[13] Still, there are faint echoes of those ideas in the Genesis 1 description of God having a female earth[14] "bring forth" plants (Gen. 1:11–12) and animals (Gen. 1:24): "and she/the earth brought forth green vegetation" (Gen. 1:12).[15] The prominence of the earth here is striking, particularly since the word for earth in Hebrew, *eretz*, is a feminine noun. Other creation myths often feature a prominent focus on a female earth goddess as the source of life. Even Genesis 1, so focused on the creation of all things by the one God, deviates to have the earth—not God directly—bring forth plants and animals. At these points, God does not create alone but through connections with another part of creation—the earth.

These parts of the text contrast with the broader emphasis of Genesis 1 on God's and humans' royal power. Much of Genesis 1 speaks of God's royal decrees creating the world, and it is tempting to interpret all of it as a cohesive description of the one God creating humanity for absolute rule over the earth.

Yet, the chapter is not so cohesive.[16] It contains other concepts of creation as well. Echoing ancient creation myths, the God of Genesis 1 works through the earth to bring forth plant and animal life. And the text diverges again from its focus on the one God to describe God's consultation with the divine council to create humans—male and female—in their image. Finally, this God calls on men and women to "be fruitful and multiply," thus sexually exhibiting God's power of life, much like they are also to exhibit God's authority over creation.

These strains of Genesis 1 suggest that human sexuality is a key way in which we embody God's creative power, a power that is still faintly erotic in Genesis 1.

Concluding Reflections

Ancient interpreters saw the significance of humans being created in the divine image but were incorrect in separating that image and likeness from the body and sexuality. Yes, humans are presented in Genesis 1 as God's representatives on earth. Yes, humans have a godlike dominion over the earth and its creatures. Yet these verses in Genesis 1 suggest that men's and women's bodies, including their sexuality, are the very mark of their godlike dominion over creation. Just as King Hadadyisi put his statue in front of the god Hadad in the sanctuary, just as the Egyptian god Amun created King Amenopolis in his image as his representative on earth, so also the God described in Genesis 1 creates all human beings in God's image as God's royal representatives on earth and as reflections of God's generative power to create life.

Let me be clear. The focus here is on the visionary elements of the text that transcend its time and place. We need not swallow Genesis 1 whole. Its authors wrote a story of the origins of the universe out of traditions given to them and their idea of how things "must have" happened. They did not know, nor have access to, modern methods for measuring the age of the universe or perceiving the unfolding of life. But they did have an idea of how their world worked, and they built their picture of creation on that. Weaving together ancient concepts, they told a story about origins built around their deepest convictions. We can listen for and engage those convictions, or we can get lost in pointless debates about the scientific value of prescientific stories. I choose the former.

So, despite the uncertainties involved, we must be selective. Certainly there are many prescientific elements, such as the idea that the cosmos was created in six days. Also, we need to balance the emphasis of the text on subduing creation with an emphasis on the care of creation. Even the focus of this chapter on reproductive sexuality has limits, limits already recognized in the garden of Eden story, to which we will soon turn. Finally, we can no longer assume, as the text's authors did, that God had a body. The Bible itself emphasizes this idea much less than many texts of its time. And even Genesis 1—in shifting to plural language at the crucial point ("let *us* make humanity in *our* image")—averts its eyes from God's body. The focus is not on God's body. That is assumed. Instead, the focus of this text is on the creation of male and female embodied humans as the climax of creation and the extension of God's power and blessing.

That being said, there is at least one crucial idea in this first chapter that undercuts sex-hostile Bible readings of the past: human male and female bodies, including our sexualities, are a reflection of divinity. Contrary to later church fathers, human bodies are not polluting flesh nor imperfect vessels of the spirit. At least in terms of God's original conception, we were not made "slaves" to our "flesh." Instead, this ancient Israelite text suggests that our flesh, our body in the divine image, is one of the primary things that is "very good" about us. *This is how the Bible begins.* Having set this tone, we turn now to a different account of human origins: the story of the garden of Eden.

3

The Eden Garden, Part 1

CREATED FOR EROTIC CONNECTION

> She indeed who was given to Adam as a help meet for him,
> because it was not good for man to be alone, instead of an
> assistant became an enemy, and instead of a yoke-fellow, an
> opponent, and beguiling the man by means of pleasure,
> estranged him through the tree of knowledge from the tree
> of life.
>
> —Gregory Nazianzen, Oration 18,
> "On the Death of His Father"

This chapter begins our look at the first garden text of the Bible: the garden
of Eden story in Genesis 2:4–3:24. Perhaps no other text in the Old Testament is so universally recognized, remembered, and pervasive in Western
culture as this story of the first human pair and their eating of forbidden
fruit. Yet the strong sexual overtones of the story are often misinterpreted
and used to repress women and sexuality. In the epigraph, Gregory Nazianzen accuses Eve of having beguiled Adam "by means of pleasure" and
"estranged him . . . from the tree of life." This is typical of many interpretations which pass right over the vision of erotic connection in Genesis 2
and give a woman-blaming interpretation of chapter 3. Here we will linger
on the vision of creation in Genesis 2 before moving on to the story of
crime and punishment in chapter 3. Both parts of this garden text have
their gifts to give us.

As we will see, Genesis 2 is distinct in many ways from Genesis 1. Where
Genesis 1 takes place on a cosmic level, the focus in Genesis 2 narrows to
a single locale. Where God in Genesis 1 is imperial and distant, God in

Genesis 2 is a craftsperson who has varied success in his efforts. Where Genesis 1 focuses on the destiny of humans to rule the earth, Genesis 2 focuses on the vocation of the first humans to till and protect the garden earth from which they were made. And where Genesis 1 emphasizes the reproductive aspect of sex ("be fruitful and multiply"), Genesis 2 emphasizes the intimate aspects of sexual eros, its role in overcoming the primal isolation of the first human. By the triumphant end of this chapter, the man sings a song of praise of his new wife who is his full peer, and the conclusion talks of how this story explains why men and women cleave to one another and "become one flesh."

These sorts of differences led scholars more than 250 years ago to recognize that Genesis 1–3 contains not one, but two creation stories. In the ancient Near East it was common for authors to write by adding to ancient traditions or collecting them.[1] In this case, a seven-day creation account in Genesis 1:1–2:3 has been beautifully joined to the garden of Eden story in Genesis 2:4–3:24. We do not know exactly when either text was written or when they were joined, but what is important at this point is this: whatever the differences between Genesis 1:1–2:3 and Genesis 2:4–3:24, the authors of Genesis apparently did not wish to give up either. So they put one after the other, and these creation stories now stand together as complementary visions of the deepest nature of reality.[2]

As a result, the story of creation, crime, and punishment in Genesis 2–3 balances and competes with the vision of creation in the divine image in Genesis 1. Though the Eden story in Genesis 2–3 serves as an extension of the story begun in Genesis 1, it also has its own integrity.

We will start with the vision of God's creation of human connectedness in Genesis 2:4b–24.[3] This will be a touchstone for reflections on sexuality and spirituality throughout this book. Its vision not only celebrates human connections, but looks more broadly at our connection to the earth and to our work. We will look at what this vision has to teach us about "work from the heart" and the relation of such work to eros and relationships. Then, in the next chapter, we will move to the next scene in the Eden story, the unraveling of human connectedness in Genesis 3.

Broadening Our Concept of Ourselves: Entering the Garden of Eden

When the Lord God created heaven and earth, no shrubs were on the earth, nor had grass grown on the field, because the Lord God had not brought rain and there was no human to work the earth . . . And the Lord God

God's

crafted the human out of the dust of the earth, and breathed the breath of life into his nostrils, and the human became a living being . . . And the Lord God made sprout from the earth every beautiful and tasty tree, and God placed him [the human] in the paradise garden to cultivate and guard it. — Excerpts from Genesis 2:4–15

World literature is full of primal myths describing the origins of the world, each of which make different claims about the nature of humanity and its place in the cosmos. The ancient Near East had its share of these myths, many of which describe creation at the site of the city temple of the people who told the creation story. The story in Genesis 2–3 builds on elements of such myths. Indeed, parts of it seem based on the Jerusalem temple in ancient Israel. For example, the story mentions that an obscure "Gihon" river went out from the garden (Gen. 2:13). This is probably an echo of the Gihon spring in Jerusalem (1 Kings 1:33–48). The myth ends with God expelling the humans from the garden and setting cherubim guards at its eastern end to guard it (Gen. 3:24). Such mythical creatures often guarded temple entrances, and this eastern entrance to the garden probably corresponds to the major eastern entrance to the temple sanctuary. These and other associations would have been obvious to ancient readers.[4] Ancient Israelites reading the garden of Eden story would have heard it telling them that the world was created in a setting much like the temple they knew well. But as in most such creation stories, the main point of the tale was *purpose* to tell them about who they were and how they fit into the broader cosmos.

Like many ancient creation myths, this familiar story is more a mythic description of the dynamics of present human life than an attempt to reconstruct early history. The language is general. Even the "Eden" that appears later in the story is merely a common word for paradise. The story's main characters are given typical names. The first person is called "the human," *haadam* in Hebrew. Soon it becomes evident that this first "human" is, in fact, male.[5] The woman is named "life" (Hebrew *havah* = *Eve = life* English Eve), and her and her husband's actions reflect how the ancient storyteller saw men and women relating to each other, the earth, and God.

That said, the first thing to stress about this story is the way it highlights the earthiness of the first human and (by implication) humanity as a whole. After describing how the earth lacked rain because there was no human to cultivate it, the crucial verse describes God's creation of humans out of that ground: "And the Lord God crafted the human out of dust from the earth, and breathed the breath of life into his nostrils, and the human became a living being" (Gen. 2:7). Using Hebrew wordplay, this text has God create a human "earth creature" out of the "earth." The Hebrew word for "hu-

earthling

man" here, *adam*, is not the proper name of a person, Adam. Rather, it is a statement about how "our [earthly] bodies" are "ourselves." The word *adam* means "human being." The word for earth here, *adamah*, means fertile, farmable ground, ground that gives forth life. Through connecting the two words in a story about creation, the text asserts that a crucial aspect of being human (*adam*) is being made of "fertile earth." An English-language equivalent would be to say that the word for "human" comes from being made out of the fertile "humus" of the earth. There is no negative connotation whatsoever to human embodiment here. Instead it reflects our original connectedness to the earth and our destiny to work it.

Yet this story also indicates that humans as living beings are more than our earthy forms. For in and of itself, dust feels nothing. Instead, this form is animated by a divine breath. It is this one breath that distinguishes a living, desiring, feeling, thinking being from a corpse. This one divine breath courses through each one of us in all of our intellectual, spiritual, emotional, and bodily senses and sensibilities. In other contexts, Hebrews refer to this life breath, this spark, as a *nephesh*, a word derived from the back of the throat through which breath goes. Although this word, *nephesh*, is often translated as "soul," it refers just as much to a person's bodily vitality and intellect, their life force. This *nephesh* is an almost electric energy that powers a person's thoughts and desires. According to this concept, I do not have an animated, pushy body on the one hand and a relatively emotion-free intellect or spirit on the other. Instead, my material body is an earthy form energized by one divine power, one that encompasses all of my desires, feelings, and thoughts.

Finally, this text implies that humans were not just made *from* the earth, but also *for* it. God's first act with the humans in this story is not to speak to them nor give things to them, but to put them in the garden, "to cultivate and protect it" (Gen. 2:15). Quite a contrast to human domination of the earth in Genesis 1.

In short, human bodies are an essential aspect of our relationship to earth and to God. We were made of fertile earth by God in order to work and cultivate it. God formed humans for this task through shaping them like a potter and breathing a divine breath into them, the *nephesh*. Now, with this divine energy coursing through us, the earth of which we were made feels, hungers, thinks, moves, and engages the world—we are living beings. Just as Genesis 1 affirms human bodily form and sexuality as reflections of God's image and blessing, Genesis 2 affirms that God crafted human bodies and enlivened them with a divine breath that is in us as long as we live. Our inner, electric energy, the part that moves us and feels passion, is God's enlivening breath.

Embodied Relationships

And the Lord God said, "It is not good for the human to be by himself, I will make for him a helper corresponding to him." And the Lord God crafted from the ground every wild animal and every bird of the sky and brought them to the human to see what he would call them, . . . but for the human, no helper corresponding to him could be found. So the Lord God made a deep sleep fall on him, and he slept, and the Lord God took one of his ribs and closed the flesh up after it. And the Lord God built the rib which God had taken from the human into a woman and brought her to the human. —Excerpts from Genesis 2:18–22

After God has created this earthy human and put him in a garden for him to tend, the whole next portion of the story focuses on a preeminent example of earthy longing—the desire for human connectedness. God notes a problem in creation so far—the human whom God has created must work the garden alone. So God sets out to create "a helper corresponding to him."

This is apparently more easily said than done, for God creates the entire animal kingdom in a failed attempt to create a helper corresponding to this earthy garden worker. The first human names each animal, but none are his equals. God only succeeds when God tries a new tack—taking a piece of that human's own body, his rib, and "building" a woman out of it. Once again, the story stresses the extent to which "our bodies are ourselves." The only way for God to create an equal of the first human was to begin with a bodily part of him.

The first human then sings the first song of the Bible in celebration of this act:

This is it:
  bone of my bone, flesh of my flesh
  This one will be called woman, for she was taken from man.
    (Gen. 2:23)

Again, the story plays on the sounds of the Hebrew language, this time to assert the connectedness of the "man" and "woman" to each other. The Hebrew words used here are *ish* (man) and *ishah* (woman). This connectedness is underlined by the end of the creation story: "Therefore, a man abandons his father and his mother and embraces his wife and they become one flesh. And the two of them were naked, the man and his wife, and they were not ashamed" (Gen. 2:24–25).

The story goes on in chapter 3 to talk about the breakdown of this original connectedness, and we will turn to that soon. For now, however, let us look at this vision of human possibility. Just as the first half of Genesis 2 stresses the earthy character of the first human, so this second half of the chapter celebrates the embodied character of the first human relationship. Lest we assume that this is merely a typical ancient focus on the primal couple—ready to produce the human family—note that nothing whatsoever is said yet about reproduction or fertility. There is no move, like there was in Genesis 1, toward a divine imperative to "be fruitful and multiply" (cf. Gen 1:28). Instead, the focus of this story—in contrast to many others found in ancient cultures—is on intimacy, an intimacy grounded in the bodily joining of two embodied creatures whom God has so carefully made for shared work as equals.

In this way, the story celebrates mutual love between peers. Just as Genesis 1 envisions the creation of both men and women in the image of God, so Genesis 2 stresses that the woman, and only the woman, was the garden "helper" who fully "corresponded to him [the first man]" (Gen. 2:18, 20, 22–23). This is because she is made of the same flesh and bone as he is. Soon we will read texts that assert the man's destiny to rule over the woman in the patriarchal family, but there is little trace of that here. Yes, the word *helper* does not measure up to modern standards of gender equality. Nevertheless, the hint of hierarchy present in the helper language is balanced by the intense emphasis in the story on how the woman fully corresponds to the man and thus contrasts with the animals. God tries and tries again to create a helper for the first human out of the ground, but none are his full equals. It is only when God builds the woman out of part of the first (hu)man that he can joyfully recognize the arrival of a partner in the garden work who fully corresponds to him: "This is it: bone of my bone, flesh of my flesh."

Elements like this in Genesis 2 provide an implicit critique of abusive sexual relationships built on the domination of one partner by the other. This vision of non-reproductive, joyful sexuality can be applied by extension to various forms of intimate, tender sexuality between partners who "correspond" to each other: male-female, male-male, female-female.

To be sure, as the conclusion makes clear, the author of this story envisions such intimacy as being found in the love between a man and a woman in heterosexual marriage: "a man abandons his father and his mother and embraces his wife and they become one flesh."[6] In an ancient agricultural world that was intensely focused on maximizing reproduction, it is hard to conceive how an ancient narrator's imagination would have worked any other way. Men and women were paired shortly before or after maturing sexually, and then enjoyed together but a fairly brief period—often only about ten to fifteen years—before one partner died, often the woman in childbirth.

Given that background, it is surprising that more of this ancient story does not explicitly emphasize the issue of having children. Many other ancient creation myths certainly do. But this story emphasizes a sexuality that is not focused initially on having children. The stress is not on the idea that this first man and woman are the parents of humanity, though that is presupposed (see especially Gen. 3:20). Instead, Genesis 2 emphasizes that these first two humans are intimately bound together by an erotic, bodily connection.

This original connection resembles the early humans of the cosmic myth that is spoken by Aristophanes in Plato's *Symposium*.[7] In that myth, male and female humans were created through the splitting of an originally round, whole, male-female human. As a result, men and women are forever drawn toward each other by their sense of incompleteness and the primal magnetic power of their original bodily connection to each other. So also, in the Biblical story of the garden of Eden, men and women were created out of the same body, and this is used to explain the way a man leaves his parents' house to "embrace" his wife so that they become "one flesh" (Gen. 2:24). Humans were created for erotic connection with one another, a connection without any focus on having children. In a contemporary world where sexuality is increasingly distinct from reproduction, this Biblical vision of sexual connection is a major cultural resource.

Eros Expanded: Eros and Work

This story, though created in a society focused on reproduction, is not limited by that focus. Instead, its picture of original sex unconnected with children anticipates the growing prevalence of nonreproductive sex in the contemporary world. This is another place where there is a surplus of experience in the Bible. Although the author and audience could not have envisioned the climax of the story any other way than heterosexual marriage, the Eden vision suggests a more powerful concept, namely, that humans can be drawn to each other in many ways that go beyond traditional male-female relations. Where the description of the creation of males and females in Genesis 1 (1:26–27) moves quickly to God's command that humans "be fruitful and multiply" (Gen. 1:28), Genesis 2 does not go there first. Instead, humans are created out of a combination of earth and a divine breath that drives our every passion. There is no division of erotic passion from other passions.

Sexual eroticism is certainly present. The climactic outcome of the text is the embodied relationship between these humans. The end of the section reads: "therefore a man . . . embraces his wife and they become one flesh" (Gen. 2:24). This example of embodied connection is the first and most important expression of the broader passion that drives humanity, a superlative example of human interconnectedness. Erotic intimacy is the final answer to God's initial concern that "it is not good that the human be by himself" (Gen. 2:18). There will also be shared work in the garden (and outside), a passion for tasty fruit, and other desires of these earthy humans, powered as they are by God's breath. But the first and foremost expression of joy in the Bible is that of the first man/human when he recognizes his erotic partner and how much she corresponds to him: "This is it: bone of my bone, flesh of my flesh."

Through having this initially nonreproductive, sexual relationship be the first, paradigmatic image of human connectedness, Genesis 2 expresses the insight that human relationships are always embodied. As Guindon in his book *The Sexual Language* points out:

> There is no such thing as an a-sexual relationship between living human beings. All concrete relations are those of sexed men and women who have, it is to be hoped, real, sensuous bodies which are existentially implied, one way or another, in all transactions. The ideal presence of human persons to each other in any exchange is never that of two marble statues or that of two angels.[8]

Thus, human embodiedness—including sexuality—is an important part of all interactions. Although we must recognize the particular power (for good and evil) of the most intense forms of erotic sensuality, much of life is structured by a language of touch and bodily presence.

This is not to suggest that we do or should sexualize all of our relationships, nor that all life should be seen through the lens of genital sexuality. Instead, this text's words about human earthiness, the divine breath in us, and human intimacy can encourage us to broaden our appreciation of the role of passion in human life as a whole. This text can help us recognize the myriad ways in which our relationships and longings in life are, to varying extents, already erotic. *Core desires*

Make no mistake: the concept of the erotic that we are discussing here is much broader than that which is dominant in much of the West. So often, much of Western culture has separated sex from personhood, making "sexuality" be an affair of the genitals, which must be carefully circumscribed and controlled. Whereas Genesis 2 depicts humans as enlivened by a single divine breath (*nephesh*), which includes sexual feelings, Christians in particular have tended to see sex as something completely different, almost radioactive. As Augustine and many others argue, "sex" is a nasty thing one has to do in order to have children. It is a lot like having to go to the bathroom, only it is more dangerous to your soul. Even later church affirmations of sexuality are focused exclusively on heterosexual sex within marriage, a sex that is carefully separated from the rest of life. The last thing such theologians wish to do is to allow sexuality out of the protective structure of such marriages. Thus loosed, it could pollute the world with its seaminess.

This is where a broader concept of eros can be useful. What if we are not divided between bodily urges and spiritual urges? What if this story is right about us being clay enlivened by a single, passionate spark of the divine? This spark does not just impel us toward others. Indeed, the first thing the creator God does with the human is not put him in relationship, but place him in the garden to "work and protect it" (Gen. 2:15). God creates the woman not only as an answer to loneliness, but as a helper in this garden work (Gen. 2:18). Thus, the first humans in the garden are two things intertwined, workers and lovers.

This part of the story can prompt us to consider how erotic love and work might be deeply interconnected. For although many find themselves lost in the grind of meaningless jobs, there can be a deeply erotic dimension to work that coincides with what is deepest in ourselves. As Lorde in her essay on eros points out,

> And yes, there is a hierarchy. There is a difference between painting a back fence and writing a poem, but only one of quantity. And there is, for me, no difference between writing a good poem and moving into sunlight against the body of a woman I love.[9]

Here is a vision of work from the heart. Even if some might not go as far as Lorde in affirming "no difference" between passionate work and erotic touch, her reflections are aimed at breaking down the high wall often set up between passionate intimacy and other forms of passion in life, including passionate work: art, struggling for justice, tending the earth.

The rest of the garden story in Genesis 3 will acknowledge the reality that much of our work is not like this. Nevertheless, Genesis 2 preserves the vision that work *can* come from our core. Many of us find ourselves caught at least sometimes in oppressive or addictive work. Yet there is another type of work that we may have tasted too, whether in our jobs or outside our jobs—creating art, volunteering, working a garden. Such work filled with eros is an expression of what Lorde describes as "what is deepest and strongest and richest within each of us, being shared." Genesis 2 asserts that this is part of what we were created for.

Indeed, the garden of Eden story sets the first human erotic relationship in the context of just such work. God begins the process of creating the second human by saying, "It is not good for the human to be by himself, I will make for him a helper corresponding to him" (Gen. 2:18). Reflecting on this story, Sölle and Cloyes in *To Work and to Love* argue that Genesis 2 promotes a vision of erotic relationship in the context of a shared project.[10] Though many would identify the shared project of erotic relationship as the birthing and raising of children, Genesis 2 actually has a wider vision. First and foremost, the man and woman in the Eden garden share in working the ground from which they were made. In addition, there is other erotic work from the heart that people can share, around which they can build a relationship: the raising of children, of course, but also a shared cause, a shared spiritual quest, and so on. It is in the context of such sharing of our deepest vocations that our relationships can become sacred and joyful, when we move from the sensation of sexuality disconnected from our personhood to the shared ecstasy of erotic connection between our bodies and our lives.

Genesis 1–2 and Eros

When we put the Eden creation in Genesis 2 with creation in God's image in Genesis 1, we can see how the Bible starts with a decisive "yes" to human passion of many sorts. Genesis 1 insists on the idea that humans—both males and females—are made in the bodily image of God, and it suggests that human sexual reproduction is likewise a reflection of God's power to give life. Genesis 2 describes how the human life force, including our sexual passion, is God's breath in us—enlivening our bodies and making us living beings. Unlike Genesis 1, sexuality in Genesis 2 is a mode of human connection, an expression of the way humans are made from the same flesh and drawn toward each other. By the end of Genesis 1 and 2, we have two humans who cleave to each other and "are one flesh" (Gen. 2:24). Made in God's bodily image, given life by God's passionate breath, fleshly creatures bound by deep connections to the earth and to each other—these humans are created for love.

As I mentioned before, such ancient creation stories are not scientific accounts of actual events, but theological statements about human identity. I have read them here as implying an initial decisive call to humans to love. This is an important "yes" with which the Bible starts. Whatever no's we need to say about erotic love should occur in the context of this overarching yes to human passion.

Both the Bible and its readers have often focused on the no's to different sorts of sexual passion. No in the Old Testament to any female sexuality outside of heterosexual marriage. No in the New Testament to sexuality in general, unless one has to have sex with a spouse to avoid burning with passion. No to most forms of sex in the early and medieval church, which saw sexual passion as a prime reflection of sin in the garden. And no to all forms of sex outside marriage in Protestant Christianity, especially in the Victorian period and later. Though most strains of Judaism have long endorsed passion in marriage as a created good,[11] only recently have major portions of Christianity begun to celebrate sexuality even within the family.

The culture of the Bible was so focused on reproduction that its writers hardly could have anticipated modern sexual shifts or said yes to them. Nevertheless, both the Genesis 1 and Genesis 2 creation accounts say a decisive yes to the major forms of sexuality those writers knew. As we saw, the Genesis 2 story even goes beyond many contemporary accounts in affirming sex as a way of joining one earthy human to another, rather than first as a means of reproduction. Both Biblical accounts describe sexuality as part of the divine within us: male and female bodies made in the image of God, sexuality as a reflection of God's life-giving power, passion as part of God's life-giving breath within us, and erotic intimacy as the crown of creation. Put together, these first two chapters of the Bible say a decisive yes to humans as lovers, enlivened by a single divine spark that drives our work and relationships.

Perhaps, this yes could be an initial basis for a sexual ethic, an ethic where the first sexual commandment would be to avoid wounding the God-given eros of another. Since humans are created for erotic connection with each other, it is imperative that human passion be embraced and nurtured, not denied; it should be cultivated and not abused. Not every erotic longing can be satisfied, especially when it involves damaging another person's capacity for sexual intimacy. Yet this sexual imperative also means recognition of the diverse ways in which people "become one flesh" (Gen. 2:24) and overcome the loneliness that God recognized at the outset of the Eden creation story.

Yet, insofar as Genesis 2 is about more than sexual intimacy, perhaps this yes can impel us to look more broadly at ourselves as passionate beings. For Genesis 2 does not envision humans just in joyful embrace of one another, but also as joined in common work. And society does not just shut down humans sexually, but it also forces people to engage in crushing work that alienates rather than enlivens them. Though this is not a sexual issue, it is an erotic issue in the broader sense. This is a way that we are alienated, day by day and hour by hour, from our core passions and dreams. We may be tempted to assume that this is just the way things are, that we just need to grin and bear it. Yet this ancient text at the outset of the Biblical tradition suggests otherwise; it suggests that the God of the cosmos originally formed us for another destiny—for shared work and love. This creator God started not with rules nor judgment but with a decisive yes to us as workers and lovers.

Let those who have been alienated from passion by the no's of the religious past, those who feel they have had to choose between a spiritual path and their erotic selves, those who have been told by churches that they are not welcome if they practice sexual intimacy with the wrong sex—let these and others hear this yes to eros at the outset of the Bible. Insofar as the Bible has been used to drive a wedge between our erotic and our spiritual passions, may these chapters help bring those parts of our selves together again.

4

The Eden Garden,
Part 2

THE TRAGIC LOSS OF CONNECTEDNESS

Do you not know that you are (each) an Eve? The sentence of
God on this sex of yours lives in this age: the guilt must of
necessity live too. You are the devil's gateway; you are the
unsealer of that (forbidden) tree; you are the first deserter of the
divine law; you are she who persuaded him whom the devil was
not valiant enough to attack. You destroyed so easily God's
image, man. On account of your desert—that is, death—even
the Son of God had to die.
> —Tertullian (c. 202 C.E.), "On the Apparel of Women,"
> addressing his "best beloved sisters"

How sin perverts human relations: it makes out of the obedient
wife a directress of the husband, out of the helper a temptress,
out of marriage a fountain of mischief, out of the man's call to
watchfulness an easy corruptibility, out of Paradise itself a state of
guilt.
> —J. P. Lange, *A Commentary on the Holy Scriptures* (1869)

So far we have focused on the yes to eros in Genesis 1–2, but the fact is
that our world—including sex—is not always good. Many experience repression, not freedom; slavery, not authority; patriarchy, not mutuality. Feeling that things are not the way God meant them to be, humans throughout
the ages have looked for an explanation of how creation might have gone
wrong.

Centuries of Christian theologians have found their answer in the second part of the garden of Eden story, Genesis 3. No matter how a scholar defined the human problem, he could find it discussed here. Past interpreters like Tertullian influenced centuries of Christians by arguing that the sin of the garden was sexual transgression: the "forbidden fruit" was sex, and "shame" was the inevitable consequence. Others, like Augustine, saw the sin of pride: humans were tempted by the snake to eat the fruit and become like God. The epigraph by Lange comes from the Victorian period and locates the sin of Eden in a basket of ills: a woman taking charge of her husband, the corruption of marriage, the corruption of humanity. Whatever the ill, most Christian interpreters found some sort of original "sin" instigated by Eve in the garden of Eden.[1]

We will find that a closer reading reveals that traditional interpretations are not supported by the text. The forbidden fruit is not sex, but human wisdom, the knowledge of good and evil. In Genesis 2, God directs the life of humans through a single, clear prohibition—"from the tree of knowledge of good and evil you may not eat" (Gen. 2:17)—but gives permission to eat of all other fruits. Once humans eat of this tree of knowledge, everything becomes more complicated. They do not immediately die, as God had promised (on this, the snake is right). Instead, they are alienated from God, the earth, and each other. In a tragic twisting of created goodness, the man rules the woman and works the earth with the sweat of his brow. Eros is disrupted, as it is in so many ways in the contemporary world. Moreover, the text depicts God as permanently closing the way back to simplicity and clarity, however much humans might long for it. God expels the humans from the garden and places guards there to prevent a return.

Choosing Wisdom and
Leaving the Garden

And God commanded the human, "You may certainly eat from any tree of the garden, but from the tree of knowledge of good and evil you must never eat, for on the day you eat from it you will certainly be put to death."
—Genesis 2:16–17

Now the snake was more clever than any of the animals which the Lord God had made, and he said to the woman, "Did God actually say that you should never eat from any tree of the garden?" And the woman said to the snake, "We can eat of the fruit of the trees of the garden, but as for the tree which is in the middle of the garden, God said, 'You must never eat of it nor touch it lest you die.' " And the snake said to the woman, "You

most certainly will not die. For God knows that on the day you eat from
it, your eyes will be opened and you will be like God, knowing good and
evil."

she decided

And the woman saw that the tree was tasty, pleasant to the eye and good
for wisdom, and she took from its fruit, and ate, and she gave some also to
her husband, and he ate.—Genesis 3:1–6

This final chapter of the Eden story starts with the entry of a clever snake
into the picture (Gen. 3:1). Later Christian and Jewish interpretations identify the snake as Satan, but there is no hint of that in the text itself. Instead,
the snake is an ancient symbol of immortality and wisdom.[2] Here, he enters
stage right, as God exits.

The snake starts by leading the woman to question God's motives and
intentions in forbidding the humans to eat of the tree in the midst of the
garden, a tree previously identified as the "tree of knowledge of good and
evil." Earlier, God used stern, legal language to forbid the humans from
eating of the tree of knowledge of good and evil and threatened execution
if/when they disobeyed: "on the day you eat of it you shall certainly be
put to death" (Gen. 2:17). The snake asserts, "You most certainly will not
die. For God knows that on the day you eat from it, your eyes will be
opened and you will be like God, knowing good and evil." The woman
is faced with two perspectives: God says she will die if she eats of the fruit,
while the clever snake says God only said that for fear of the wisdom she
would get if she ate from it. She looks again at the tree, sees that its fruit
is pretty, tasty, and good for wisdom. She eats it, shares the fruit with her
man as well, and he eats (Gen 3:6).

> And their eyes were opened, and they knew that they were naked,
> and they made loincloths for themselves out of fig leaves. Then they
> heard the sound of the Lord God walking around in the garden like
> a day breeze. The man and his wife hid themselves from the Lord
> God amidst the trees of the garden. And the Lord God called out to
> the human and said to him, "Where are you?" And he said, "I heard
> your sound in the garden, and I was afraid, because I was naked. So
> I hid." And God said, "Who told you that you were naked? Did
> you eat of the tree which I commanded you not to eat from?" And
> the human said, "The woman whom you gave to be with me, she
> gave to me from the tree and I ate." The Lord God then said to the
> woman, "What did you do?" And she said, "The snake deceived
> me, and I ate." (Gen. 3:7–13)

The eating of the fruit sets in motion an unraveling of the connected web
of relationships that God had woven earlier. The first thing to go is the

humans' unashamed sexuality—they see their nakedness and clothe themselves with flimsy fig leaves (Gen. 3:7). The next thing gone is intimacy
with God. When God comes walking in the garden, they hide themselves
for fear of their nakedness (Gen. 3:8–10). This shame at nakedness then is
the key for God to realize that something has gone horribly wrong. God
questions the man and woman, and the interrogation reveals not only that
the man and woman have eaten of the forbidden tree, but that the man's
original celebration of God's gift of the woman (Gen. 2:23) has been replaced by his blame of her and of God for his role in the garden crime. In
excusing himself, he says, "The woman *whom you gave to be with me* . . .
gave to me from the tree and I ate."

Ironically, centuries of interpreters, mostly male, have echoed this tradition of blaming the woman for the garden crime. The Hebrew of the story
makes clear that the man was present for every moment of the woman's
dialogue with the snake and did not say a word. Yet through the centuries,
interpreters have attempted to shift the blame to the woman, reflecting the
same loss of male-female connectedness that was reflected in the first man's
speech.

> And the Lord God said to the snake, "Because you did this, you are
> more cursed than any of the farm and wild animals. You will crawl
> on your belly and eat dust all your life. I will put a hostility between
> you and the woman and between your children and the woman's
> children. He will wound you on the head, while you will wound
> him in the heel."
> To the woman the Lord God said, "I will greatly multiply your
> toil in childbearing as you bring forth children with exertion. Your
> desire will be for your husband, but he will rule over you."
> To the man God said, "Because you listened to your wife and ate
> of the tree I commanded you not to eat from, the fertile land is
> cursed because of you. With toil you shall eat all your life. Thistles
> and thorns will spring up for you, and you shall eat the grass of the
> field. With the sweat of your brow you shall eat bread until you
> return to the earth from which you were taken. For you are dust,
> and to dust you shall return."
> And the human called his wife, "Life," because she was the
> mother of all life. And the Lord God made skin tunics for the
> human and his wife and dressed them.
> And the Lord God said, "Look, the human is now like one of us,
> knowing good and evil. Now, lest he reach out his hand, take from
> the tree of life, and eat and live forever." . . . And [before God could
> finish the thought] the Lord God sent the human out of the garden
> of Eden to work the ground from which he was taken. And God
> expelled the human, and God put the winged sphinxes and a

whirling sword east of Eden to guard the way to the tree of life.
(Gen. 3:14–24)

Things get worse in this part of the story. God pronounces the consequences of the snake's, woman's, and man's actions, and expels the humans
from the garden. Now that the original, untroubled intimacy between the
man, the woman, and the earth is gone, the woman must toil in childbirth
in the context of a patriarchal family (Gen. 3:16).[3] As we will see in more
detail in the next chapter, ancient Israelite women did have to deal with a
constant stream of pregnancies, from when they reached puberty in their
teens until they died in their twenties or thirties. God goes on in the story
to tell the man he must work his entire life at raising food out of resistant
earth (Gen. 3:17–19). This too matched the lived reality of the ancient
Israelites. After this, Adam names his wife "Life" because she will become
the mother of all humanity (Gen. 3:20), and God dresses the humans (Gen.
3:21) before expelling them from the garden to work the earth outside it
(Gen. 3:22–24).

Where once the human made from earth tended and guarded a paradise
orchard, now he must live and die wrenching food from barren ground.
Where there once was a human and a partner fully corresponding to him,
now the man rules over the woman. As if to put a final stamp on this shift,
the narrator at the end of the story simply says that God "sent *him* from
the garden of Eden" (Gen. 3:23) and "expelled *the human*" (Gen. 3:24),
without even mentioning the woman God had so carefully crafted to share
in his life and the garden work.

Obviously, by this point, Genesis 3 reflects how imperfect the world now
is. We might wish that humans could freely act on their passions, but the
fact is that life is fraught with domination, compromises, and sacrificed
goods. People cannot freely pursue objects of desire and still honor significant commitments to partners, children, work, and so on. Even the best
erotic connections are incomplete in a broader perspective. What measure
of fulfilled work some people find is built on the travail of many others
who must toil endlessly. What measure of erotic relationship is achieved is
unavoidably influenced by the inequalities and violence of our society and
constrained in a multitude of ways by social structures having to do with
reproduction.

Good Eros, Beguiled Eros

Taken as a whole, the Garden of Eden story evokes both the potential and
the tragedy of such erotic relationships. On the one hand, it describes hu-

man beings as intensely embodied creatures, physically (and verbally) connected to the earth and one another. Further, it lifts up erotic relationship combined with shared work—a relationship not necessarily connected to reproduction—as the ultimate realization of human relational potential. On the other hand, the story recognizes ways in which our present reality does not reflect that vision. Humans are no longer "naked and not ashamed." Many are compelled to hide their bodies and sexualities from God. Men and women often deal with alienation from God by blaming each other (and implicitly God), where they might celebrate each other instead. Most women must still live out their sexuality in a patriarchal context and are bound by both biology and culture to the reproductive task. And many men and women are bound to endless, alienating work. The Eden story of Genesis 2–3 combines all these elements—the potential of erotic connection and the frequent human failure to realize that potential—into one highly evocative whole.

One might think that there is no more erotically oriented culture than the sex-saturated, consumeristic society of North America. Yet I am suggesting otherwise. If one understands eros to refer to "what is deepest and strongest and richest within each of us, being shared," as Lorde affirms, then eros does not encompass the majority of things that are advertised, sold, sung about, and longed for in our culture. Instead, much of our culture is devoted to channeling the eros of consumers toward things they did not originally want: luxury cars, jewelry, liposuction, media, and so on. The advertising that powers our economy has developed manipulation of people's desires into a high art, grabbing people's attention, using sexually charged images to sell nonsexual things. If asked what I want on a deeper level, it is difficult to extricate myself from this web of forces that have helped define my passions for me. Genesis 2 suggests that humans were created for shared work and love, but that is not a given in the North American context, any more than it is in other cultures. Instead, both we and the world are not perfect, we betray each other and our deepest loves, and major cultural forces aggravate this process.

Although we can work to minimize these realities, we cannot, in the final analysis, avoid them. The first step toward realizing full human potential in such a situation is to recognize and mourn these ways in which we cannot fully reach the connectedness that we most desire, even as we then work to build a society in which it might be easier for our children to work and love in years to come.

As Martha Nussbaum suggests in her discussion of tragic compromise in Aeschylus, there are right and wrong ways to respond to situations in which we cannot do a "right" thing because we must choose between two wrongs.

When faced with the choice between letting his shipload of warriors starve and sacrificing his daughter, Agamemnon's mistake is to sacrifice her without remorse, as if she were a beast. In another tragedy by Aeschylus, Eteocles, son of Oedipius, errs in eagerly seeking the opportunity to fight his brother Polynices and save the city. Both actions serve a greater good. Nevertheless, the tragedies also depict the error of making such choices without mourning and feeling the agony of the lost connection.[4]

We are so deadened by media overload that it is easy to ignore ways in which we have lost opportunities for deep connections with work, friends, and intimates. And this is not even a choice of giving up a loved one to save a ship or city. Instead, this Eden story suggests that whatever deadness we feel is a case of forgetfulness. But things were not always this way. We were made for deep connection with God, each other, and the earth. The way things are now is only a reflection of how things went wrong in the wake of the garden crime.

The Garden Crime

This complex story has proven immensely powerful over the ages, often not for good. Early Christians took it as a tale of original sin: Eve tempted Adam into sexual sin, and then God punished her by giving her pain in childbirth and making the man rule over her, partly to control her troublesome desire. But this ancient interpretation tells us more about how our forebears viewed women and sex than it does about the story itself. The word *sin* never occurs in the story. The man is present throughout every conversation with the snake. And the Genesis 3 story is not about punishment for sex. Yes, the story is saturated with sexual imagery—the creation of humans for each other, human nakedness, and so on. And yes, eating—such as eating the fruit—can be a metaphor for sex. We will see that again in the Song of Songs. Yet sexuality long precedes the eating of the fruit in this story. Remember, the story talked of the man and woman embracing and becoming "one flesh" from the first moment they saw each other (Gen. 2:24).

If we read the text itself, the forbidden fruit is not sex, but wisdom. As the story says, this was the fruit of the tree of knowledge of good and evil (Gen. 2:17; cf. 3:6). "Knowledge of good and evil" is a phrase often used to describe wisdom (1 Kings 3:9, 11–12), indeed a godlike wisdom possessed by only a few (2 Sam. 14:17, 20). Proverbs calls wisdom "a tree of life to all who take hold of her" (Prov. 3:18), and the tree was a frequent symbol of wisdom in the ancient Near East.[5] The snake, described as extremely "clever" here (Gen. 3:1), was likewise a symbol of wisdom in the Near East. The woman is described as seeing the fruit of the Eden tree as "good for wisdom" (Gen. 3:6).[6] All of these clues suggest that the central crime in Eden is this: seeking a human knowledge of right and wrong rather than trusting God's simple law, the one prohibition God had given at the beginning, not to eat from the tree of knowledge of good and evil. The "clever" snake should know: eating of a tree of knowledge will bring wisdom; their eyes will be "opened" (an expression for enlightenment in the ancient world).

So, having been led by the snake to think for herself about God's prohibition, the story asserts that the woman looked at the tree, made her own decision, and shared the fruit with her man. The startling thing is that the snake turns out to be right: their eyes are opened, God gets worried (Gen. 3:22), and yet they do not die, at least not "on the day" that they ate of it. Though God had promised to put the human to death if and when he ate of the fruit (Gen. 2:17),[7] God does not kill anyone. Yes, God does bar the way to the tree of life out of concern that the humans might become more like him (Gen. 3:22–24). The snake anticipated this too (Gen. 3:5). But the first human and his wife still go on to have children and live long lives (Gen. 4:1–16; 5:1–5). As a result of correct human reasoning, things would never be uncomplicated again.

The story may have been written to make us judge this development negatively, but it can also be read as an accurate reflection of the painful process of maturing. On the one hand, the text features legal genres like law, disobedience, interrogation, and pronouncement of punishment. These have led centuries of interpreters to convict Adam and, especially, Eve of the "crime" of introducing toil and suffering into the world. On the other hand, this story might help people see current suffering as part of what it means to be mature adults. One might complain, but the story seems to say, "Grow up, this is what it means to see clearly."

As the story says, there is endless toil, and the lives of many women are still dominated by the demands of childbirth and childrearing. Yet the main point of the story does not lie in an explanation of those realities. Instead, one truth of this final part of the Eden story is this: thanks to an ancient human decision to grow up and seek wisdom, we are now faced with the uncertainties and suffering of choices. We are out of the garden forever, and nothing will be simple again. Divine certainties are gone. The enchantment of childlike existence in the garden is past. Now we live in a world where we must forage for ourselves and think for ourselves.

Uncertainty amidst Contemporary
Shifts in Sexuality

To some extent, this lack of certainty opens up possibilities. As circumstances change, we can use our minds to think through what is "good and evil." Having eaten the fruit and left the garden, we cannot settle in the security of a single prohibition, but must use our reason to discern wisdom in the present day.

Yet uncertainty can also be difficult, especially amidst rapid contemporary shifts in the basic infrastructure of sexuality. Where sex always involved the possibility of children in the ancient world, now sex is increasingly separated from reproduction. Young adults become sexually mature long before they are emotionally or economically ready for marriage. This prolongs the period of potential premarital sexual activity. Marriage itself is loaded with higher demands. Husbands and wives often expect a high level of intimacy from each other, and longer life expectancies mean that they must sustain a good marriage two or three times longer than most ancient couples did. Before, an ancient marriage would have lasted an average of about fifteen years. Now, "til death do us part" often is a commitment of forty-five years or more. Meanwhile, people are constantly exposed to more sexual stimuli and more sexual options than any ancient Israelite would have faced. Men and women work in close proximity to each other, there are many private places to pursue a relationship (cars, motels, private bedrooms), and new means of keeping in contact (for example, e-mail). Many use virtual sex— erotic romance novels, Internet chat rooms, pornography—to get romantic or sexual excitement without the obstacles, hazards, and disappointments of sex with partners. According to a recent report by Forester Research in Cambridge, pornography is now a bigger business in the United States than professional basketball, baseball, and football put together.[8]

This details only the shifts in sexual eroticism. When we add to this the impact of advertising on our other desires, the picture becomes even murkier. We are constantly bombarded with claims on our passions—sexual, physical, social, and so on. Amidst all of these claims, it is tempting to try to return to a time when answers seemed clearer.

But the garden of Eden story implies that simple laws will not suffice now that we live outside the garden. Because of an ancient human decision to grow up, we must figure out what is right and decide to do it, even if we use ancient traditions in the process. We must reason about what is wrong and avoid it.[9] We must decide whether and how to follow or adapt ancient Biblical rules about sex, including norms that are highly disturbing when we take a close look at them. So far I have talked a lot about eros broadly defined, a passion including but not confined to sexual intimacy. In the next chapter, however, I focus more narrowly on sexual eros, specifically Old Testament rules surrounding sexuality. This will prepare us for our journey through the Prophets, where figures like Hosea apply these sexual rules to the divine-human relationship.

5
The "Rules"

BIBLICAL SEXUAL MORALITY

> CWA believes the traditional family consists of one man and one
> woman joined in marriage, along with any children they may
> have. We seek to protect traditional values that support the
> Biblical design of the family.
>
> —Concerned Women for America, Statement on
> "Definition of the Family"

Biblical "Family Values"

Judging from the "family values" platform of religious conservatives, one
might assume that the Bible condemns all forms of premarital or extramarital
sex and all forms of homosexual sex. Actually, at least with regard to the
Hebrew Scriptures, the Biblical perspective on sex is far from what any
political party would want to endorse now. Some rules are harsher. Many
things are not covered. In either case, as soon as we take a closer look at
Biblical "shalt nots" and permitted behaviors, it quickly becomes apparent
that "we aren't in Kansas any more."

Ancient Israel, like many ancient agricultural societies, depended heavily
on families having lots of children. Paleo-osteological analyses of remains
in Israel and similar societies indicate that only a minority of live births
survived into the second year. Even those who survived early childhood
lived only an average of twenty-five to thirty-five years. Women tended to
die about ten years earlier than men, often during childbirth or as the result
of complications attending frequent pregnancy. Within this context, every

fertile woman needed to produce more than five live births during her adult life in order for the next generation to take the current generation's place.[1] As we can see from the Bible, not all women were fertile or lived through many birthings, so the reproductive potential of fertile women was highly valued. For example, in the Genesis narratives, the central Israelite matriarchs—Sarah, Rebecca, and Rachel—are all initially barren, and Rachel dies in childbirth.

Men and women had quite different roles in this system. Men were seen as the bearers of seed and guardians of their women. Women received the seed and bore children to inherit the land.[2] As a result, many Biblical traditions aim to ensure that the proper women become vessels of Israelite seed. Men were seen as the owners of their wives' and daughters' sexuality, while a woman's role generally was to be the obedient wife and mother promoting the dynastic line. Generally, men are presented in Biblical stories as the proper initiators of sex. Women who initiate sex are depicted as either prostitutes or otherwise sexually wayward. To be sure, some women, like Tamar of Genesis 38 or Ruth, are depicted positively for their sexual initiative. But in these cases, the women's seduction of their future husbands promotes royal dynastic lines.

Outside of such special cases, women are depicted as passive participants in sex, and a woman who initiates sex is depicted as a dangerous adulterer. We see an example of this in Proverbs 7, where the speaker warns his "son" to avoid the "strange woman" whom he saw seduce a foolish youth by inviting him to share her perfumed bed:

> At the window of my house
>   I looked out through my lattice,
> And I have seen among the simple,
>   I perceived among the youths
>   a young man without sense. . . .
>
> And look, a woman meets him,
>   dressed like a harlot, wily of heart. . . .
>
> She seizes him and kisses him,
>   And with daring she says to him:
> "I had to offer sacrifices,
>   And today I have paid my vows;
> So now I came to meet you,
>   to seek you eagerly, and I have found you.
> I decked my couch with coverings,
>   colored spreads of Egyptian linen;
> I perfumed my bed with myrrh,
>   aloes and cinnamon.

Come let us take our fill of love till morning
 let us delight ourselves with love.
For my husband is not at home;
 he has gone on a long journey;
he took a bag of money with him;
 at full moon he will come home." (Prov. 7:6–7, 10, 13–20)[3]

The speaker goes on to warn that this woman's "house is the way to Sheol, going down to the chambers of death."

This warning in Proverbs about a woman out of control grows out of a set of rules that protected men's "honor" as sexual aggressors and owners of women. In this context, it is helpful to remember that there was no reliable contraception in ancient Israel, let alone a way to trace the paternity of a disputed child. As Carol Meyers points out, adultery is serious enough in a modern context, but it has added implications in an ancient world where a man married to an adulterous wife might end up devoting scarce resources to raising the children of another man.[4] This risk of illicit reproduction does not excuse rules that enforce violence on married women who have sex outside of marriage, but it helps provide a context for the ancient idea that men somehow owned the rights to their wives' and daughters' sexuality and could punish anyone who violated those rights.

One key place where this dynamic of possession is exemplified is in the laws against adultery. Today, many think of adultery as when married people, male or female, have sex with someone besides their spouses. That has not always been the case. The Bible and most other ancient Near Eastern traditions define adultery as when a married *woman* has sex with someone other than her husband. This is seen as a violation of her husband's rights[5] and carries with it strict punishments for both the wife and her partner.[6] Take the following law from Deuteronomy as an example: "If a man is found lying with another man's wife, both of them—the man with the woman—shall be executed. In this way you shall burn evil from Israel" (Deut. 22:22). The issue of ownership is so emphasized in the adultery regulation in Leviticus that many have supposed some kind of scribal error:

If a man commits adultery with the wife of a man,
committing adultery with the wife of his neighbor,
both the adulterer and the adulteress shall be put to death.
(Lev. 20:10; emphasis added)

Finally, this logic of possession is reflected in laws about pre-marital sex. A man who has sex with a nonbetrothed woman—whether consensual or

premarital sex

not—becomes functionally married to her (without the possibility of divorce) and has to pay her father the bride price that the father would have received from a more conventional marriage (Exod. 22:15–16; Deut. 22:28–29).[7] Apparently, at the discretion of the husband, adultery with a married woman could likewise be handled by payment by the offending man.[8]

The idea of men as sexual owners and aggressors plays a role in the famous Old Testament laws against homosexuality. The longest of these two laws reads: "A man who lies with a male the lying down of a woman has committed an abomination. The two of them shall be put to death. Their blood is on them." As Saul Olyan argues in a pivotal article, this "lying down of a woman" does not refer to homosexual acts in general: kissing, oral sex, and so on. Instead, it refers specifically to one man's sexual penetration of another male—anal intercourse. The other regulation in Leviticus uses the same terms and is even clearer about the issue: "*and with a man* you shall not lie down with the lying down of a woman. It is an abomination" (Lev. 18:22; emphasis added). Men in Israel were penetrators, not penetrated. In the Bible, men "lie with" women.[9] Only in extreme circumstances do women "seize" men (for example, Isa. 4:1), and never do they then lie with them. Even when Potiphar's wife grabs hold of Joseph, she tells him to "lie with me" (Gen. 39:12). Building on this concept, these laws in Leviticus presume one man lying with another as a fundamental violation of his status as sexual actor. Such intercourse with another man was seen as a violation of the cosmos much like sex between humans and animals. As in that case, both participants, including the passive one, were executed (Lev. 20:15–16).[10]

On the female side, the Bible proclaims harsh punishment for any engaged or married woman who has sex with a man not her husband. At the very least, she is liable to be divorced or publicly stripped by her husband.[11] Genesis 38 describes the patriarch Judah as sentencing his daughter-in-law Tamar to be burned to death for seemingly having sex outside of marriage (Gen. 38:24).[12] And the two laws quoted above proclaim the death penalty for any engaged or married woman who has sex with a man other than her husband.[13] The only named exception was if an engaged woman was raped in open country where she could not have called for help. "If a man comes on an engaged girl in the open country, seizes her and lies with her, only the man who lay with her shall be executed. You shall do nothing to the girl. . . . He came upon her in the open; though the engaged girl cried out for help, there was no one to rescue her" (Deut. 22:25–27*). In contrast, if a man succeeds in having sex with a betrothed girl in town, both are executed because it is presupposed that she did not cry out for help (Deut.

22:23–24). Finally, a series of laws forbade Israelites from allowing their daughters to be prostitutes (Lev. 19:29; Deut. 23:18).[14]

Other than these, the "rules" of ancient Israel were affirming of sex, particularly for male Israelites. One law says that a newly married Israelite man should be exempt for one year from military service "so he can make the wife he has taken happy" (Deut. 24:5). A wisdom saying urges men to "enjoy life with the wife whom you love all the days of your life," alongside other pleasures in life, like bread and wine (Eccles. 9:7–9). As we saw, the Eden story celebrates the creation of woman as the first man's companion and their becoming "one flesh" (Gen. 2:24).

Though Biblical laws forbid bestiality,[15] incest,[16] and sex during a woman's menstrual period,[17] the Bible does not condemn many of the sexual behaviors that people think it does.[18] The story of Sodom and Gomorrah (Gen. 19) is not a condemnation of male-male sex, but a condemnation of a town that violated hospitality by trying to rape guests in one of its homes. The only law regarding divorce dictates that a man may not remarry a prior wife who had married another man since he divorced her (Deut. 24:1–4).[19] Finally, the one text often used to condemn masturbation (Gen. 38:9) actually judges a man who practiced *coitus interruptus* by spilling his "seed" on the ground "whenever he came to his brother's wife." By doing so, he was avoiding his legal obligation (Deut. 25:5–10) to have children with his dead brother's wife in order to continue his brother's line.

As in many ancient societies, both married and unmarried Israelite men were free to have sex with prostitutes, war prisoners, widows, and any other unmarried, nonprotected women they wished. The woman's consent was not even a legal factor, as long as the woman was not under the control/ protection of a father or husband.[20] Yes, it is true that the Bible has multiple stories about ancient Israelite men loving their wives,[21] and one prophet condemns Israelite men for divorcing their Israelite wives in order to marry foreign women (Mal. 2:10–16).[22] In addition, several proverbs praise the benefits of having a good wife,[23] urge men to be faithful to their wives,[24] and caution against the problems that could arise from patronizing prostitutes.[25] Yet all of these are just recommendations. And the texts encouraging married love stand alongside another proverb that argues that patronizing a harlot is less risky than adultery:

For the fee of a prostitute is only a loaf of bread,
But the wife of another stalks a man's very life. (Prov. 6:26)

Genesis includes a story about Judah's attempt to have sex with a prostitute that does not include any judgment of the patriarch for seeking extramarital sex (Gen. 38:15–18). And not one law specifies a punishment for a married man having sex with an unmarried woman.

Imagine a political party that adopted a set of Biblical "family values" that included rules like the following as part of its platform:

Free sex (consensual or not) between men and unmarried women who are not under the protection of a male relative.

Requirement that the male pay the father a bride-price after sex with a marriageable woman (and marry her without the possibility of divorce).

An obligation that, if a man dies before having children, his brother must have children with his widow.

No comment on sex between women or sex between men that does not involve anal intercourse between men.

This does not sound exactly like the religious right. The Promise Keepers would have fewer promises to keep if they adopted the rules discussed here, and a married president could have as much sex with interns as he liked, as long as they were unmarried females and he was prepared to pay the bride-prices if required.

Of course, most people now advocating "Biblical" family values are Christians who mix laws from the Hebrew Scriptures with materials from the New Testament, particularly Paul. Certainly in Paul you find texts that condemn some ancient forms of sex between men or sex between women (for example, 1 Cor. 6:9; Rom. 1:26–32). But as we saw in the introduction, Paul is also against sexual passion *in general*, whether inside or outside of marriage. If one is a Christian and counts writings like Paul's in the picture of what counts as Biblical, then one needs to contend with Paul's hostility toward marriage, his condemnation of all forms of nonreproductive sexuality, and his endorsement of general celibacy in texts like 1 Corinthians 7. Paul's sexual system and the rules of other New Testament writings are profoundly different from both the Hebrew Bible and any contemporary positions.

The point here is simply that the sexual rules of the Hebrew Bible (and the New Testament) revolve around sets of values that are alien to most people in modern, industrialized societies. In the harsh agricultural context of ancient Israel, the men owned the women and the fields (often associating the two), while women were required to be wholly devoted to their one husband/fiancé on penalty of being stripped, abandoned, stoned, or burned to death.

Moving beyond the Garden

So what are we to make of family values as they are found in the Hebrew Bible? The garden of Eden story provides us one key. The essentials of Biblical morality are described there as a reflection of the breakdown of created connectedness. After the man and woman ate of the tree of knowledge, God proclaimed the following consequence to the woman before going on to condemn the man to endless agricultural labor:

> I will greatly multiply your toil in childbearing
>> as you bring forth children with exertion.
> Your desire will be for your husband,
>> but he will rule over you. (Gen. 3:16)

We saw this image in the other Biblical texts discussed: male rule over women and sexuality focused on producing children. It is a picture deeply shaped by the harsh conditions of agricultural life in ancient Israel: high infant mortality, short life expectancy, and so on. Yet Genesis 3 does not endorse this vision. It is not how God meant things to be. Instead, endless pregnancy and male rule over women is depicted in this garden text as part of the tragic postwisdom world. As Phyllis Trible suggests, these pronouncements in Genesis 3 "show how intolerable existence has become as it stands between creation and redemption."[26] In sum, ancient male-centered family values are depicted in this text as a reflection of just how far from our created goodness we have fallen. They are not what the creator God intended, but a sad consequence of the growth of human wisdom and civilization.

Must we read these texts as a new set of commands? Should the Biblical rules outlined here have a similar status to God's earlier command not to eat of the garden fruit? Certainly, many have read these texts this way. At the same time, as I argued in the previous chapter, we can also read the garden story as a myth proclaiming the impossibility of ever returning to a childlike existence of rules and regulations. Even if we choose to perpetuate a system of gender hierarchy, which the Bible itself describes as tragic, that is still a choice. As a result of human wisdom, creation has been broken open to the possibilities and compromises of human moral reasoning.

These choices are more open now, in the West of the twenty-first century, than at any other time. Fewer people endure lives of endless toil; not all women must toil with childbirth and childrearing; and now, more than ever, we are the ones who must determine what is good and what is bad. As God at the end of the story says, "See, the human has become like one of us, knowing good and evil" (Gen. 3:22). There is no return to a time—

if there ever was one—when humans just did what we have been told to do.

As the Eden story suggests, the resulting uncertainty can lead to shame, hiding from God, blaming of each other, and dishonesty. Our eyes are opened, and we are aware, if we let ourselves be, of how tenuous, how fragile, human values are, perhaps especially regarding sex and gender. Even when we peel away centuries of oppressive misreadings of Biblical traditions, they still portray a sexual system geared for maximum reproduction and a gender system where men are privileged. Now, we must make decisions about how to respond to these ancient traditions, and this can be a difficult process. There are no ongoing, direct revelations from God to help us. Men and women can and often do blame each other, especially as different communities in modern, pluralistic, and globalized societies make different decisions: from evangelical Christians to the most secular intellectuals.

Though some might long for a simpler time when a rule was a rule was a rule, it will never return. We can pretend that we are back in the garden, but that does not put us there. Many fundamentalist movements in our world seek to answer the uncertainty of this life outside the garden with a false certainty of secure rules and stories. They only clothe human judgments in divine garments.

So we must live fully in the postgarden reality, recognizing the brokenness of relationships that happened there and making choices about how to respond to that brokenness. From the man's blaming of the woman for the garden crime to God's proclamation of the coming of patriarchy, we see how God's originally intended connection between the genders has been wounded. Yet, as we saw in the humans hiding from God and blaming, the connection to the divine is not whole either. This is clear in the prophetic texts to which we turn next. In our broken world, not only are women terrorized by men, but the suffering ancient people of Israel sometimes felt like a "woman" terrorized by God, a God now experienced as the ultimate "male."

II

Isaiah's Vineyard Garden and the Prophets

Naaman — Aramean (Abram)
cured, land

Each God · own soil-place
"" Worshipers - people of that
soil,
≠ terms of covenant Land
People
me-mine

6

Marriage to God

ISAIAH'S VINEYARD AND OTHER IMAGES
OF DIVINE-HUMAN SEXUALITY p68 Hosea

Let me sing now for my beloved,
   a song of my beloved about his vineyard.
My beloved had a vineyard,
   On a hillock abounding in olives.

—Isaiah 5:1

We turn now from garden to vineyard, to a vineyard song. In ancient Israel a vineyard is one of the most precious possessions a family can have. It provides refreshing drink during the summer drought and is a place of feasting and rejoicing. Though the vineyard is often associated with gardens in general, it is distinguished from them by two things. The first is that vineyards require sustained care over a period of years. Unlike grain fields, they cannot be left fallow and later seeded. Rather, they must be lovingly terraced, pruned, trained, and protected, much like a sustained erotic relationship.[1] The second major thing that distinguishes a vineyard from many gardens is that such loving cultivation produces something intoxicating: wine.

This product-producing dimension of vineyards is present in Isaiah's song for his "beloved" about a vineyard. Once again, sexuality moves into the foreground. But as we will see, this is a sexuality that has consequences, a sexuality that produces children. Before, we saw how many sexual rules in ancient Israel revolved around the fact that any sex by a married woman could result in her having children by a man not her husband. In this text, Isaiah plays upon that fact but takes the image further. He starts with typical images of the loving cultivation of a vineyard (clearing, planting, building). Yet soon we must adjust our expectations and adjust them again. What first seems to be a parable about a vineyard seems next be an accusation about a wayward human woman, but the song ultimately turns out to be about a wayward people and their lover, God.

This vineyard song introduces a group of prophetic texts that are difficult and yet important. From the outset, it will be clear that this is not love at its best. Instead, this vineyard song introduces a series of texts that envision love at its worst: painful, jealous, violent. Yet, once we have surveyed these passages in this chapter, the next chapter will argue that these texts help us in at least two ways as we reflect on sexuality and spirituality. First, they balance a frequent tendency to romanticize love, to assume that if it is pure enough, it is always good. They envision how love can go wrong. Second and more important, these prophetic texts are central Biblical witnesses to the idea that passion matters *in general*, not just sexual passion. Though Isaiah's vineyard song can be read on one level as about sexual unfaithfulness, it turns out to be about the deeper issue of divine-human eros. It can be a clue to turn our gaze more broadly, to look at how a passion for God might be related to and envelop other human passions.

Isaiah's audience starts out on one level and ends up on the next. Let us turn to his song and see where it takes us.

Isaiah's Vineyard Song

Imagine yourself as a male Israelite, standing at a bustling gate in the wall of Jerusalem, capital of Judah, the southern part of the land of Israel. Such gates are a city's main public place, a place where legal cases are discussed, business is conducted, and prophets preach. Isaiah, a prominent citizen, begins to present what sounds like a legal case on behalf of a beloved friend of his. The language is veiled, and we, the ancient audience, do not yet know for sure who his beloved is:

> Let me sing now for my beloved,
>   a song of my beloved about his vineyard.
> My beloved had a vineyard,
>   On a hillock abounding in olives.
> He dug around it and cleared it of stones
>   And planted it with choice red vines.
> He built a tower in its midst,
>   and even hewed out a wine press in it.
> And he waited for it to make grapes.
>   Rotten berries were all it made. (Isa. 5:1–2)

On one level, Isaiah's beloved appears to be a disappointed vintner. He put a lot of work into his vineyard and got bad results. Yet, if we are ancient Israelites, we quickly see another level of the song, where the "vineyard" of the prophet's beloved is, in fact, a woman. Women and their genitals have been imaged as fields and vineyards for millennia in the Near East. An ancient Egyptian love song has the singer say:

> I am your favorite sister.
>   I am yours like the field
> planted with flowers
>   and with all sorts of fragrant plants.[2]

Another partially preserved love dialogue from ancient Sumeria has the woman proclaim:

> The vulva it is . . .
> Like a horn it . . . at the large wagon . . .
> It is fallow land, in the plain . . .
> It is a field, which the uz-bird . . . the uz bird,
> It is a high field, my . . . ,
> As for me, my vulva is a . . . hillock,—for me,
> I, the maid, who will be its plower?
> My vulva is . . . wet ground for me,
> I, the queen, who will station there the ox?

To this the king replies:

> Lady, the king will plow it for you,
> Dumuzi, the king will plow it for you.

And she says, "Plow my vulva, my sweetheart."[3] This Sumerian dialogue includes the imagery of both field and hillock found in Isaiah's vineyard song.

Ancient Israel also used such imagery. We see it in the Song of Songs, where the male lover speaks of his female love as a lush garden of spices (esp. Song 4:12–5:1). She speaks of him coming down to "his garden" and of herself as a vineyard (Song 1:6). She invites him to come visit the vineyards[4] or be like a gazelle or stag climbing her "mountain of spices."[5]

Obviously, Isaiah 5:1–2 is not such a happy love story. Although it is hard to know how far to take the imagery of the song, it sounds on one level like a description of a frustrated, even betrayed male lover. Just as an ancient male Israelite owned his wife, this "vintner" owned a "vineyard," a fertile "hillock." This husband did all he could to clear and protect his "vineyard." He planted it with choice seed, put a "tower" and "wine press" in it, and waited for his wife, his "vineyard," to produce grapes. But she produced rotten berries instead. The children just do not look anything like him. Did his wifely "vineyard" have them with another lover?

Certainly, the next part of the song suggests such intense betrayal. Isaiah takes on the persona of his beloved friend. Perhaps we, as an ancient audience of his, know him as a prophet and realize he speaks on behalf of God. Or maybe we are still trying to figure out what is going on. In either case, the wronged vintner—God?—now calls on the audience, us, to join in a legal judgment against his adulterous vineyard:

> And now, citizens of Jerusalem
>   and men of Judah,
> Judge now between me
>   and my vineyard
> What more could I have done for my vineyard
>   that I did not do?
> Why did I wait for grapes
>   And it produced rotten berries instead? (Isa. 5:3–4)

By this point we realize that this is not about a literal vineyard. Ancient Israelites did not typically take their unproductive fields to court and ask for judgments against them. Instead, the beloved is engaging in a legal process against his vineyard/wife, asking his male audience, asking us, to join him in condemning her betrayal of him.

Without waiting for an answer from us, the wronged husband, Isaiah's "beloved," rushes on to proclaim his plans to remove his manly protection from his female "vineyard," and he calls on us, his male compatriots, to support his righteous judgment:

> Now, let me tell you
>   What I am about to do to my vineyard.
> Remove its hedge,
>   so that it is stripped bare.
> Tear down its wall,
>   so that it is trampled over.
> I shall give it over to ruin.
>   It shall not be pruned or hoed.
>   It shall be overgrown with briars and thorns. (Isa. 5:5–6a)

As we saw in the last chapter, Israelite women accused of adultery were punished by being stripped, stoned, or burned. The beloved here announces his plans to strip his "vineyard" of its "hedge" and "wall," letting her be ruined.[6] At this point, however, we begin to see him reveal his identity. His last promise of destruction is the following:

> I will command the clouds,
>> Not to rain anymore on it. (Isa. 5:6b)

In Israel, God alone had such power over weather. Isaiah's beloved is Yahweh, the God of Israel.

Before we, the prophet's audience, have a chance to catch our breath, we soon realize something surprising about the vineyard too:

> For the vineyard of Yahweh of hosts is the house of Israel,
>> And the men of Judah are the planting of his pleasure. (Isa. 5:7a)

We thought we were joining in the condemnation of an adulterous wife of Isaiah's friend. In fact, we ourselves—the men of Judah—were the vineyard/woman while our God, Yahweh, was the betrayed husband. Just so the point of the previous parable is made clear, the prophet, using a clever wordplay (the Hebrew is in italics below), translates the final part about grapes/rotten berries for them:

> He [God] waited for justice (*mishpat*),
>> but look, lawbreaking (*mispah*).
> For social solidarity (*tzedeqah*),
>> but instead, cries of helplessness (*tseᶜaqah*). (Isa. 5:7b)

On one level, this appears to be a straightforward prophetic judgment. After all, this is not the first time a prophet tricked his audience into joining in judgment before making clear that they were judging themselves. The prophet Nathan does the same in having King David proclaim a judgment on someone who stole a shepherd's only lamb. Only after David has proclaimed a sentence of death does Nathan make clear that David is the thief in question, having stolen Uriah's wife, Bathsheba (2 Sam. 12:1–10). Yet where Nathan's speech used a nonsexual allegory to condemn a sexual misdeed, Isaiah's speech involves sex on two levels. On one level, the audience is tempted into viewing Isaiah's speech as a condemnation of human sexuality gone wrong: a caring husband cheated on by an ungrateful wife. Yet by the end of the poem it is clear that another level of behavior is at stake: a caring God being cheated on by his ungrateful people.

What a striking move across levels of gender! So far we have looked at human gender and divine gender separately, but Isaiah moves fluidly from one to the other. Moreover, the same disturbing power dynamics operate on both levels. Just as ancient women were subject to stripping and starvation when they had sex outside of marriage, so Isaiah sees God as stripping and starving Israel for its "unfaithfulness." Isaiah was not isolated in seeing this analogy. Let us look at other, often disturbing examples, starting with the crises out of which they arose.

Ancient Israelite Suffering

As we have seen, everyday life could be quite harsh for ancient people like the Israelites. Even for those who survived early childhood, life was comparatively short and dominated by childbirth (for women) and intense agricultural labor (for women and men). Israelites often starved as winter stores ran out, especially during a drought, which occurred every three or four years. Furthermore, untreatable epidemics often decimated huge sections of the population. Fire was common and catastrophic in the close quarters of walled cities. Earthquakes, such as the one mentioned in Amos's prophecy (Amos 1:1; 9:5) devastated the towns and villages.[7]

Perhaps most significant of all, ancient Israel was often under attack or domination by the various superpowers of the area. Lying as it did on crossroads connecting the river cultures of Egypt and Mesopotamia (ancient Iraq), Israel was in a strategic position. The major civilizations of the area often seized control of the area and forced treaties on the local peoples, treaties that required them to offer allegiance solely to the superpower king and pay large amounts of tribute to him. Egypt was the dominant power of the area in the period just before King David and King Solomon. Later, the Mesopotamian kingdoms of Assyria and Babylonia were more prominent.

Especially in the 800s and 700s Before the Common Era (B.C.E. = B.C.), the northern and southern kingdoms of Israel were almost constantly dominated by one or the other superpower, although they occasionally rebelled and were brutally suppressed. Israel was caught between a rock and a hard place. Scholars estimate that subject nations were often forced to pay huge amounts of tribute, often up to 20 percent of their produce in a subsistence culture. If they joined with other subject nations and tried to rebel, however, they usually suffered even more. The ruthlessly efficient armies of ancient Assyria or Babylonia would cross the borders, kill large numbers of people, and ravage the land. Not only would many die through starvation either in besieged cities or because of famine caused by destruction of crops, but the Assyrians specialized in terrorizing ancient populations with their brutality. Take for example, the following boast from an Assyrian king, describing his conquest of a rebellious people:

> 3000 of their combat troops I felled with weapons. Many of the captives taken from them I burned in a fire. Many I took alive; from some of these I cut off their hands to the wrist, from others I cut off their noses, ears and fingers; I put out the eyes of many of the soldiers. . . . I burnt their young men and women to death.[8]

Here is another example: "I fixed up a pile of corpses in front of the gate. I flayed the nobles, as many as had rebelled and spread their skins out on the piles of corpses."[9] Ancient Israel often had to choose between paying a tribute it had no money to pay and risking these sorts of brutality through forming a coalition with Egypt or other neighbors suffering the same sort of oppression.

It was in the midst of exactly these kinds of crises—earthquake, drought, and invasion—that prophets like Isaiah experienced their God as a vengeful husband. The idea of God as vengeful was not new even then. It is as old as ancient flood myths and as recent as Jerry Falwell's blame of the September 11, 2001, terrorist attacks in New York and Washington on a sexually permissive culture. What was new was the vision of this vengeful God as *sexually* jealous. The texts that unfold this vision emphasize the bleakest, most disturbing parts of the ancient Israelite experience of sex. More specifically, the prophets of Israel saw battered Israel as the "woman" in the divine-human relationship, experiencing a woman's harsh treatment at the hands of the angry divine husband she had betrayed.

The Origins of Divine-Human Marriage Imagery in Hosea

Hosea's Image of Love between God and People/Land

The eighth-century prophet Hosea provides what is probably the earliest example of this. In a poetic speech dated just a few decades before Isaiah's, Hosea describes God speaking to the "children" of Israel, divorcing their (female) land as a whole:

> Go to court, take your mother to court
> For she is not my wife
> And I am not her husband. (Hos. 2:2a [Hebrew 2:4a])

Next, God threatens the land with the same stripping that we saw before as a punishment for adultery:

> She must strip away her sexual waywardness from her face
>   and her adultery from between her breasts,
> Lest I strip her naked,
>   And display her like the day she was born,
> Make her bare as the desert,
>   and make her dry like parched earth,
>   And let her die of thirst. (Hos. 2:2b–3 [Hebrew 2:4b–5])

Hosea's God goes on to say that he will have no pity for the land's children, since they are the children of her unbridled sex (Hos. 2:4 [Hebrew 2:6]). Just like the "rotten berries" produced in Isaiah's vineyard, these children are proof that the wife has engaged in illegitimate sex.

This then leads to God's description of the character of Israel's "adultery," and here we may hear the prophet inverting love poetry that later found its way into the Biblical Song of Songs.[10] In the Song of Songs, the female lover speaks of "seeking and not finding" her lover until she locates him and takes him to the house of "my mother" and the room of "she who conceived me" (Song 3:1–5). The only other place this language about the mother "who conceived" appears in the Bible is in Hosea's speech against the land of Israel:

> Yes, their mother has been promiscuous.
>   She who conceived them has disgraced herself.

Next, the prophet attacks this mother's active seeking of sex and of lovers' gifts:

> For she said, "Let me go,
>   after my lovers,
> The ones who give me my bread and water,
>   My wool and linen,
>   My oil and drinks." (Hos. 2:5 [Hebrew 2:7])

The Song of Songs contains a similar reflection of love gifts. In one poem, a male lover says he has "gathered my myrrh with my spices, I have eaten my honeycomb along with the honey, I have drunk my wine with my milk" (Song 5:1). But Hosea's God here claims that female Israel has made a big mistake. The three pairs of gifts that she thought were from her

lovers—"my bread and water, my wool and linen, my oil and drinks"—
were actually from God. So God promises to block her way so that, like
the woman in the Song of Songs, she will "seek" and "not find" her lover(s)
(Hos. 2:7 [Hebrew 2:9]; cf. Song 3:1–2). Then, she will return to him, her
husband.

As in the case of Isaiah's vineyard song, the language is veiled. Most think
the issue here is Israel seeking fertility from gods other than Yahweh, particularly the Canaanite god, Baal. This would explain the focus of much of
the text on the gifts that the wife sought from her lovers. Israel was worshiping gods like Baal in search of bread, water, wool, and so on, when
actually it was Yahweh, Israel's husband, who gave those gifts. For Hosea,
Israel's worship of other gods was as "unfaithful" to Yahweh as a wife having
sex with men other than her husband.

Hosea's God responds accordingly, and he is not done yet. He adds another threat. He will take away the vegetation that used to clothe the land
and expose Israel's genitals to her lovers (Hos. 2:9–10 [Hebrew 2:11–12]).
Only then does the prophet, or a later editor, add a divine promise of
reconciliation. By this point, the people of Israel are no longer the illegitimate children of the land. They have become God's lover themselves:

> Therefore, look I will seduce her,
>   and I will lead her in the desert,
>   And speak tenderly to her.
> I will give her vineyards from there,
>   and the valley of Achor as a gate of hope.
> She will respond there as in her youthful days,
>   As when she came out of the land of Egypt.
> Then, you will call me "my husband"
>   And not call me "my lord" [="my Baal"] anymore.
> For I will remove the names of the Baals from her mouth,
>   And they will never be heard of again. . . .
>
> And I will take you for my wife forever,
> I will marry you in solidarity and justice
>   loyalty and compassion,
> And I will marry you to me in faithfulness,
>   And you will know Yahweh. (Hos. 2:14–17, 19–20 [Hebrew 2:16–
>   19, 21–22])

The metaphor of betrayed love grounds both God's rage and God's intent
to take Israel back, while preserving God's honor. The same strong husband,
the same "manly" God, can feel both emotions. Meanwhile, the female

image of Israel helps explain how the victim is to blame for her own battering. In Hosea, this female image subtly wavers between being the "land"
at some points and being the "people" at others. The book does not seem
to sharply distinguish between land and people in the way we would. In
either case, this "woman"—whether land or people—comes to understand
the sin of seeking other divine lovers, to see the disasters that have overtaken
her (invasions, famine) as just punishment, and to expect the same divine
husband to eventually take her back and marry her forever (Hos. 2:15b–20
[Hebrew 2:17b–22]).[11]

This series of texts sounds a lot like the abuse cycle seen in battering
relationships: the husband flies into a jealous rage and beats his wife, calms
down, and takes her back—only to repeat the cycle again. Feminist interpreters have raised important concerns about how Biblical texts trade on
the idea that such violence against women is OK. God in this ancient text
does not even seem to feel remorse, and this reflects the sexual system we
discussed already: within ancient Israel, such beatings were seen as the natural prerogative of a husband. As if that were not enough, Biblical texts use
this picture to justify divine abuse of God's people. The people of ancient
Israel were suffering, and unlike modern people who readily attribute pain
to bad luck or "nature," the prophets attribute all to God. They ask, "Why
is God battering Israel?" and "Is there any hope?" The image of betrayed
divine-human love provides an answer to both questions. Hosea explains
the present disasters as a result of Israel worshiping gods other than its own
God, Yahweh.[12]

So now, in Hosea, gender and love have become key concepts for describing the relationship between God and God's people. God is the divine
male and the human community (or the land) is the female partner. At least
as far as this theological image goes, the gender world has become a continuum defined by power, with God at the top. Yahweh, the one God of
Israel, is the male compared to whom all are "women." Furthermore, Israel's belief in male ownership of women and the right to brutally punish
their sexual behavior is now extended to the theological level.

The Origins of Hosea's Love Imagery

Hosea and others who followed him may have been spurred to think of
God as the ultimate man through international treaties that used the language of male-female love to describe political relations.[13] Just as a wife
was to "love," "walk after," and "cleave to" her husband, so these treaties
called on subject nations to "love," "walk after," and "cleave to" the king
who had imposed the treaty on them.[14] For example, a famous Mesopo-

tamian legal text specifies that a woman choosing between a former husband and a new one may "go after him whom she loves."[15] Ancient kings adopted this language in insisting that their (male) subjects "go after" them.[16]

Meanwhile, if a subject nation failed to act the part of a good vassal, it was sometimes threatened with feminization or rape. For example, Ashurnirari, a king who dominated Israel, wished the following on his vassals if they rebelled:

> May the aforesaid indeed become a prostitute, and his warriors women. May they receive their hire like a prostitute in the square of their city. May land after land draw near to them.[17]

Here military conquest by "land after land" is imaged as the rape of a woman. The Bible contains this kind of violent feminization of other nations as well. The prophet Jeremiah predicts that foreign mercenaries in the army of Babylon will "become women" (Jer. 50:37), and he prophesies the same fate for the Babylonian army (51:30).[18] Other Biblical texts image the military conquest of a city as the stripping and humiliation of a woman.[19] In Israel and elsewhere, whole peoples could be subjugated as "women" in addition to the subjugation of actual human women.[20]

This combination of commands and threats presented nations like Israel with a choice of what kind of "woman" they would be: faithful wife or stripped and raped prostitute. They could act the part of the good wife, faithfully "loving," "cleaving to" and "walking after" a superpower king like Ashurnirari. Or, if they rebelled, were politically promiscuous, and "walked after" another lord, their misbehavior would be punished by the military equivalent of rape: being penetrated and stripped by a foreign army. In this way, ancient rulers used the age-old virgin-whore dichotomy to control their vassals, much like husbands used/use this dichotomy to control their wives and daughters.

Within this world of genderized power, it was but a small step to put Yahweh in place of such kings, with Israel as Yahweh's woman rather than the wifelike subject of an Assyrian king. Indeed, exactly such considerations may have been part of Hosea's thinking. As the Israel of his time shuttled from nation to nation, trying to build a coalition to resist Assyria, Hosea saw such power politics as analogous to the worship of other gods. For him, going after such treaties with other nations was like going after other lovers.[21] Much like tyrants sometimes threaten their subjects with rape or sexual humiliation, so God in Hosea threatens Israel with similar punishments.

Hosea's Heirs: Law, Violence, and Reconciliation

Hosea probably did not get much of a hearing in his day. But as catastrophes multiplied for the kingdoms of Israel and Judah, more and more Biblical writers—in addition to Isaiah—adopted Hosea's image of divine gender terror and a husband's call for exclusive, wifelike faithfulness.

A Law of Love

Already there may be faint echoes of this image in the book of Deuteronomy and the historical texts that follow it. Although this book probably started as an ancient law code, unknown authors adapted that code into a full-blown replica of one of the international treaties already discussed. But whereas the international treaties had a superpower king imposing his will on a vassal nation, God in Deuteronomy imposes his will on Israel. Ancient treaties commanded subject nations to love, walk after, and cleave to their superpower king much like a human wife was to do for her husband. Deuteronomy applies the same language of wifely devotion to God. Speaking to Israel, Moses says: "After Yahweh, your God, you shall walk; it is he you should fear; his commandment you should observe and his voice you should obey, it is he you should serve and to him you should cleave" (Deut. 13:5).[22] Here and elsewhere, Israel is told not to "go after" other gods, much like a human wife is not to pursue other lovers. Yahweh is a "jealous" god.[23] One text closely related to Deuteronomy, Exodus 34:14, even asserts that "jealousy" is God's name.

Yet Deuteronomy goes beyond the international treaties in using love language to describe Israel's relationship to God. Indeed, at one crucial point, the book of Deuteronomy describes God's passion for Israel using the same Hebrew word, *hashaq*, that other Biblical texts use for a man's passionate desire for a woman (Deut. 7:7).[24] Consider the Shema, a central part of the introduction of the law in Deuteronomy: "Hear, Oh Israel, Yahweh, our God, is one Yahweh. You shall love Yahweh your God with all your heart, life force [*nephesh*], and might" (Deut. 6:4–5). The *nephesh* mentioned here is the same life force that Genesis 2 describes God as breathing into the first human: "[God] breathed the breath of life into his nostrils, and the human became a living being" (Gen. 2:7). Later we will see that a woman in an ancient Israelite love song could speak of her lover as the one whom her "life force [*nephesh*] loves" (Song 1:7; 3:1–4). Perhaps some form of this love poem was already known by the author of Deuteronomy.[25] In Deuteronomy, however, we do not have a man and a woman. Instead, the people of Israel are told to love God with such passionate, female love. So far, however, the feminine imagery present in these exhortations is implicit, and the extensive threats of punishment given at the end of Deuteronomy carry no explicit tinge of gender terror.[26]

Gender Violence in Jeremiah and Ezekiel

Jeremiah and Ezekiel intensify Hosea's image of divine-human marriage and sexual shaming. The kingdom of the north, Hosea's home, had been destroyed by the Assyrians, and now Babylonia, another Mesopotamian power, threatened to do the same to the southern kingdom, Judah, which was Jeremiah and Ezekiel's home. As Judah's problems became more intense, so also did the prophets' threats of rape and gender violence.

Jeremiah proclaims God's permanent divorce from God's promiscuous wife, Judah (Jer. 3:1–5). She had been even more promiscuous than her northern sister, Israel (Jer. 3:6–10).[27] Therefore, Jeremiah predicts that God will strip her and remove her wall/crown (Jer. 13:18–22). He does not focus on a reconciliation between God and God's wife. According to him, she is irredeemably polluted. Instead, he predicts that her faithless children, her "sons," will confess their guilt and return to God.[28]

Shortly after Jeremiah, the prophet Ezekiel develops the sexually violent imagery even more in chapters 16 and 23 of his book. If anything, the crises have worsened by Ezekiel's time. The southern kingdom of Judah is poised just before its total destruction. In chapters 16 and 23 of his book, Ezekiel shifts to the imagery of the city, Jerusalem, as woman and draws on every possible resource to depict her as unclean, permanently polluted. According to him, Jerusalem did not become promiscuous but was born that way, just like her pagan parents and wayward sisters, Sodom and the northern capital, Samaria. Though God had sex with her, claimed her as his bride, and clothed her, Jerusalem responded with indiscriminate "harlotry"—seeking other gods and alliances with other nations (Ezek. 16:1–34; 23:1–21). As a result, Ezekiel prophesies that God will allow her lovers to strip her, stone her and cut her to pieces for forgetting God's gracious marriage to her (Ezek. 16:37–43; 23:11–49). By this point, Ezekiel has almost nothing to say about God's reconciliation with his wife.[29] She is too irredeemably polluted. Indeed, Ezekiel so associates female imagery with pollution that his final vision of restoration has no images of a female city or people whatsoever.[30]

Late Isaian Images of Divine-Human Reconciliation

Ezekiel did not have the last word on this divine-human marriage imagery. A few decades after Ezekiel, as Israel was emerging from near-total destruc-

tion by Babylon, a set of anonymous prophets spoke words of encourage-
ment that are now found toward the end of the book of Isaiah. As if to
neutralize the earlier prophecies from Hosea to Ezekiel, these anonymous
prophets focus exclusively on God's promise to take the community of Israel
back as wife. In a text addressed to the Israelite people in exile, one promises
that God will marry them and liberate them from captivity:

> Fear not, you shall not be shamed;
>> Do not be ashamed, you shall not be disgraced.
> For you shall forget the shame of your youth,
>> And you will not remember any more the dishonor of your widow-
>> hood.
> For he who made you will marry you,
>> Yahweh of armies is his name.
> The holy one of Israel will buy you free,
>> He is called the god of all the earth. (Isa. 54:4–5)

So far, it sounds as if the earlier wife battering has been forgotten. Yahweh
is finding, marrying, and buying free an Israelite people who had been
enslaved. Yet this is a people who have heard divorce speeches from prophets like Hosea and Jeremiah, and so we see a prophecy of hope addressing
their despair:

> Like a wife who was abandoned and forsaken——
>> Yahweh has called you back.
> Can one cast off the wife of his youth?
>> Says your God?
> For a little while I abandoned you,
>> But with abounding compassion I gather you back in my arms.
> In slight anger, I hid
>> my face from you for a moment.
> But with everlasting loyalty I have compassion on you
>> Says your liberator, Yahweh. (Isa. 54:6–8)

This imagery continues into a portion of the book of Isaiah that is usually
dated after the period of exile (Isa. 56–66). A few small waves of exiles had
returned and were attempting to rebuild the temple and the community to
their former glory. We know from many sources that this task was not easy,
that there were severe conflicts over religious and political issues. In the
midst of this, a prophet added yet another poem about God loving Israel
to the Isaiah tradition, promising even more emphatically that the bad days
were gone forever:

Nevermore shall you be called "deserted"
  Nor shall your land be called "desolate."
Instead you shall be called, "My desire is for her,"
  and your land "married."
For Yahweh does desire you,
  And your land will be married.
Like a young man marries a young woman
  So the one who rebuilds you will marry you.
And as a bridegroom rejoices over the bride,
  So will your God rejoice over you. (Isa. 62:4–5)

Once again, this late text in Isaiah has no memory of Israel having done anything wrong. Instead, the marriage image stresses God's delight in Israel and God's intent to reverse the nation's past misfortunes.

God as Male Beloved?
Israel as Woman?

This survey from Hosea to after the exile helps explain early Isaiah's opening description of God as his "beloved" in the vineyard song with which we started. Some scholars have had trouble interpreting Isaiah's vineyard song as a sexual allegory. One commentator arguing against this approach declares: "No evidence needs to be provided to show that Isaiah is not using the language of a mystic."[31] Yet one does not have to be a "mystic" to image God as a spouse of the people or their land. Ancient prophets, whether mystics or not, saw Yahweh as Israel's passionately jealous husband. Hosea, who prophesied only a few miles away from Isaiah, describes God as Israel's betrayed beloved. A bit later, Jeremiah speaks of God "seducing" and "overcoming" him: "you seduced me and I was seduced; you seized me and I was overpowered" (Jer. 20:7).[32] For prophets like Hosea and Jeremiah, Yahweh could be seen as theirs or their people's male beloved. Israel was Yahweh's often unfaithful lover, punished for her unfaithfulness, hoping to be taken back.

As we have seen, the latest examples of this imagery found in the book of Isaiah are relatively positive. Yahweh takes his wife back and promises never to hurt her again. Yet it is difficult to forget the images of gender terror from prophets like Hosea, Jeremiah, and Ezekiel. In each case, the promise of comfort is linked to a description of the people as a rightfully humiliated woman, lucky to be taken back by her God. How can they be sure that the judgment cycle will not continue, that their God/husband will not again reject them?

Within the texts themselves there is no guarantee that the cycle will not continue. In the next chapter, we will look at the assumptions behind this imagery and what these texts might have to tell us about a way forward.

7
Unromantic Eros

DIVINE–HUMAN GENDER TERROR, RELIGIOUS EXCLUSIVISM, AND LOVE GONE WRONG

> I'd go home and he'd be quiet. It was a very loud quiet. I'd always say, "Are you okay? Is anything wrong?" He'd always say everything was okay, but I knew I was in trouble. Sometimes, the quiet would last awhile—2, 3 days, a week. And sometimes, it would end quickly, with an ugly remark or yelling or worse. But that quiet was like the "quiet before the storm," a signal telling me I had been bad and would be punished.
>
> —Annie

The epigraph to this chapter comes from a woman who survived the cycle of spousal abuse. Unlike the prophetic polemics of the last chapter, we hear from a woman here. She is the human counterpart to the "vineyard" of Isaiah's song. There, Isaiah's "beloved," a vintner, prepares to expose and starve a female vineyard for suspected infidelity. The beloved turns out to be God. Ultimately, in Isaiah (and in Hosea 2), God turns to woo his wife back to him. In the epigraph, however, a woman who has been wooed back describes her wait for a new cycle of violence. The abuser here is her human husband.

In this chapter, we will discuss how we may work with these prophetic gender terror texts. If we accept them, must we affirm their picture of God as an abusing spouse and us as women subject to his "jealous" demands? Given this, can these texts teach us anything about love gone right?

These questions are relatively new. In the past, texts like Hosea were taken as prime examples of the Bible's testimony to God's loving mercy.

cities

Take, for example, the following conclusions regarding Hosea in one of the best and most widely used introductions to the Old Testament:

> Yahweh's "wrath" is not capricious, vindictive, and destructive; it is the expression of a holy love which seeks to break the chains of Israel's bondage and to emancipate them [sic] for a new life, a new covenant. According to Hosea, this new freedom will come only when God acts to destroy the idols in which people place their trust so that the "wife," Israel, may stand naked and humiliated in the presence of her lovers (see Hosea 2:2–13).[1]

This quote, like virtually all such discussions up through the early 1980s, uncritically presents the picture of an unfaithful wife as an image of an idolatrous people. The author does not express discomfort with Hosea's picture of the stripping and public humiliation of this "woman."

More recently, feminist scholars have raised compelling questions about whether texts like Hosea are good for women or, indeed, for men. In the mid-1980s Gracia Fay Ellwood showed how the image of divine-human marriage in Hosea and elsewhere depicts God as a violent husband caught in a cycle of spousal abuse of Israel, his wife: becoming jealous of his wife, violently abusing her, and then wooing her back.[2] At about the same time, Drorah Setel argued that Hosea's negative depiction of female sexuality and his celebration of female degradation involved a "pornographic" caricature of female identity.[3] Still others have shown that such texts force women to adopt the male's standpoint in reading, making them sympathize with and endorse his rage and violence toward "his" woman.[4]

Some have tried—unsuccessfully—to limit the damage. They argue that things in the Bible are different because the promiscuous women it depicts are communal constructs and not real women, while the God who violently responds has far more right to do so than do real men. Nevertheless, the metaphor was built on a presupposition of the legitimacy of male possession of and violence against women. If the male God of the Bible has the right to brutally punish his unfaithful wife in the Bible, it is harder to argue that human husbands do not have the same right as well. The model depends on the legitimacy of gender power, in which husbands—whether human or divine—have specific rights and violent power over their wives.

The problems do not stop there. Not only do these texts negatively depict women and caricature female sexuality. Not only do they violate female readers and function in actual society to legitimize spousal abuse. But the prophets also introduce a larger sexual-theological framework whose image of God and people has profoundly problematic implications, a framework in which God is the most manly man, while the community is subject to him as his (often unfaithful) female spouse.

This system has had long-lasting effects, both influencing male-female relations and warping spirituality. We cannot move beyond it without first recognizing its crucial elements and how this system influences our views of God, sexuality, gender, and other people.

Divine-Human Gender in Ancient Israel and Beyond

As we have seen, the prophets' image of divine-human marriage had many precursors, but their particular version of it involves a major shift in how gender is conceived. Where before human men and women might relate in various ways to male and female deities, the texts just surveyed freeze that relationship into a patriarchal bond between a male deity and his human people/city. Previously, male and female gods married in parallel to male and female humans (with humans sometimes acting out divine marriages). Yet ancient Israel bridged this divine-human divide by positing a marriage between a divine Yahweh and human Israel/Jerusalem.

This meant that gender and divine power were identified on a level they had not been before. Already men had extensive power over their wives and daughters. Already ancient Near Eastern kings echoed male-female language in describing the subjugation of their subjects to their supreme maleness. But the divine-human marriage metaphor extended the gender continuum in a new way up to God. God became the most manly man of all, while all men and women of Israel played the part of "woman" in relation to him.

Thus divinity, power, maleness, and "love" were bound together in Israel.[5] It is difficult to describe exactly how this worked. It is not that maleness became precisely identical with divinity, power with love, maleness with power. Nevertheless, these realms overlapped in subtle ways. In a way that was not true before, being subject to God meant adopting a femalelike stance in a patriarchal marriage.

This meant women's roles were consistent, although oppressively so. Just as they were socialized to be good wives vis-à-vis their human husbands, so also they were required to be good wives to God. In later years, the roles were often melded, so that the New Testament letter of Ephesians tells wives "to be subject to your husbands, as to the Lord." The human men in their lives were to stand in for the ultimate divine "man." In turn, the same text calls on men to "love your wives, as Christ loved the church," acting the part of the divine "men" vis-à-vis their human women (Eph. 5: 22–24).

At the same time, men in this system had to perform an identity switch. At one moment, they were semidivine men vis-à-vis their subject wives, but they also had to act the part of "women" in a patriarchal society vis-à-vis God. To some extent, men were socialized into such a role of submission as children, slaves/servants, or subjects of rulers and other authorities. These metaphors too are used for the human-divine relationship in Biblical texts. Nevertheless, whatever a man's role vis-à-vis such authorities might be, usually he was also a man who "had" (in the sense of semi-ownership) a wife/woman and authority over her.

The gender system was no longer something that encompassed just humans. Now it organized the cosmos as a whole. God, men, and women all stood on a single continuum. Their different positions on this continuum separated them, while the claims of patriarchal love defined their relationships. Women had to offer exclusive, all-consuming love to their husbands (and God). Men had to offer exclusive, all-consuming love to God. And both women and men were to expect and understand when the "man" in their life—whether divine or human—brutally shamed and punished them for failing to be faithful.[6]

Certainly not all relationships of power were equally defined by this gender paradigm. The ancient texts talk frequently of people as "slaves" or "children" of their rulers/masters/gods. Nevertheless, one key indicator that a patriarchal gender-sex paradigm is being applied to the divine-human or other relationship is the extent to which the subjects in the relationship are required to have *exclusive* "love" for the one who has power over them, with unfaithfulness punished by shame and violence. Though the more powerful partner may likewise "love" the less powerful one, this patriarchal gender paradigm mainly focuses on his provision for and protection of her. Mutual love cannot be assumed. Rather, "women" in this system are required to be faithful to their "men," while "men" provide for their "women" *and* shame and brutally punish them for being with others.

This system requires men to respect each other's rights over their women, but a problem arises when a woman opts out of the system and actively seeks love outside her marriage. In chapter 5, we saw the text in Proverbs that warns youths to avoid the "strange woman," who might seduce them while her husband is away, and we have seen many more depictions of female sexuality as chaotic in the Prophets. Within this broadened gender system, such passionate "lawless women" are not only images of moral problems. Their failure to buy into the cosmic gender system calls the whole hierarchy into question. Insofar as power is imaged in such a gendered way, a woman of unruly sexual initiative symbolizes the subordinate person getting out of control, not knowing her place. That is what makes the image of the sexually proactive "adulterous woman" so potent as a symbol of a rebellious Israel—because it accuses Israel of ignoring this broader cosmic hierarchy.

Holy Jealousy

For love is strong as death, jealousy is harsher than the grave. —Song of Songs 8:6

This system trades on a primeval sense of jealousy, which is present in many love relationships but particularly in men's attitudes toward women. Such jealousy is characteristic of animals where the males are not sure of the paternity of the children they are raising. From birds to human men, we see males striving to control the sexuality of females. Across the animal world, males often drive other males away from females with whom they wish to have offspring. This is particularly intense in humans, where the male invests significant effort in providing for and protecting the young of his mate—hoping that he is providing for his own young.[7]

These dynamics are manifest in a widespread sexual double standard in many cultures. While societies have attempted to guarantee to men the paternity of certain children by enforcing virginity on daughters and sexual fidelity on wives, men in such societies, including Israelite and Christian societies, are often free to have sex with unmarried women, usually slaves or prostitutes. Such men jealously guard their wives from competitors and brutally punish their wives for having sex with other men. Meanwhile, wives are urged to tolerate their husbands' sexual infidelity, as long as the husbands keep providing adequately for them and their young.

In this way, most cultures make jealousy a particularly male trait. Clearly, women of ancient cultures also felt jealousy and many do now. Nevertheless, particularly within the ancient world, including Israel, it was men who were socialized to feel such jealousy, it was expressed violently (also a trait particularly connected to men), and such jealousy and its attendant violence were socially sanctioned by the broader society.

This male sexual jealousy is attributed to God in the Old Testament, in both narratives and prophetic texts. The legal texts announce God's intolerance of any competitors for Israel's attentions. In them, Israel is called on to worship God alone and not "go after" other gods. The God of these texts describes other peoples as possible tempters into infidelity and is described as brutally destroying them. When Israel goes after other gods and nations, the Prophets threaten divine destruction, and the narrative texts describe such threats being carried through.

Throughout, "women" are envisioned, whether individual human women or the collective community, through the lens of male anxiety and jealousy. The theological and social efforts of the community go into securing control of such women, ensuring that they do not stray after other lovers and punishing them if they do.

Religious Exclusivism in a Cosmos Dominated by a Male God's Jealousy

If we uncritically adopt the world of these Biblical texts, we—whether biologically women or men—become "women" subject to a masculine deity jealous of his sexual prerogatives. Insofar as our world is chaotic and violent—like the world of the ancient prophets—we interpret that violence as judgment against our infidelity to a terrorizing deity. That deity, despite his passion for us, will not stop at anything, including shaming and violating us, to bring us back to him. Moreover, he loves us with a jealous love. Others who are outside his beloved community fall into only two categories: (a) candidates to be absorbed into the community and (b) potential tempters to apostasy/infidelity.

Many other religious people use erotic imagery to envision the divine-human relationship: Sufi mystics, Hindu devotees of Krishna and Shiva, practitioners of Tibetan tantrism, and so on. Yet these traditions did not develop the theme of jealousy in the way the Bible did. Whereas all of the—largely mystical—world religious traditions focus on the erotic union of the *individual* believer with God, the prophetic traditions of the Old Testament focus on God's marriage with God's entire *community*. This involves at least two unique elements. Rather than using the metaphor of lovemaking to envision ecstasy and union, the prophetic tradition uses models of patriarchal marriage to envision a passionate and jealous divine response to human freedom. Moreover, whereas the other world religious traditions generally focus on the individual believer, the "lover" in the Prophets is generally the community as a whole.

Within the mystical traditions, there is an explicit openness to God having the same kind of ecstatic relationship with multiple believers, but the marriage focus and communal orientation of the Prophets does not allow for such inclusion. Rather, we see a hostility toward non-Israelites precisely in the texts that most focus on the divine-human marriage paradigm, including Deuteronomy, Hosea, Jeremiah, and Ezekiel. These are the texts that use marriage and related (treaty) imagery to call on Israel not to intermarry with foreign nations and fiercely to eliminate any threat to the purity of Israel's devotion to God.

This becomes more intense as Israel comes to believe not only that as a community it must worship Yahweh alone, but that Yahweh is the only true God. Once God is the only God with whom one might be in a beloved relationship, the rest of the world is faced with a decision of whether it is in—that is, part of the beloved community—or out. Hence it should be no surprise that some of the most striking examples of religious intolerance have occurred in "religions of the book" (Judaism, Christianity, Islam), which combine the imagery of sexual jealousy with a belief in monotheism.

These texts join the human tendency toward jealous love with the inclination to solidify feelings of community through excluding others. Nations gain unity through opposing an "enemy." High schools gain unity through opposing a football rival, and friends often deepen their feeling of connection through criticizing an acquaintance. A study that organized children into opposing summer camp groups of "rattlers" and "eagles" found that these groups solidified around depictions of the other group as fundamentally different and bad.[8] Sadly, people often form their social groups through treating excluded groups as bad. Imagine how potent this dynamic becomes when those outside groups are also depicted as potential tempters away from God or rivals for God's love. The Prophets not only push their people toward exclusive love of God, but they encourage the creation of national unity around caricature and exclusion of other peoples, now seen as dangerous lovers.

Thus, we see in ancient Israel the birth of an erotic religious exclusivism. People had long fought over various issues, including ethnoreligious divisions. Humans have fought over issues in areas of the world relatively untouched by Judaism, Christianity, or Islam. Nevertheless, there is something different about such fights in these three religions of the book. Together, they inherited from ancient Israel the idea of one God bound in an exclusive relationship with his people—whether the Jewish people, the church, or Muslim *Umma* (people). Together, they inherited the idea that God's people were called to the sort of love that ancient women were to give their husbands: loving their husbands with all their hearts and resisting all others. Together, they inherited an ambivalence toward people outside that relationship. Judaism has tended to struggle over various forms of separation from non-Jews, while Christianity and Islam have looked toward ultimately incorporating all others into their special relationship with the one God. In each case, the link of the primal emotion of jealousy with the idea of divine-human marriage has produced often explosive results.

This may help us understand the forces of religious fanaticism and violence that manifested themselves in the September 11, 2001, terrorist violence and many other times in world history. This is not just a problem with the misguided idea of religious exclusivism. It is a problem with religious cultures that meld the primal emotion of erotic jealousy with a belief in monotheism. The shadow side of an erotic longing for deep connection is a jealous anxiety about losing that connection. The theology of exclusive, marriagelike love is deeply interwoven with such jealousy and anxiety. We will not see a world free of violent intolerance in Judaism, Christianity, and Islam until leaders in each tradition successfully promote new ways of envisioning intimacy with God, ways that are not plagued with such erotic-religious anxiety.

Summary of the Problem

As we have seen, the broad gender/sex system of prophets like Hosea has significant implications on both human and divine levels. Certainly, its implications for women are acute. Those who endorse this system must at least provisionally endorse its negative depiction of female sexuality and its assumption of husbandly rights to violently control it. Insofar as actual human sexuality is influenced by this system, it is damaged by it.

Moreover, this system subjects the community of God to the same violence. Not only are human women subject to the violence of their jealous husbands, but Israel/Jerusalem is subject to the claims, passion, and violence of its jealous male-husband God. The religious person or community in this system is an unfaithful woman, rightfully abused on occasion by her divine husband. Imagine this as a message addressed to you. You are, at core, bad and impure, as are all women in this system; you are chronically prone to religious adultery. Your prayers for mercy are prayers for relief from this cycle of abuse.

Finally, the world as a whole is organized differently by this theological marriage system, divided as it is between God's community and potential converts/potential tempters. Sometimes the balance in a given era or context shifts toward absorption of the religiously Other into the beloved community through conversion or alliance. At other times the community leans toward destruction of the noncommunal Other. In both cases, the erotic gender code makes it profoundly difficult to encounter the Others on their own terms. The passionate, jealous male God envisioned in this code—whether expressed in narrative or prophecy—has limited patience for the ongoing presence of potential threats to the "love" he shares with his wayward "woman."

Is Go(o)d to Be Found
amidst These Texts?

Given all of this, it is possible that we should just dismiss these prophetic divine-human marriage texts, openly repudiate them, cut them out of our Bibles, and warn our children away from them. They enshrine broken gender relations on the divine level, characterize human apostasy as female promiscuity, and depict God as a divine abuser, who cycles between wrathful strippings of his lover and reconciliation with her. For many people, these texts will be forever unredeemable. Could any competent pastor or rabbi recommend these texts to an abused woman as an image of divine punishment and grace? The answer is almost certainly "no." When working with such people, we can set those texts in social context and balance them with better texts. But sometimes, even when we do this, such texts are still irredeemably harmful.

Divine-Human Marriage as an Image of
God Infected with Postgarden Patriarchy

If we are to find any way forward with these texts, one place to start is to recognize how these prophetic texts are a reflection of the loss of connectedness seen in the garden of Eden. Read in light of what I said earlier about the Eden garden, these prophetic texts witness to the fact that even God has been infected with the patriarchy that God proclaimed on humans. We have already seen how the garden of Eden story depicts male rule over women as a sad reflection of a broader breech in creation. The Eden text also describes the human impulse to hide from God as a reflection of the same breech. Perhaps we can interpret the prophetic impulse to image God as a terrorizing male as part of the same wound.

On a prosaic level, life was so harsh for ancient Israelites that their picture of God as male tyrant was harsh as well. On a mythic level, God "himself" did not emerge from the garden events untouched. God was tragically transformed into/confirmed in being a violent patriarch requiring reformation. This picture of God as patriarchal male is as much a reflection of the divine-human relationship gone wrong as the patriarchal males this God appoints over women (Gen. 3:16). Even the Biblical God is not immune from the virus of violence and patriarchy.

Prophetic Texts as Testimony
to the Destructive Side of Love

These prophetic divine-human marriage texts testify to the fact that love is not always good. They depict a love relationship characterized by hierarchy, not mutuality; terror, not tenderness; betrayal and jealousy, not trust. Though ancient, the picture of divine-human marriage in these texts is reminiscent of all too many life-damaging relationships in the present world. To be sure, gender violence is not as sanctioned as it once was. Nevertheless, spousal abuse is still a widespread problem in North America and abroad, and jealousy and betrayal remain persistent realities in many people's lives.

Meanwhile, it is tempting to romanticize love, including sexual love, arguing that if it is pure enough, uncorrupted by patriarchy or repression, such love is always good. Strong streams in our society encourage such a view. Think of sayings like "love is the answer" and "all you need is love." And we see reflections of such romanticism in many scholarly studies of the garden of Eden story and the Song of Songs, in which writers—myself included—have exclaimed about the pure, mutual love to be found there. This love is seen as a balance to the abusive love depicted in the Prophets.

We will turn soon to the benefits of such affirmations of love, especially for groups such as gay and lesbian people, whose sexuality has been systematically stigmatized. Yet I am reminded of the instances in which erotic love, even with the best of intentions, does not always build up, but also destroys people. We might wish that erotic love in its purest form only brought the best for our beloveds, but many who love find themselves joined to another by an almost organic bond, a bond that can be broken only with profound pain. When the relationship ends, the breaking of that bond can be catastrophic. Such agony is also part of the experience of love, not just the happiness of anticipated/fulfilled desire. To some extent, all love is imperfect. All love involves inequity of power, suffering, and missteps.

In this connection, I am reminded of a character, Maya, in a beautiful novel by Kyoko Mori, *Stone Field, True Arrow*, who—after hearing of how her best-friend's husband is leaving her for another woman—thinks back on her mother claiming to be in love for the first time when she left her husband, Bill, to be with her new lover, Nate. Her mother said at the time, "When I'm with him, I feel like we are the only people in the world. Nothing else matters." A month after her mother left, Maya "visited Bill, who looked ten years older, his eyes sunk in their sockets, his hair gone gray. If this is what love does to other people, Maya thought then, love should be outlawed. . . . even if feelings blow across the horizon, as large and unpredictable as tornadoes, people should know when to take shelter and wait out the disaster."[9]

Maya, by the way, is on her way toward opening up to love. Nevertheless, these reflections are right in suggesting that forms of erotic desire are like atomic forces—potentially harnessed for good, but also easily able to explode and overturn lives. Love is no guarantee of good.

Death-Dealing Desire

The Biblical texts we have been discussing criticize anyone loving anything earthly as if it were God. The book of Deuteronomy calls on people to love God with all their heart/mind, life force, and might (Deut. 6:5). Prophets like Hosea and Jeremiah judge Israel for loving material images of God, the ancient worship of things called "idolatry." Idolatry came to designate trusting other gods or nations to provide the protection and gifts that only God could give.

Such idolatry is present today in other forms. Many people love things with "all their heart/mind, life force, and might": alcohol, romance, work, gambling, and even sex. They give up who they are, their values, and their future for the thing to which they are addicted. They sacrifice more and more things to this idol—money, time, friendship, moral values like honesty and empathy, and eventually career, health, financial security, and other goods in life. Ironically, even the loved/worshiped thing itself—such as sex—can lose its luster if it is used to fill an ultimate need it is not suited to satisfy. For example, it takes more and more alcohol or other drugs to get the same fix. As a result, there is a progression in the bondage to a drug, sex, or any other contemporary "idol," as a person seeks more and more of the thing they crave in order to get the same charge from it. There are ways that groups can be stuck in such idolatry/addiction too. Certainly, many outside the Euro-American West are struck with our preoccupation with ever-increasing consumption, no matter what the cost or consequence for the environment.[10] This too is love gone wrong. It is an example of a broader eros going bad. Any time you put your passion into something or someone transitory, you open yourself to addiction or loss. This is what Maya in *Stone Field, True Arrow* is responding to when she thinks, "if this is what love does to other people, . . . love should be outlawed."

Many religious and philosophical traditions have done just that: outlawed or discouraged love. The Platonic philosophic tradition especially (and its heirs) has dealt with this problem by denigrating the love of transitory things and elevating the love of the eternal. So also, the Buddhist tradition advocates achievement of freedom from suffering (dukka) through the disciplined loss of attachment to things. And these are just two ways that eminent ancient traditions have coped with the reality that a life lived with love can go horribly wrong.

The Biblical tradition, particularly the Hebrew Bible, holds love of God and love of things *in tension*. On the one hand, the prophetic traditions sharply critique idolatry—loving something earthly as if it were God—and proclaim its destructive consequences. On the other hand, the early creation stories and the Song of Songs celebrate the richness of love. The Biblical tradition is fully aware of how people can become compulsively bound to things, loving some things (or people) too much. The Prophets describe how people and communities can be broken by such idolatry. Although the prophets' image of the consequences of such idolatry is faulty (God as righteously violent husband), their insight into the destructiveness of such bondage is sound. At the same time, the Bible never lets go of its image of humans as lovers, made in God's bodily image, created for connection to each other.

Christianity often has dealt with this tension by denying earthly desire. Yet suppression of desire all too often contributes to its emergence in compulsive and twisted forms. Dieters often have the most trouble eating healthily. One of the largest groups of alcoholics is those people brought up in homes where alcohol was completely forbidden. This is true for sex too. Those brought up in sexually repressive homes often have the most trouble living honest and healthy sexual lives. Intense sexual denial breeds pornography. Certainly not all of the world's sexual problems can be blamed on repression. That was a mistake of the 1960s and 1970s. Nevertheless, the denial of desire creates many of the problems it is intended to prevent.

The Prophets

Looking back, the prophetic divine-human marriage texts help us see a multitude of ways that love can go wrong. They counter contemporary tendencies to romanticize eros. They witness to the often tragic, painful, and even evil side of love. They can prod us to identify ways in which we, as individuals and society, love things other than God with all of our hearts, souls and minds. And these prophetic texts suggest that God—or our picture of God—is not immune. Even God can be infected with the same virus of violence and patriarchy with which we humans are infected on the other side of the Eden garden.

Is there a way to move beyond this picture of love gone wrong? The broader Biblical tradition suggests one way forward, one that avoids the either-or of much religious tradition. Texts like the creation story and others affirm human desire, and they occur in a Bible that ultimately calls on Israel to "love Yahweh, your God, with all your heart, life force and might" (Deut. 6:5). So also, in the New Testament, when Jesus is asked about what the greatest commandment is, he answers with two commandments of love (Mark 12:28–31).[11] First, he recites Deuteronomy's call to love God with all your heart, soul, mind, and strength, and then he adds the call from Leviticus to "love your neighbor as yourself" (Lev. 19:18). Put together, texts like these suggest that we need not choose between earthly passion and spirituality. Rather than completely affirming or denying our desire, we could set our earthly loves in the context of a broader and deeper passionate connection to God. Earlier I suggested defining *eros* in a broad way, as the core longing of a person for deep connection. Now I am proposing that such eros be grounded first and foremost in a love of God strong enough to provide direction for other loves.

If we were to cultivate such a deeper love for God, what more powerful symbol for an all-encompassing longing than the image of erotic connection? To be sure, our associations with sexually erotic imagery may be mixed, depending on our own experience of sexual violence and intimacy. Yet human cultures through the ages have found no other metaphors with such potential to image the deepest and most intense experience of union that anyone could hope to achieve. This is the grounding of erotic mysticism in Hinduism, Sufism, and other world traditions.

That said, let us be clear: the specifics of the prophetic texts are not loving. Though they depict an erotic God, this God is an abusive male who is filled with jealousy. He images the worst in the cosmos and elicits the worst in us. Though the Prophets depict some sort of love relationship between God and God's community, the relationship is too abusive to be helpful. We must ask ourselves: just how evocative of love is the picture of a male God stripping God's people/wife naked, displaying her before others, starving her, divorcing her and disowning the children, hacking her into pieces, or burning her? How interested should men or women be in taking on the sexual/spiritual identity of such a woman humiliated and punished for breaking the double standard of a patriarchal culture? Even if one looks at the later passages, which promise redemption, they only work as promises to a wife, a community, who was rightfully shamed and punished earlier.

We must look elsewhere. We must look in the tradition for a picture of love not so dominated by violence, in which God can be male or female, an evocative drama of love that we might wish to enter.

Luckily, the Bible has *multiple* pictures of sexual eros. So often people presuppose that the Bible has only one perspective on these matters, or that ancient Israel worked with just one set of rules. But as we will see, both Israel and the cultures around it had divergent depictions of sexual love. These depictions found expression in different sorts of texts. On the one hand, there were the dominant mythic and legal systems, often oriented around issues of honor and reproduction. Much of the Torah and the Prophets—the rules and divine-human marriage—reflect that dominant system. On the other hand, each of these societies has a major body of love poetry, which expresses a different vision of eros, men, and women. We turn to those different visions now.

III

The Garden of the Song of Songs amidst the Writings

8

Other Gardens

WOMEN'S WORLDS AND ANCIENT
LOVE POETRY

Patience brought no fulfilled wishes,
I wearied and hope's door closed.
                    —Bedouin woman's lament

So far, we have explored a set of perspectives on eros in the Torah and the Prophets, perspectives that focused on the rights of "men" (whether God or human males) and the link of sex and reproduction. The main exception was the garden creation story in Genesis 2.

This chapter begins our search for an alternative vision of love later in the Bible. We will see how an apparent consensus on issues like this can be misleading. Just as people in our society do not all agree on sexual issues, so ancient peoples disagreed as well. On one level, it might seem as if the Bible or another ancient culture had a single perspective on eros: male-centered, focused on having children, and so on. Yet this is not true, especially for cultures like Israel's, which preserved different spheres for men and women.

Insofar as we might be tempted to assume that the Bible says only one thing about eros, we need to tune our ears to the *different* voices in these ancient cultures. People are all too prone to think that a given ancient culture had only one perspective on these issues. When one turns to the Bible, this temptation is even more pronounced. Sometimes people read the Bible as presenting a system of values that they like: for example, family-centered and emphasizing monogamy. Others read the Bible as all-oppressive, presenting only patriarchal, violent images of sex. The Bible still has such importance in our culture that many cannot hear the diversity within it.

This chapter prepares us to hear the various voices in the Bible as truly different. We will see how cultures around Israel preserved divergent visions of love and gender. These ancient, alternative visions will sensitize us to the truly alternative view of love in the Song of Songs. They highlight the way that ancient love poetry often involves an intricate interweaving of human and divine elements, the sexual and the spiritual. Finally, our look at these ancient love poems will show how the Song of Songs is part of a stream of ancient visions of love, visions often centered not on the world of men but on the world of women.

Veiled Sentiments: The Discovery of Hidden Songs among the Egyptian Bedouin and Others

Before turning to those ancient love literatures, let us consider the discovery of alternative women's songs in more recent societies, particularly societies that preserve separate spheres for men and women. The song quoted at the outset of the chapter comes from just such a society, the 'Awlad Ali Bedouin, who live in Egypt.

Lila Abu-Lughod, an anthropologist, heard the song used as the epigraph to this chapter in the middle of a two-year stay with the 'Awlad Ali people, during which she observed their lives and taped their poetry. As part of her study, she taped hours of women's songs, yet it was this song ("patience brought no fulfilled wishes") that women of the tribe asked to hear over and over. It began an exchange between two women who were sewing a tent together. One woman, 'Aziza, had sung the song to express her sorrow at being abused and eventually divorced by her husband and living with a poverty-stricken brother. She did not write it. It was an old *ghinnaawa* poem, which expressed her deepest feelings. Her friend replied with another *ghinnaawa* song about replacing love with patience. 'Aziza answered with a poem about how memories last. Her friend replied with another such poem, this time about forgetting those who cause pain.[1] At every point, these women were singing songs that had long preceded them. But the traditional poetry expressed their most personal feelings.

It took Abu-Lughod quite a while to decipher the significance of these brief poems. The honor-oriented, dominant culture of the Bedouin is quite hostile to expressions of sorrow or vulnerability. Those who openly express pain suffer social consequences. Members of the group strive to present an appearance of endurance and resolve to each other. This is all that most outside observers see.

Yet, after living for months with the group, Abu-Lughod discovered that many, particularly women, express deep feelings through traditional poetry. Like 'Aziza and her friend, they sometimes converse with each other by way of these short poems, poems that are often connected to larger heroic epics esteemed by the group. Sometimes, men and women use such poems while courting. Abu-Lughod was told that sometimes lovers use such poetry to express their desire for each other. In all such cases, traditional poetry offers a way to sing one's emotions in the form of words written by others. It is often interdependent with the values of the dominant culture, affirming the suffering people have gone through to uphold those values, even as the poetry violates some of the values of that culture in bringing pain and passion to expression.[2]

Abu-Lughod's work is important because it is one of the best demonstrations of the way seemingly monolithic cultures often contain multiple microcultures. In the late 1960s, anthropologist Elizabeth Fernea discovered an entire world of women's gatherings and discourses in a small Iraqi village, a world that had been completely invisible to her anthropologist husband, Richard Fernea.[3] This was followed by many other studies that documented women's networks and women's cultures in gender-segregated Muslim cultures.[4] Often these networks and cultures produce alternative discourses about love, sorrow and gender. Anthropologist Unni Wikan documented how women of Oman have consistently different ideas about honor from that of the broader, male, "honor-shame" culture often encountered in other studies.[5] Kaveh Safa-Isfahani found Iranian women engaging in folk dramas that mocked their husbands and confronted the problems of their lives.[6] Teri Joseph documented how teenage Riffian Berber girls sing daring songs in the liminal situation of their wedding celebrations.[7] Such gender diversity in a culture is hardly limited to the modern muslim world. John Winkler found traces of similar alternative female discourses about sexuality and power in ancient Greek traditions.[8]

Cultural Complexity in Ancient Israel and Elsewhere

Modern examples like Abu-Lughod's are helpful because we cannot send an anthropologist to ancient Israel to explore the secret songs of love. We must content ourselves with clues hidden amidst a literature gathered and sifted by those in power. But having read the work of Abu-Lughod and others, we can look harder for traces of such diversity in ancient cultures. Like the cultures studied by Abu-Lughod and others, ancient Israel appears monolithic at first. So far, I have been discussing the sort of sex and gender rules that would have impressed an outside observer, rules focused on reproduction and male/God rights. But might there be more? Indeed, might the cultural diversity in ancient Israel be based in a difference between women's and men's discourses? Abu-Lughod's study suggests that, though men sometimes sing *ghanaawy*, it is women who are the primary singers of feeling among the 'Awlad Ali Bedouin. Other studies have shown that women's discourses often contrast with male values particularly on topics of gender roles and sexual morality. To be sure, men's and women's discourses overlap with each other and interlink. They are not completely separate. Yet Abu-Lughod's and other studies suggest that, particularly when it comes to issues of sexuality and gender, societies like Israel's are more complex than they appear.

This picture of hidden conversations is important because it keeps us from avoiding a typical oversimplification of the Biblical picture of sex. Those who cherish the Bible most all too often want it to say only one thing on a given subject. Many will say it is critical of various sexual behaviors. Others will argue that it is more affirming of sex. In either case, people are seeking a single set of norms by which to judge modern behavior. That is a temptation of people who read the Bible as Scripture.

As we will see, both ancient Israel and the cultures around it were complex. Alongside the major chords of the dominant cultures, there were other melody lines played by subgroups within those cultures. Mythic images of gender terror and reproductive sex contrasted with more tender and sensual love poetry. As in the case of the Bedouin studied by Abu-Lughod, these different perspectives on sexuality were not wholly separate. They overlapped and were probably interdependent in complex ways. Nevertheless, they were distinct.

This pluralism is easier to see initially in the non-Biblical cultures of Egypt and Mesopotamia. We are not as tempted to depict these two cultures as saying only one thing about sexuality. People are not prone to seek a single perspective on eros in ancient Egypt or Mesopotamia. We do not read the love songs of these ancient cultures for a single "word of God."

As we will see, both ancient Egypt and Mesopotamia were complex like the 'Awlad Ali Bedouin studied by Abu-Lughod. Both cultures have a dominant discourse about sex amidst the public monuments of the culture, but both also have an alternative discourse about sex in love poetry. In both cases, this alternative discourse about sex is particularly connected to women, whether priestesses or female singers. Finally, the love poetry of both ancient cultures parallels specific aspects of the Song of Songs in the Bible.

Sacred Marriage and Other Love Poetry in Ancient Mesopotamia

We start with love poetry from ancient Sumer, a set of city-states in southern Mesopotamia (now Iraq). Much scholarship about ancient love poetry has focused on the Sumerian rite of "sacred marriage," which was celebrated for a few centuries leading up to 2000 B.C.E. In this rite, a king, representing the god Dumuzi, would have sex with a priestess, representing the goddess of love, Inanna. Toward the end, the priestess would bestow a blessing on the king, proclaiming him "eligible" for victory in combat, rule on the throne, and a long life. This royal blessing appears to have been a main point of sacred marriage in ancient Sumer. Contrary to older scholarship, sacred marriage did not stimulate fertility in general. Instead, the rite was focused on the king.[9] By being accepted as the divine spouse of Inanna, the king gained blessing and legitimacy.

Most interesting for us are texts that give a script of what the stand-ins for Dumuzi, and Inanna and a chorus say to each other during such a ceremony. The give and take between the lovers and their praise of each other anticipate a similar give and take in the Song of Songs. For example, one text opens with a choir of women, who speak in the Sumerian *emesal* dialect (a women's dialect) and describe how a man is arriving at a woman's house: "When the moonlight has entered its 'house,' when the stars have become small (lights) in their 'houses,' . . . Then you draw the bolt from the door to come to the girl." Next, the lovers great each other with the family epithets—"brother" and "sister"—that are used throughout the Near East:

Man: My sister.

Woman: My sweet, my beloved.

Man: My first spouse.

Woman: My brother of fairest face.

A few lines later, the woman praises the man's body as if he were a statue, and the man replies with the invitation "Come, my beloved sister" and adds (with typical Sumerian sexual explicitness) "like her mouth, her vulva is sweet." The text ends with the woman's wish for the man/king to have a long reign.[10]

Other sacred marriage texts emphasize the importance of a garden as a site of loving, a major theme of the Song of Songs. For example, one text, "The Manchester Tammuz," starts with a description of how Dumuzi "brought joy into the garden, into the garden of apple trees he brought joy, into the garden of grapes he brought joy." After the lovers praise each other and Dumuzi brings offerings, Inanna cries out: "Let me go, let me go, to the garden let me go! Me, the lady, let me go, let me go to the garden. . . . in the garden dwells the man of my heart!"[11] The text goes on to describe the joining of their families and Inanna's final blessing on Dumuzi/the king that we have seen in the other texts.

Though actual kings probably stopped participating in this rite about 1900 B.C.E.,[12] it continued to be celebrated throughout Mesopotamia for more than another millennium.[13] There are even isolated references to sacred marriage rites in Persia (2 Macc. 1:13–17) and Egypt.[14] By this point, however, both the ritual and the players are different.[15] For example, several texts describe how the scribe god, Nabu, and his consort, Tashmetu (1) visit a "bedroom" and have sex there; (2) move out of the bedroom either alone or together; and (3) go to a garden. Though the king was occasionally present, he did not consistently play the part of Nabu or other male gods.[16] Instead, priests or priestesses had statues play the parts of the two deities. In addition, these texts do not end like the others with the goddess blessing the king. Instead, these rituals ensure blessing for the king by having Tashmetu become intimate with Nabu and intercede for the king with Nabu. A king in one text describes Tashmetu to Nabu in this way: "Tashmetu, the great lady, your beloved spouse, who intercedes [for me] before you in the gentle bed, who never ceases demanding you to protect my life."[17]

Despite the move from persons to statues, these later sacred marriage texts have the same give and take, the same garden setting, and other characteristics that parallel the Song of Songs. For example, a Mesopotamian text from around the time of the Bible parallels the Bible in having the female (Tashmetu) invite the male (Nabu) to join her under "the shade of the cedars" (Song 1:17) before calling on him to adorn her:

My lord, put an earring on me,
let me give you pleasure in the garden!
[Nabu] my lord, put an earring on me,
let me make you happy in the tablet house.

Nabu replies, "My Tashmetu, I will put on you bracelets of carnelian!" and then praises her:

Let me provide a new chariot for you . . .
whose thighs are a gazelle in the plain!
whose ankle bones are an apple of Siman!
whose heels are obsidian!
whose whole being is a tablet of lapis lazuli!

Tashmetu enters the bedroom, bathes, and dresses. Upon her emergence, the chorus tells Nabu, "Thither, ask, ask, question, question!" and he asks her, "For what are you adorned, my Tashmetu?" She replies, "So that I may go to the garden with you, my Nabu," and she goes on to say, "Let me go to the garden, to the garden." In the following lines, both deities wish to see "the plucking" of their lover's "fruit."[18]

So far, I have been concentrating on texts about divine marriage, but there are other texts that focus more on human passion. Take, for example, one woman's invitation to King Shu-Suen (Shulgi's son) to come water her "lettuce" or "wool":

My "wool" being lettuce he will water it,
it being box lettuce will water it
and touch the *dubdub* bird in its hole! . . .
Let him come! Into my "wool," it being the most pleasing
   of lettuces,
I shall with arousing glances
induce the brother to enter
I shall make Shu-Suen—all ready—
show himself a lusty man,
Shu-Suen to whom my [allure] be without end!
[Shu-Suen, whose allure to me] will [never cha]nge![19]

There is little in this poem about marriage, royal blessing, or divinity. Instead, this and several other love poems focus on the woman's erotic passion for the king[20] or (later) human passion in general.[21]

   This is not to say that one can sharply distinguish secular and sacred love in ancient Mesopotamia. Poems about human love draw on the dialogue form and other themes from sacred marriage poetry. There are some dialogue songs of Inanna that presuppose the sacred marriage rite and mention gods, but do not appear to have functioned in the cult. In these poems, the divine characters do not act out a ritual, give blessings, or otherwise exercise their divine power. Instead, the poems elaborate possible subplots to the famed marriage of Inanna and Dumuzi: Dumuzi's sister tells him of how Inanna aches for his love, Inanna unknowingly taunts her future husband when he comes to call on her, and we hear of the delicate attempts of

Inanna's brother to break the news of the wedding to her.[22] In these texts, the ancient sacred marriage idea and the deities in them serve as a framework for a drama of love in which gods act the parts of humans. In ancient Mesopotamia, human love poems often echo divine love, while some divine love poems image human as much as divine love. Divine and human eros interpenetrate each other.

These Mesopotamian love poems provide a distinctive, perhaps particularly female, perspective on sexuality that contrasts with depictions of sexuality elsewhere in Mesopotamian literature. Recent studies have argued that many of the earliest songs were written by Sumerian women and that almost all of them were meant to present a women's voice regarding love and sexuality.[23] We know that some women in Sumeria could write. One of the most famous Inanna hymns is attributed to the priestess Enheduanna.[24] Indeed, most of the Sumerian love texts are particularly connected to the cult of Inanna, a cult in which priestesses played a prominent role. Furthermore, women were known as singers in ancient Sumer. The Dumuzi character in one love dialogue seems to presuppose such a link of women and song when he urges Inanna to tell her parents:

> My girlfriend was strolling with me in the square,
> to the playing of tambourine and recorder she danced with me,
> our sad songs were sweet—she crooned to me—
> the joyous ones were sweet—and time went by.[25]

Perhaps this link of women and song is why all but one of the published Mesopotamian love songs feature a prominent female voice, and almost half of them are exclusively in a woman's voice. To be sure, some love poetry was spoken by men, especially in later periods, which lack any documentation of female authors. Nevertheless, because later periods preserve the themes of earlier literature, even later love poems are often strikingly informed by the different, woman's voice of earlier literature.

Whatever the amount of love poetry actually written by women, Sumerologist Jerrold Cooper argues that it offers an unusually female perspective on sexuality.[26] Building on cross-cultural studies of female fantasies, Cooper argues that the focus on interior feelings and relationships in Sumerian love poems reflects ancient female sexual inclinations. In contrast, dominant Mesopotamian myths and incantations correlate with ancient male sexual fantasies. They focus on the phallus and reproduction, describe sex in a graphic and perfunctory way, and often link sex with power. For example, several myths describe how Enki, the god of sweet waters, masturbated to produce the Tigris and Euphrates rivers, dug irrigation ditches with his penis, and impregnated the goddess Ninhursag, before raping the daughters who resulted. In another myth, Enki stimulates human sexual reproduction and then calls on the goddess Ninmah: "Let now my penis be praised and serve as a reminder to you!" This kind of link of sexuality and power occurs in Mesopotamian love incantations for males as well. An incantation for male impotence reads:

> At the head of my bed I have tied a buck!
> At the foot of my bed I have tied a ram!
> The one at the head of my bed, get an erection, make love to me!
> The one at the foot of my bed, get an erection, caress me!

Such imagery for sex contrasts sharply with the depictions of sex in the Mesopotamian love poems. Indeed, even male sexuality is depicted differently in the love poetry. Consider, for example, how much more subtle the Dumuzi of the love poems is than the male of the incantation above. He says to his Inanna:

> Let me spread for you the pure sweet couch of a prince,
> let me loosen your combs for you,
> and let me pass a sweet time with you in joy and plenty!

This is just one of many examples in which love poetry contrasts with the myths. The love poems describe an extended period of foreplay, frequently use evocative rather than explicit terms for body parts (references to the "vulva" are the main exception), and focus on the feelings of the female lover. In contrast to the myths, none of the love poetry ever uses the Sumerian terms for intercourse or ejaculation.

These characteristics lead Cooper and others to conclude that Sumerian love poetry renders a "woman's voice" about sexuality.[27] Although men certainly wrote much of this poetry and expressed their experiences through it, it appears to be unusually influenced by themes characteristic of women's ways of talking about love as seen in a variety of cultural settings. Some of this may be due to the fact that women played an unusually prominent role in singing this poetry, especially in the formative stages of the Mesopotamian love poetry tradition. But the emphasis of love poetry on feelings, desires, and relationships certainly would have spoken to both males and females and been continued by authors of both sexes.

The point of discussing male and female voices here is to anchor and sharpen our insight into the different ways that ancient Mesopotamians talked about love and sex. Though one might be tempted to harmonize these perspectives as the expressions of the same people in different settings, the traces of female (versus male) voices in the different literatures about love suggest that—at least at some point—there were distinctively different perspectives on sex in different subgroups in Mesopotamia. The distinctive language about love in Mesopotamian love poetry is in part because it was more informed by women's experiences and intended to express them.

To be sure, we need to be careful about generalizations about differences between male and female sexual experiences. Men and women like more than one kind of fantasy, and there is a lot of variation among individuals. Linking female sexuality with relationships and feelings can promote pictures of the "virtuous female," which reflect more of the Victorian ideal of the passionless woman than the diverse sexual realities and potentials of actual women. Nevertheless, as Cooper argues, studies of men's and women's sexual fantasies have suggested some long-term, widespread differences in the types of fantasies preferred by men and by women. Insofar as these differences hold, Mesopotamian myths and incantations more closely match the typically male voice. They talk graphically about male body parts and connect sexuality with power and reproduction. In contrast, Mesopotamian love poetry is closer to a female voice, evoking passionate sex in the context of a relationship.

Love Poetry in Ancient Egypt

Ancient Egyptian literature has a similar contrast between myths in a male voice and love poetry that is more evocative of women's experiences and feelings. The examples of the former are more scarce than in Sumeria, but follow similar patterns. In one set of creation stories, the sun god creates the first two gods by masturbating, which begins a process of procreation that continues to the creation of Osiris and other main gods through the intercourse of Nut (the sky goddess) and Geb (the earth).[28] Another myth, the divine contest between Horus and Seth, features a story where Seth pursues a transformed Isis in order to force sex with her and—in one version—later forces sex with his brother Horus.[29] Like their Sumerian counterparts, these Egyptian mythic texts link sex to power and reproduction, and say almost nothing about the feelings of the divine participants.

In contrast, there is a series of about thirty-five Egyptian love songs that elegantly depict the desire of male and (especially) female lovers. Unlike the Mesopotamian sacred marriage texts, these poems are not attributed to divine, or even royal, figures. They are anonymous, evoking the ordinary experience of love, and as in Mesopotamia, women's voices predominate. Poems describing women's passion outnumber poems of male passion by almost two to one.[30]

Women appear to have been the predominant singers of love poetry in Egypt. During the time these poems were written (approximately 1300–1070 B.C.E.), we start to see tomb pictures of naked young women at banquets, often playing instruments for the guests (figure 8.1).[31] These were sensuous events in ancient Egypt. As can be seen in figure 8.2, the guests have incense cones on their heads, are wearing lotus flowers, and are having drinks poured for them. Apparently the tomb pictures were meant to bring renewed vitality or diversion to the deceased occupant(s) of the tomb. Several are labeled as scenes of "entertainment."[32]

The Egyptian love songs appear to have been sung by young women at such banquets. Indeed, several of the Egyptian love song collections are labeled as "songs of entertainment," using the same term for *entertainment* that is used to label the banquet scenes. One collection of love songs even includes a harper's song to encourage merriment at the banquet, calling on the hearers to listen to the singing women:

Put songs of singing girls before you,
Cast aside all evil,
and think of joy.[33]

Moreover, these young women probably specialized in songs of love. Hathor, the goddess of love, was the patron of female singers, and several depictions of the young female musicians show them bearing the tattoo of Bes, a deity closely associated with Hathor, sexuality, and reproduction. Likely these are the "songstresses of Hathor" to which many texts refer.[34]

Many of these motifs come together in the love songs of the Chester Beatty Papyrus. The manuscript includes a copy of the myth that was discussed in chapter 4, where Hathor revives Osiris by revealing her genitals to him. But here we are interested in a cycle of love poems on the same papyrus that are attributed to a "great female entertainer." The first song opens with a man praising a woman using the same "sister" epithet that we saw in Mesopotamia:

One alone is my sister, having no peer:
    more gracious than all other women.
Behold her, like Sothis [a star] rising
    at the beginning of a good year:
Shining, precious, white of skin,
    lovely, the look of her eyes,
Sweet, the speech of her lips,
    She has not a word too much.
Long of neck, white of breast.[35]

Fig. 8.1. Musicians at banquet. From the tomb of Nakht, mid-fifteenth century B.C.E. Photograph courtesy of the Metropolitan Museum of Art (15.5.19d).

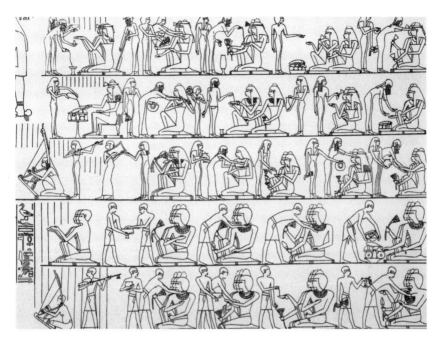

Fig. 8.2. Rejoicing at Thebes on the return of Rekhmire from greeting Amen-hotef II. Detail from a banquet scene in the tomb of Rekhmire, fifteenth century B.C.E. Source: Norman de G. Davies, *The Tomb of Rekh-mi-Re at Thebes* (New York: Plantin, 1943), plate 26.

The man's praise of her beauty continues down to her thighs and lovely walk. She then replies by describing her love for him and how she wishes her parents and others would affirm their love:

> My brother torments my heart with his voice,
>   He makes sickness take hold of me;
> He is neighbor to my mother's house,
>   And I cannot go to him!
> Mother is right in charging me thus
>   "Give up seeing him!"
> It pains my heart to think of him,
>   For love of him has captured me. . . .
> O brother, I am decreed for you
>   by the Golden One [Hathor].
> Come to me that I may see your beauty!
>   May father and mother be glad!
> May all people rejoice in you together,
>   rejoice in you, my brother![36]

The stanzas go on with the woman and man aching for each other and sometimes invoking Hathor, the "Golden One." Yet, unlike the Sumerian poems, they do not speak directly to each other. Indeed, this poem ends with the lovers apart and ill from desire. The man's and woman's words are dueling monologues, showing the banquet audience how the love of one lover is balanced by the love of the other.

This and other Egyptian poems share striking themes with their Mesopotamian counterparts and the Biblical Song of Songs. These include:

The lovers address each other often as "brother" and "sister."

They mention their mothers frequently as intermediaries for their love (and never mention fathers by themselves).

They often describe their beloved as the "love" of their "heart."

They occasionally praise their lover's body as if it were a statue.

Lovemaking is "sweet" as "honey."

The garden is a prominent place for love.

Yet there is at least one way in which the Egyptian poems are even closer to the Biblical Song of Songs than are the Mesopotamian poems: the Egyptian love poems focus on the drama of human desire, rather than the fulfillment of semidivine love. To be sure, all of Egyptian society was religious, and so the divine permeates human love in various ways: Hathor is invoked; the primeval flood waters are a setting for love; a woman describes her man as resembling Re, the sun god ("my god, my lotus"); and the man talks of adorning Menqet, the goddess of beer.[37] Nevertheless, despite this interpenetration of divine and human in Egyptian love poems, the lovers in these poems are never actually deities or even royalty, and there is no parallel to the royal blessing that concluded many Sumerian sacred marriage texts.

Indeed, in the Egyptian songs, marriage is only anticipated. Lovemaking rarely happens, and when it happens, the lovemaking is described in elliptical terms. Even children are rarely envisioned in these poems, though they were a regular consequence of sex in a world without reliable birth control. The poems, after all, are "entertainment." They are a fantasy of love, not an accurate picture of it. Rather than emphasizing the reality of family life, these poems are far more focused on the drama of early love: the passion for a lover, the drive to overcome all obstacles to love, and the pain of separation.

Ancient Israel and These Alternative
Visions of Love

So far, we have focused on alternative visions of love in cultures outside of
Israel, visions often hidden to the initial observer. I described how anthropologist Lila Abu-Lughod took months to discover the world of passionate
women's poetry among the 'Awlad Ali Bedouin. Before that, she was more
exposed to the dominant, male-oriented honor culture of the tribe. So also,
the Egyptian and Mesopotamian love poems show that there was more to
love in the ancient Near East than one might have supposed from studying
the myths of each culture. Though the love poems link to the broader
culture, they present a dream of love embedded in relationship and driven
by desire. Moreover, just as the alternative discourse that Abu-Lughod discovered was dominated by women, both the Mesopotamian and Egyptian
poems appear to express women's experiences, and many were written or
performed by women.

Such alternative discourses are crucial in helping us search for and recognize potential alternative discourses about love in Israel. Those who seek
a single norm from the Bible often take the dominant sexual ethos of ancient Israel or the early church and assume that one or the other is the sole
Biblical picture of eros. Yet the materials we have looked at in this chapter
suggest a more complex view. Although major parts of the Bible affirm a
sexual-religious system in which men claim exclusive power over their
women's sexuality and God claims exclusive power over the devotion of
God's people, we have seen that such broad affirmations in other cultures
are often only part of the story. If we look, we may find resistance and
alternatives hidden in orally transmitted songs or filtered through the dominant myths.

In the case of Israel, our main source is the Bible, a written text. Yet
even here we can find traces of alternative visions of love. Might ancient
Israel have had an alternative discourse about love like that found in other
cultures? Might it have featured prominent female singers or at least a prominent female voice?

Certainly, both the art of ancient Palestine and the Bible itself suggest
that women were the main musicians in ancient Israel.[38] A passage in Ezekiel even suggests that Israel knew of the sort of entertaining love songs we
saw in Egypt. In it, God predicts that the prophet Ezekiel will experience
the same lack of reaction from his audience that a love song would:

> My people will come to you as to a public gathering and sit before
> you. They will listen to your words but not do them. For they have
> a taste for erotica. . . . As far as they're concerned you're just a [singer

of] erotic songs, who sings nicely and plays well. So they'll hear your words—but do them they will not! (Ezek. 33:31–32)[39]

Here Ezekiel seems to understand Israelite love songs as being the same sort of entertaining erotic fantasy as the Egyptian love poems: nice for diversion, but not implemented in real life.

Within ancient Israel, women would have been more likely than men to provide such diversion. Take, for example, a "prostitute's song" that is quoted in Isaiah:

> Take your harp, walk the town,
>   oh, forgotten prostitute!
> Play it well,
>   create many songs,
> so that you will be remembered. (Isa. 23:16)

This text presupposes that prostitutes did not just sell sex, but were also musicians, a probable combination of jobs in ancient Egypt as well.[40] We see the same sort of combination of song and sex in a much later text, Sirach. He includes the following in a series of sexual warnings: "do not dally with a singing girl, or you will be caught by her tricks" (9:4 NRSV). These texts suggest that ancient Israel would have known singing female entertainers of the sort seen in ancient Egypt.[41]

Women, however, are not the only love-song singers recorded in ancient Israel. We already looked in depth at the violent "love song" sung by Isaiah about his vineyard (Isa. 5:1–7). We have not yet discussed another text, which the Bible itself labels as a love song: Psalm 45, which was to be sung to the king at his wedding. In it, a scribe begins by praising the beauty, power, and justice of the king:

> You are the most beautiful among human beings,
>   grace has been poured over your lips,
> Therefore God has blessed you forever.
> Gird your sword to your thighs, Oh hero.
>
> Your throne, oh divine one, stands forever and ever.
> (Ps. 45:2–3a, 6)[42]

The poet then turns to the wedding itself, exhorting the bride to "forget your people and your father's house, and may he desire your beauty, for he is your Lord" (Ps. 45:10–11). The final part of the poem resembles some of the Sumerian sacred marriage ritual texts; the poet describes the bringing of gifts and the procession of the bride and her servants before the king (Ps.

45:14–15). Like those poems, this one ends with a blessing for the king (Ps. 45:16–17).

The depiction of the king as a semidivine figure, the focus on marriage, and the movement of the poem toward a royal blessing all link Psalm 45 with the Sumerian sacred marriage tradition with which we started. As one commentator said, "There is no parallel to Psalm 45 in the OT [Old Testament]—not even anything approaching it."[43] That being said, this is no sacred marriage. Where the goddess was a major figure in all of the sacred marriage texts, the bride here is subordinate to the king and clearly human. This scribe was influenced by non-Israelite traditions, but the resulting text is a thoroughly Israelite poem.

Perhaps within the strict gender system of ancient Israel, it would have been too radical to compose divine love poetry that was close to the goddess/god love poetry of ancient Mesopotamia. Although Israel once may have had a mythic system in which Yahweh was paired with a goddess consort, by the time of the prophets many worked with a gender system in which God's spouse was the people of Israel (or the city of Jerusalem). Within this goddess-absent system, women were even more identified with submission than they were in patriarchal cultures like Mesopotamia. In Israel, being a woman increasingly meant being subject to a divine or human male "lord." In such a culture, few poets would have composed poems describing the mutual love of god and goddess. Existing poems along those lines would have been discarded. This may be why the thoroughly male-oriented Psalm 45 is the only such "sacred marriage" text to have survived.

Be that as it may, we do have some love poetry in the Hebrew Bible that is closer to the female orientation of the love poetry in the ancient Near East: the Song of Songs.

9
Come to the Garden

A WALK THROUGH THE SONG OF SONGS

In the last chapter, we entered the special world of love poetry in the ancient Near East: Mesopotamian songs of royal-divine love and entertaining Egyptian love poetry. Often these love poems feature gardens, whether gardens of lovemaking or the female lover imaged as a garden. Now we enter a different garden, the Biblical Song of Songs.

Like much other ancient love poetry, the Song of Songs presents an alternative vision of love. It links with the garden of Eden story in envisioning humans in a garden of love, but it asserts that the possibility of such eros has not been lost. It parallels motifs from prophetic divine-human marriage texts, but focuses on love between humans. It recognizes the reality of ancient Israelite sexual rules, but envisions a woman and man resisting them. The writings of the Hebrew Bible include other texts that affirm love and passion, including calls for male students to love wisdom (for example, Prov. 8 or Sir. 51), a psalm where the speaker passionately longs for God like a hart longs for ever-flowing streams (Ps. 42), calls to enjoy one's wife (for example, Eccles. 9:9), and other depictions of life's passions.[1] Nevertheless, no text comes close to the Song in providing a sustained poetic exploration of erotic love, a love that breaks out of the spiritual-sexual categories that would bind it.

The following tour uses major sections of the Song to illustrate central themes that are present throughout it. Though there is no consensus on the book's major divisions, most proposals preserve the coherence of a dramatic interchange toward the middle of the book (5:2–6:3), while also orienting themselves around a series of refrains that occur throughout (2:7; 3:5; 8:4).[2] Those will be our place markers as we walk through the Song. After touring the first section (1:2–2:7), we will look at how the Song of Songs heightens its eroticism by depicting desire in an elusive, indirect way. This will prepare us for discussions of the Song's focus on forbidden love, its unique depiction of male and female lovers, and its melding of the lovers with the natural world and with the divine.

Entering the Song: 1:2–2:7

First, let us set the scene. Michael Fox has argued persuasively that the Song of Songs, like the Egyptian love songs, was written to be sung at a banquet. Egyptian depictions of banquets show people drinking, enjoying incense ointment pouring down their heads, and surrounded by lotus flowers, which symbolize vitality and rebirth. From its outset, the Song of Songs is infused with these images: wine, incense, lotuses, and so on. We know that ancient Israelites enjoyed feasting and drinking, and such occasions would be a major event where nontheological love poetry, like the Song of Songs, could be sung. The Song appears to have continued to be popular at such celebrations for many years. As mentioned before, Rabbi Akiba condemned people for singing the Song of Songs in banquet houses as if it were just "one of the songs."[3]

Imagine yourself at such a banquet. You are an ancient Israelite man or woman, probably in your "mature" twenties. Your everyday life is dominated by the labor of cultivating living things, whether crops, livestock, or the large number of children required for an agricultural society. But now you are taking some time out for a banquet. Perhaps someone is getting married, someone important died, or the community is celebrating the change of seasons and the coming of life to the earth again.

There is abundant food and wine, and the scents are incredible: cinnamon, myrrh, cardamom—all the most exotic spices. You and some of your companions may even have put cones of spiced oil on your heads, and these cones are dripping their pungent scents down your body as the banquet proceeds. Then, as a special attraction, the singers arrive, mostly women, maybe a man as well, to perform dramatic love poetry for the festive audience.

The Song of Songs opens with the voice of the female lover, who speaks in more than two-thirds of the book. She begins by addressing a group, saying one of the most famous lines of the song, "Let him kiss me with the kisses of his mouth!" Then, as if impelled by her desire, she turns to her lover and continues:

For your lovemaking is better than wine.
In fragrance, your oils are exquisite.

Fig. 9.1. Ancient Syrian cylinder seal, c. 1750 B.C.E. Source: Figure 24 in Othmar Keel, *The Song of Songs*, trans. Frederick Gaiser (Minneapolis, Minn.: Fortress, 1994). Reprinted by permission.

> Your reputation is poured out oil.
> That's why the young women love you. (Song 1: 2–3)

She goes on, but already the first two verses illustrate how the song moves from speech by each lover *about* the other to speech *between* them. Note also how the poetry engages and awakens the senses: *hearing* of his reputation, *feeling* the intimate touch of his mouth kiss, *tasting* wine, and *smelling* his exquisitely fragrant oils.[4]

The only sense missing up to this point is sight, but that comes soon and repeatedly as the dialogue heats up a little later in chapter 1. The male lover exclaims,

> Oh, you are so beautiful, my friend
> You are so beautiful, your eyes are doves! (1:15)

Here the man is not speaking just of his love's anatomy, but of the associations she and her whole body have come to have for him. Othmar Keel has argued on the basis of images like figures 9.1 and 9.2 that the dove is not only associated with goddesses like Ishtar, but that the dove in these pictures symbolizes the lovemaking that the disrobing goddess is offering the male figures.[5] Thus, the ancient audience may have heard in the lover's words his female beloved has melded partially with the dove, reflecting in her eyes the way she has become an emblem of love and lovemaking for him.

She responds to his praise by echoing his words and speaking of their outdoor bedroom, probably meant to evoke scenes of outdoor lovemaking, lovemaking outside the bounds and limits of normal society:

Fig. 9.2. Ancient Syrian cylinder seal, c. 1750 B.C.E. Source: Figure 25 in Othmar Keel, *The Song of Songs*, trans. Frederick Gaiser (Minneapolis, Minn.: Fortress, 1994). Reprinted by permission.

> Oh, you are beautiful, my love, yes lovely!
>   Oh, our bed is luxuriant leaves,
> The beams of our houses are cedars,
>   Our rafters are cypresses. (1:16–17)

She shifts to speak of herself. Now she is a lotus flower, an Egyptian image of divine/human sensuality:

> I am just a crocus of Sharon[6]
>   A valley lotus. (2:1)[7]

The man echoes her words and intensifies them:

> Like a lotus among thorns,
>   So is my friend among the young women. (2:2)

The woman then uses this pattern to praise him:

> Like an apricot tree among the trees of the wood,[8]
>   So is my love among the young men.
> In his shade I often delighted and lingered,
>   And his fruit was sweet on my tongue. (2:3)

Evoking the banquet setting once again, she tells the audience, "He has brought me to the wine house, and love is in his eyes" (2:4). At this point she shifts to speak to a group of women, calling on them to

Fig. 9.3. Ancient Syrian cylinder seal, c. 1750 B.C.E. Source: Figure 45 in Othmar Keel, *The Song of Songs*, trans. Frederick Gaiser (Minneapolis, Minn.: Fortress, 1994). Reprinted by permission.

Lay me down among fruit clusters,
   Spread me out among apricots.[9]
   For I am faint with desire.
His left arm under my head,
   His right arm embraces me.
I make you swear,
   Oh daughters of Jerusalem,
By the gazelles or wild does,
   To not ever awaken or arouse love[10]
   Until she is ready. (2:5–7)

The feminine gender of the Hebrew *love* ("until *she* is ready") is important because the gazelles and wild does mentioned here are frequently associated with goddess figures in ancient Near Eastern art. This is demonstrated in a number of images that the scholar Othmar Keel has linked with this text, such as the Syrian cylinder seal in figure 9.3, on which copulating gazelles and a nursing doe stand alongside a goddess figure while she offers fruit to a royal figure; another Syrian cylinder seal in figure 9.4, on which a running gazelle is to the right of a disrobing goddess figure; and the goddess figure from pre-Israelite Canaan in figure 9.5, where a goddess breast feeds humans while gazelles feed around her pubic area.[11] This does not mean that the book's audience worshiped a goddess, though we now know that figures like Asherah and Ishtar were prominent in the worship of ancient Israel up to a remarkably late point. Perhaps the author of the Song of Songs merely assumed the audience would know of these associations between a largely

Fig. 9.4. Ancient Syrian cylinder seal, c. 1750 B.C.E. Source:
Figure 46 in Othmar Keel, *The Song of Songs*, trans.
Frederick Gaiser (Minneapolis, Minn.: Fortress, 1994).
Reprinted by permission.

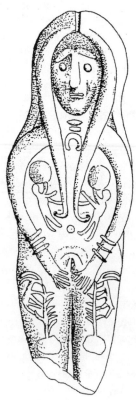

Fig. 9.5. Composite drawing by Hildi Keel-Liu,
1997, based on three fragmentary terra-cotta
plaques from pre-Israelite Canaan, c. 1300–1150
B.C.E. Source: Figure 82 in Othmar Keel and
Christoph Uehlinger, *Gottinen, Götter und
Gottessymbole: Neue Erkenntnisse zur
Religionsgeschichte Kanaans und Israels aufgrund bislang
unerschlossener ikonographischer Quellen*, 4th ed.
(Freiburg, Germany: Herder, 1998). Reprinted by
permission.

abandoned goddess figure and these wild animals. In either case, the effect of the combination of gazelles and wild does with the female-gendered love of the refrain might be paraphrased as follows: "I make you swear, by the signs of the goddess, not to awaken or arouse love, until she is ready."

The rest of the book is unified by versions of this refrain (3:5; 5:8; 8:4), and many other parts of the Song parallel each other in wording and imagery.[12] Also, the characters seem to stay the same, as we hear again of a female lover, a male lover, and the "daughters of Jerusalem." Nevertheless, there is no clear plot or logical sequence. All attempts to create a specific drama from the Song of Songs have failed to gain consensus.[13] Some of this may be caused by the author's use of older love poems, some of which may be alluded to in Hosea and Deuteronomy. But the fractured sequence also keeps the audience from viewing the Song as a completely separate drama of love happening apart from them. This is not just two lovers acting out their own love story. Rather this book is an often illogical sequence of vignettes that offer multiple opportunities for readers to imagine themselves in the Song's poetic world(s).

The Song of Songs as Tease

Last we saw (in Song of Songs 2:7), the lovers were in each other's arms ("his left arm under my head,/ His right arm embraces me"), and their love is so powerful that the lead singer tells the women to beware of ever awakening such a force prematurely. This is about as explicit as the Song ever gets. The man and woman never actually "make it" in this poem. Yet, here, as at so many other points of the Song of Songs, the poetry tantalizes us with the probability of their embrace. She yearns for him to kiss her with his mouth. She exalts his lovemaking over wine. She tells him to take her and run with her, and he brings her into his rooms. She calls on him to join her in dancing, exclaiming "rightly [those young women] love you." The lovers converse back and forth, go out to the garden, and even lie together in close embrace, but the scene fades with a refrain before anything more happens. The poetry soon shifts to another scene, and we are left teased by these evocations of desire.

Indeed, much of the rest of the Song of Songs is a tease. It describes yearning for and celebration of lovemaking without ever clearly describing the lovemaking itself.[14] The woman drags the man to her mother's room before the scene fades again (3:1–5); she invites him to the garden, and he says he has already feasted on it (4:16–5:1), but even here the language of garden, honeycomb, honey, milk, and wine is more evocative than precisely descriptive. Later, the man sticks his "hand" through the "hole" (5:4) and the woman's insides "groan" for him and she "opens" to him (5:4, 6), yet it turns out he was already gone before she opened the door (5:6). By chapter 7, the woman is inviting the man to the garden and promising to give her lovemaking to him (7:11–14), but the poem then immediately fades to another scene where she wishes she could kiss him publicly, but cannot (8:1–2). There is a constant openness of the poetry of the Song to an ecstasy that is beyond language. It invites the reader to dance around that ecstasy.

We do not know exactly why the Song and many like it in the ancient Near East do not get more explicit. Some ancient Near Eastern art certainly does. Perhaps the decorum of a banquet setting dictated against more explicit description. Or perhaps the poet simply wished to focus more on longing than on consummation.

Be that as it may, the evocative reticence of the Song may be uniquely suited to evoking passion within our present context. As mentioned at the outset of this book, our society is prone to an ever-increasing amount of language about sex and images of it. As philosopher Paul Ricouer pointed out, this unveiling of all that is sexual often has the effect of divesting sex of its power rather than enhancing it.[15] After all, it is no accident that— whatever the variations in dress codes across different societies—it is usually the parts of bodies that are covered that are the ones with the most erotic associations. The reverse is also true. The less that bodies are covered—say, at a nudist colony—the fewer the sexual associations with parts of the body that are normally eroticized.

So it is that the Song of Songs, however explicit it will get at times about the man's and woman's bodies, never attempts to tame their sexual union (or our imaginative creation of it) with language. Instead, the Song constantly approaches their lovemaking and fades away, or teases with double entendres. It stokes the fires of erotic imagination, getting explicit enough to get the flames burning, yet not dousing them with the water of description.

In the end, the Song is more about desire than consummation. Again and again the refrain will appear, "Do not ever awaken or arouse love, before she is ready," and the Song ends not with them together, but with her telling him to flee from their garden rendezvous: "flee, my love, make yourself like a gazelle, or a young stag, on the mountains of spices."

Perhaps this focus on longing rather than on the experience of sexual pleasure is one of the things in the Song that made it so adaptable to being reinterpreted in relation to other desires, to eros more broadly conceived. We will return to this topic later as we look at how the Song was reread.

Song of Songs 2:8–3:5: Forbidden
Love That Risks Discovery

A key theme of the next section of the Song is the wildness of the lovers
and the forbiddenness of their longing. This is already anticipated in chapter
1, where the woman proclaims:

> I am black but beautiful,[16]
>   Daughters of Jerusalem,
> Like the tents of Kedar's nomads,
>   Like the tapestries of Solomon.
> Don't stare at my blackness,
>   That the sun has gazed upon me.
> My mother's sons quarreled with me.[17]
>   They set me to keep the vineyards.
>   But my vineyard I have not kept! (1:5–6)

virginity

She is no ordinary beauty, and her desire is not supported by society around
her. Her mention of being "black" after having been put in charge of
vineyards suggests that she faces disapproval for having darkly tanned skin.[18]
Such a tan was often a mark in the premodern world of being part of the
peasant class, which worked outside. Social disapproval of such tanned skin
was as common as modern forms of racism. This woman faces down such
disapproval, asserting her beauty despite the fact that her skin marks her as
part of a social underclass.

Yet there is more. The end of the poem suggests that this woman also
resists the sexual bonds put on her. In honor-focused societies, brothers—
the "mother's sons" here—are often the primary guardians of their sisters'
virginity. If we keep this and the sexual implications of "vineyards" in mind,
the conclusion of the poem gains new meaning: "[My brothers] set me to
keep the vineyards, but my vineyard I have not kept." Her quarreling
brothers may have "set [her] to keep the vineyards," both literally and
figuratively (having her guard her sexuality). She may have been marked
with dark-tanned skin from having been put outside in the vineyards. But
she resists her brothers with her body: "my vineyard I have not kept."
Recall the prophet Isaiah's song about a wayward female vineyard and God's
anger toward her. Here a similarly wayward woman gets to tell her side,
and she proclaims—despite disapproval by others—that she is "black but
beautiful."[19]

As we turn to chapter 2, this female lover sees a wildness in her male
lover as well. He does not face down societal disapproval, but he does
become melded with the wild landscape, becoming one of the stags or
gazelles that were so often associated with the goddess:

The sound of my love,
  Now, he is coming!
Bounding over mountains,
  Springing over hills.
My love is like a gazelle
  or a young stag. (2:8–9)

A move from divine to human has taken place. Where gazelles and stags were associated with the goddess, now this dark and beautiful woman imagines her man as one of those animals coming to her.

Soon he is standing outside the wall, calling on her to leave the restrictions of her house and join him in the springtime landscape, a prime place in the ancient world for illicit lovemaking. She quotes him:

Arise, my friend,
  my beautiful one, and come away.   *, Beloved*
For the winter has passed,
  The cold rains have gone away.
The wild blossoms are here.[20]
  The time of Spring singing has arrived,[21]
  And the cooing of the turtledove is everywhere.
The fig tree sweetens its young fruit,
  And the blossoming vines spread their fragrance. (2:10–13)

In the next stanza, this lover, this stag, envisions her as an animal too, the dove so often associated with eroticism:

Arise, come, my friend,
  My beautiful one, come now!
My dove, in the fissures of the cliff,
  In the hiding place of the crags,
Let me see your face,
  Let me hear your voice.
For your voice is delicious,[22]
  And your face is beautiful. (2:13–14)

At this point, a group, perhaps the "daughters of Jerusalem" chorus, joins the wish for a wild lover.

Catch the foxes for us,
  the little foxes,
Vineyard raiders,
  And our vineyards are in bloom! (2:15)[23]

The "foxes" of which they sing are images in Egypt of great lovers or womanizers.[24] Note that the chorus only wants the foxes caught; they do not want them killed. Where before one woman was not guarding her "vineyard" (1:6), now the "vineyards" of the others are in bloom, and the "foxes" are at large.

Amidst this picture of spreading desire, the woman stakes her claim on her lover, naming him as hers, at least until day breaks upon them and they must return home from their outdoor palace. She calls on him to be her "gazelle" or "young stag," mounting the famous spice mountains of Beter:

> My love is mine, and I am his
>   Who grazes among the lotus flowers.
> Until the day breathes,
>   and the shadows flee.
> Turn, my love, make yourself like a gazelle,
>   or like a young stag
>   on the mountains of Beter. (2:16–17)

These lovers belong to each other, but they do not appear to be married. Most of their meetings take place outdoors, the prime trysting place for unmarried lovers in an ancient world with no separate bedrooms, cars, or motels. Though a central part of the poem describes some sort of wedding process (3:6–11), there are still scenes afterward in which the lovers are not yet husband and wife. For example, later in the Song, the man is knocking at the woman's door and trying to persuade her to open the door (5:2). Still later, the woman passionately wishes that he was her brother so she could kiss him in public and bring him home (8:1–2). And the Song ends not with the lovers dwelling together, but with her calling on him to flee (8:14). The man calls the woman "my sister" and "my bride" at one point (4:8–5:1), but the two do not appear to be any more married (or biologically related) than the Egyptian lovers who used similar epithets to express their affection for each other.[25]

This wild longing even impels the woman repeatedly to seek her lover at night, a risky enterprise:

> On my bed night after night[26] I sought him,
>   My true love,
>   I sought him, but did not find him.
> Let me get up now, and go everywhere in the city!
>   In the streets and squares,
>   Let me seek my true love,
>
> I sought him, but did not find him.

> The guards found me,
>   making their rounds in the city.
>   I asked "Have you seen my true love?"
> As soon as I left them,
>   I found my true love,
> I caught him, now I won't let him go,
>   Until I've brought him to the house of my mother,
>   to the room of her that conceived me. (3:1–4)

Hear how the poem shifts from the repeated "I sought him, but did not find him" to the climactic "I caught him, now I won't let him go." Her search for her love is so powerful that she is impelled to risk bringing him home, to join with him in the very room where her own parents' love produced her.

Such an all-consuming love, a love intent on making a hidden love public—or risking doing so—is a dangerous thing. Later in the Song she seeks him again, only this time the city guards assault her:

> I sought him, but could not find him.
>   I called, but he did not answer me.
> The guards found me,
>   As they made their rounds in the city.
> They struck me and wounded me.
>   They stripped my shawl off,
>   Those guardians of the city wall. (5:6–7)

This female lover is vulnerable, like other ancient Israelite women. Not only is she often stuck indoors while her lover is outside (for example, 2:8–14), but sometimes she is attacked when she ventures out. She is vulnerable to other men too. Early in the Song, she says that her skin is dark because her brothers put her outside in the vineyards after she quarreled with them (1:6), and later her brothers conspire to keep her from potential lovers by "building a turret for her" and "boarding her up with cedar" (8:8–9). In each case, the woman resists (1:7; 8:10), but this is not an easy road. She is victimized and repressed like many others throughout history who have violated societal sexual conventions.[27]

This dynamic of passion and risk gives new meaning to the refrain that reappears here, calling on the daughters of Jerusalem, whose "vineyards are in bloom" (2:15) to take care before awakening such a love:

> I make you swear,
>   Oh daughters of Jerusalem,
> By the gazelles or wild does,

To not ever awaken or arouse love
Until she is ready. (3:5)

She does not tell them to avoid such love. She certainly does not tell them
to start "keeping their vineyards." Nevertheless, this refrain does underline
the risk of love, a love that may not keep within the bounds that others
deem appropriate. As we already saw in discussing the prophets, love often
involves heartbreak, violence, and loss. Here in the Song, we see that, even
at its best, love can be painful.[28]

Song of Songs 3:6–5:1:
Lovers/Garden/World

So far, we have focused on the Song's depiction of an extraordinarily powerful, forbidden love. This section illustrates how these lovers, particularly
the woman, are remarkable too. It starts with images of royal glory and
ends with a lush garden.

The section opens with the wedding scene (3:6–11). Solomon's lavish
wedding litter proceeds across the desert, guarded by sixty elite warriors,
each armed with a sword and skilled in war. A speaker calls on the "daughters of Zion" to gaze on King Solomon on the day of his wedding, on the
day of his heart's rejoicing. This scene may be one reason why the Song
was later ascribed to King Solomon, who is reported to have written more
than a thousand songs (1 Kings 4:32 [Hebrew 5:12]). But the rest of the
Song does not focus on a royal lover. For example, later someone compares
Solomon's lavish vineyard unfavorably with the female lover:

Solomon had a vineyard,
    In Baal-hamon[29]
He set keepers over it.
    Each would pay for its fruit,
    A thousand pieces of silver.
My very own vineyard is before me,
    Solomon, the thousand silver pieces are yours,
    And two hundred apiece go to those who guard its fruit. (8:11–12)

Whether the speaker is male or female,[30] this is not Solomon speaking, but
someone who has a love more precious than anything that rich Solomon
ever had. As a result of texts like this and characteristics of the Hebrew of
much of the Song, most scholars date this book long after Solomon's time.[31]
Perhaps fragments like Solomon's wedding scene predate the book as a

whole.[32] But now the picture of male Solomon's glory in 3:6–11 serves as a lead-in to an even more extraordinary figure—the female lover of the Song of Songs, the vineyard that surpasses Solomon's.

The man, whether a Solomon character or just the male lover, describes just how beautiful this woman is. Building on the earlier description of her as "beautiful, with a dove's lively eyes" (1:15), he starts:

Oh how beautiful you are, my friend,
  Oh how beautiful you are, with a dove's lively eyes.
    Looking out from behind your tresses. (4:1)[33]

His gaze descends from her hair to her face, merging her features with the natural landscape around them: goats on Mount Gilead, shorn sheep up from the wash, a ripe pomegranate (4:2–3).[34] As he continues downward, he envisions her bejeweled neck as fortified like the tower of David. It is hung with weapons that surpass those of Solomon's retinue:

Your neck is like the tower of David,
  Built in courses.[35]
Hung with a thousand shields,
  All of the warriors' weapons. (4:4)

He moves still farther downward, merging her breasts with gazelles and fawns, signs of the goddess:

Your two breasts are like two frisky fawns
  Lively gazelle twins,[36]
    Grazing among the lotus flowers. (4:5)

Earlier, she had called on him to climb the "spice mountains of Beter" at the coming of the morning (2:17). Now, impelled by her beauty, he will go to her. He will be her gazelle, her young stag:

Until the day breathes,
  and the shadows flee,
I will go myself to the mountain of myrrh,
  to the hill of frankincense.
All of you is beautiful, my friend,
  You are completely flawless. (4:6–7)

Having accepted her invitation to go to the mountain of spices, the man now extends an invitation of his own. As before (2:14), he pictures her in a mountainous, inaccessible place. This time, however, the mountains are the mountains of Lebanon (Amanah, Shenir, Hermon), ancient garden of the gods, and they are a place of wild, dangerous animals: lions and leopards.[37]

> With me from Lebanon, oh bride,[38]
>   Come with me from Lebanon!
> Come down from the summit of Amanah,
>   From the heights of Shenir and Hermon,
> From the lions' lairs,
>   From the leopards' peaks. (4:8)

Soon the man moves from the garden of the gods to his own garden, his love:

> You are a locked garden, my sister, oh bride.
>   A secured well, a sealed spring.
> Your watered fields are a pomegranate orchard
>   With choice fruit.
> Flowering henna with plentiful nard,
>   Nard and tumeric,
> Sweet cane and cinnamon bark,
>   Along with all the scented woods,
> Myrrh and aloes,
>   Along with all the best spices.
> A garden spring, well of fresh water
>   Streams from lush Lebanon. (4:12–15)

The woman, his garden, replies with her invitation to the man:

> Wake up North wind, come South wind!
>   Breathe on my garden, let its spices flow!
> Let my love come to his garden,
>   And eat of its choice fruit. (4:16)

The man replies that he has already partaken of her honey and milk:

> I have come to my garden, my sister, oh bride,
>   I have gathered my myrrh with my spices,
> I have eaten my honeycomb along with the honey,
>   I have drunk my wine with my milk. (5:1a)

Finally, the chorus, perhaps the "daughters of Jerusalem," celebrates their joining, calling on them to drink deep of that "lovemaking better than wine." Perhaps, as the audience at an ancient banquet, we hear this call coming to us in some way as well:

> Feast friends,
>   Drink til you're drunk with lovemaking. (5:1b)[39]

This is a love that radiates out from the lovers to include their world and those around them. There is a hint of this at the outset of the Song, where the woman shifts imperceptibly from picturing her lover between her breasts to her lover as a blossom amidst the vineyards of the seaside town of Ein Gedi:

> My lover is an amulet of myrrh to me,
>   Spending the night between my breasts.
> My lover is a cluster of henna blossoms to me,
>   In the vineyards of Ein Gedi. (1:13–14)

We see this again when the woman envisions her love as a stag leaping over the springtime mountains to greet her (2:8–14). And we see it repeatedly as the Song shifts from depicting their lovemaking in a garden to depicting the woman herself as a garden.

As we have seen, this association of women with gardens is quite ancient. We have seen how prophets like Hosea depict the land of Israel as the female spouse of God. This association of women and land/gardens appears in Mesopotamian and Egyptian love poems as well. But the Song of Songs creatively plays back and forth between garden and lovers to create a picture of lovers and world commingled with each other. Robert Alter, one of the earliest observers of this phenomenon in the Song, nicely contrasts this with other depictions of eroticism:

> In more explicit erotic literature, the body in the act of love often seems to displace the rest of the world. In the Song, by contrast, the world is constantly embraced in the very process of imagining the body. The natural landscape, the cycle of the seasons, the beauty of the animal and floral realm, the profusion of goods afforded through trade, the inventive skill of the artisan, the grandeur of cities, are all joyfully affirmed as love is affirmed.[40]

Thus, not just the woman, but also the man are poetically depicted as melded with the world around them. These people, made from the earth in Eden, link with their wild surroundings in the Song of Songs.

This is, indeed, an idyllic picture. In real life, the wild world is not always a garden or a lush springtime landscape. Nevertheless, the song joins with other Biblical and ancient Near Eastern texts in offering a poetic vision in which love of another person and love of the earth synergize with each other rather than being opposites. This is a love that somehow extends beyond the pairing of two human beings. The lovers, remarkable as they are, image forth the glory of the world around them.

Song of Songs 5:2–6:3: Shimmers of the Divine

Though there is no refrain at this point, the Song shifts scenes again, turning now to a nighttime sequence. Some have wanted to consider this a dream story, but there is a sense in which all of the Song of Songs, not just this poem, is dreamlike. We have already mentioned the first part of this nighttime sequence and its depiction of the woman being beaten when she seeks her lover at night.[41] The main focus here will be on her later interactions with the daughters of Jerusalem and how her picture of her lover's beauty (5:10–16) reveals its early origins in praise of the divine.

The drama begins with her hesitating to open the door to her lover and then finding him gone when she does (5:2–6a). This prompts her to seek him through the city streets like she had before (3:1–5), only this time the guards find her, beat her, and strip her (5:6b–7). Thus stripped and struck, she alters her call to the daughters of Jerusalem. No longer does she call on them not to "awaken love." Instead, she asks them to help in her search for her lover:

> I make you swear,
>   Oh daughters of Jerusalem,
> If you find my love,
>   What shall you tell him?[42]
>   That I am faint with desire. (5:8)

They respond skeptically:

> What's so special about your love,
>   Oh, most beautiful among women?
> What's so special about your love,
>   That you make us swear so? (5:9)

This then leads to the woman's praise of her lover's body. Echoing ancient love poetry, she praises him as if he were a divine statue plated with gold and fine gems, radiant with power and beauty (5:10–16). As in his earlier praise of her (4:1–7), she starts with his head:

My love is dazzling and red,
Outstanding among ten thousand.
His head is of the very finest gold. (5:10–11)

By the time she gets to his arms, he sounds like the sort of statue of a god that would have been featured in ancient Mesopotamian rituals:

His arms are cylinders of gold,
Set with Tarshish gems.
His stomach is ivory craftwork,
inlaid with lapis lazuli.
His legs are marble columns,
Set on gold foundations.
His body[43] is like the Lebanon,
Preeminent as the cedars. (5:14–15)

Toward the end, she returns to the images of sweetness so important in ancient love poetry:

His mouth is so sweet.
He is all delight!
This is my love, this is my friend,
Oh daughters of Jerusalem. (5:16)

This description of her lover's glorious body apparently has quite an effect. Having heard about his beauty, the daughters of Jerusalem are now all too eager to help find him. They ask, "Where did your love go, . . . where did he turn, that we may seek him with you?" (6:1). In reply, the woman claims him as her own, speaking of how he came down to "his garden":

My love has gone down to his garden,
to the beds of spices.
To graze in the gardens,
to gather lotus blossoms.
I am my love's, and he is mine,
Who grazes among the lotus flowers. (6:2–3)[44]

This interchange around the man's beauty illustrates a theme already seen in our discussion of non-Israelite love poetry: the interpenetration of divine and human dimensions in human love poetry. As we saw, the poem in 5:10–16 sounds at points more like a description of a cult statue than a description of a flesh-and-blood man: "His head is of the very finest gold, . . . His arms are cylinders of gold, . . . His legs are marble columns." An-

cient Mesopotamian love poems have similar elements, although they sometimes echo actual rituals of love in which divine cult statues played a role.[45]
Within the drama of the Song, however, 5:10–16 is praising a human man,
not a statue. It uses idioms and images that derive ultimately from a worship
context, but applies them to a human character. Much later, one of the
earliest Jewish interpretations of the Song of Songs understood this praise
of the man's body to actually be the people's praise of God's beautiful body
when they saw God rescue them from Egypt at the Red Sea.[46] This interpretation took the mixed images of divine-human glory in 5:10–16 and
redirected them back at the divine.

This interpenetration of human and divine may be present in the female
protagonist of the Song as well. Just as Mesopotamian poems are linked to
the love goddess Inanna and Egyptian poems to the love goddess Hathor,
so also the woman of the Song echoes goddess traditions in repeatedly
warning "not to awaken love until she is ready." As we saw, the Song
repeatedly associates this feminine love with gazelles and wild does, animals
frequently associated with goddess figures in the world around ancient Israel.
She appears at the outset of the Song as a divinely sensual "lotus" (2:1–2),
and toward the end she appears as a terrifying, almost godlike figure, gazing
down on them. Someone asks: "Who is that gazing down like the dawn?
Beautiful as the white moon disk, pure as the hot sun disk, terrifying like
armies with banners?" (6:10).

As in the case of the praise of the man's body, later interpreters sometimes
understood this female character to be an image of God. Within the drama
of the Song, she is human. But some early Jewish mystics took her to be
an image of the Shekinah, Wisdom, or Torah. Courtly love poets sometimes
sang praises to divine love using images from the Song of Songs.

During the fifteenth century, some Christian illustrators even took the
stripped and beaten woman of the Song of Songs 5:6 to be a prophetic
image of Christ stripped and beaten before his crucifixion. In a brilliant
study, Susan Smith shows how several illustrated Bibles place an image of
the bride of the Song of Songs as one of several Old Testament scenes that
surround and anticipate a central picture of Christ being humiliated,
stripped, and beaten. For example, in figure 9.6, we see an image of the
stripped Christ in the center and the stripped bride of the Song in the lower
right.[47] This is no great image for the liberation of women. Given the
presuppositions of the time, this female figure represents divinity only insofar as she anticipates the vulnerability of God in Christ. Still, this is an
example of how divinity does not just shimmer through the man of the
Song, but also through the woman.

That said, we need to be clear: the Song itself is not originally about
divine-human love nor about love between gods. God is not explicitly

Fig. 9.6. "The Disrobing of Christ" and "David Dancing before the Ark and Achior," Biblia Pauperum. Reproduced by permission of the Pierpont Morgan Library, New York (MS M.230 f. 16).

mentioned nor addressed. The Song is not placed near nor explicitly co-ordinated with other texts (Hosea, Ezekiel) that depict God and Israel's marriage relationship.[48] In contrast, Mesopotamian dialogues between gods include addresses to the deities by name.[49] Moreover, erotic religious literature from Sufism and Hinduism include explicit indicators of the fact that they are spiritual works.[50] The Song has no such indicators. Finally, when one looks closely at the Song, it becomes clear that it includes many details—flowers, places, and so on—that are part of the landscape of love, but do not have clear theological significance.[51] Though generations of theological commentators have found hidden meanings in such elements of the Song, it appears that these details were originally just integral elements of ancient Israelite poetry about human love.

It is no coincidence, however, that later interpreters took the Song further. Like other forms of love poetry in Mesopotamia and Egypt, the Song draws freely on sacred motifs as it describes human love. And the lovers themselves not only merge with the world around them, but are translucent to the divine. This is clear again in the next section, where the woman achieves goddesslike dimensions.

Song of Songs 6:4–8:4: The Rise of the Woman

By the time we get to this point in the Song, it has diverged widely from typical depictions of male-female relations. This is not a normal picture of an Israelite husband and wife in their lives after the garden, the husband claiming exclusive power over his wife's devotion, and his wife dutifully, indeed passionately, having children to continue his line. To be sure, we have already seen ways in which the female lover of the Song is depicted as confined and vulnerable to others in ways the man is not. She must stay inside, while he wanders outside. She must resist the control of her brothers, and she risks attack when she goes out to seek her lover. Yet despite this, her character is increasingly powerful, at least in her lover's eyes.[52] Meanwhile, the man finds himself ever more drawn to her.

The increasing power of the woman is illustrated at this point in the Song by a series of poems, which praise her awesome beauty. The man starts by expanding on his earlier praise of her, now highlighting the effect of her terrifying allure on him. Then, someone—either the man or someone else—speaks of her as an almost divine figure. Soon afterward, the man offers a completely new song of praise to her beauty, this time moving from her feet to her head and stressing again her imposing power. As we will see, however, this powerful beauty does not turn him away, but ultimately makes him all the more passionate for her. And his passion is returned in full by her. By the end, we will see how this picture of their relationship explicitly contrasts with those in the laws, Prophets, and even the garden of Eden.

This section starts with the man's expansion of his earlier praise of her beauty (6:4–10). In 4:1–9, he followed his description of her beauty with a statement of her power over him:

> You have captured my heart,[53] my sister, oh bride!
>   You have captured my heart with one of your glances,
>   With but one of the strands of your necklace. (4:9)

Now, in chapter 6, he has an even deeper appreciation for her. He echoes elements of the praise song in chapter 4, but prefaces this song with a description of her terrifying effect on him:

> You are beautiful, my friend, like Tirzah,
>   Pretty, like Jerusalem.
>   Awesome like armies with banners.[54]
> Turn your eyes from me,
>   For they make me tremble. (6:4–5)

After describing again the beauty of her face (hair, teeth, mouth), he asserts her incomparability to the most prestigious women of the ancient Israelite world:

> There are sixty queens,
>   And eighty concubines,
>   And innumerable young women.
> But there is only one of her, my dove, my flawless one.
>   She was the one and only to her mother,
>   Perfect to the one who bore her.
> Young women see her, and exclaim over her good fortune,
>   Queens and concubines gaze on her and trill their praise. (6:8–9)[55]

At this point, the woman is preeminent in the human world. Soon, however, she is almost goddesslike in her power. Another question comes in the Song, perhaps from the chorus, joining in the man's awe before his powerful woman. They have the woman "gazing down" like God "gazes down" from heaven,[56] the powerful sun disk, shining down from the sky. She has assumed divine proportions:

Who is this gazing down like the dawn,
   Beautiful as the white moon,
Pure as the hot sun,[57]
   Terrifying like armies with banners? (6:10)

Meanwhile, this goddesslike woman is still a lover. In the next poem, she goes down to her "nut garden," to "see if the vine had budded." In an obscure verse she says, "before I knew it, my desire [*nephesh*] had set me among the chariots of Aminadab."[58] She is both vulnerable to desire and awesome to those around her, and yet there is no indication within the text of any unease with her power and sexuality.[59] Rather, the characters in the drama praise her and are drawn to her sensual, awesome beauty.

This mix of inaccessibility and desirability is clear in the next poem, where the man uses architectural imagery to praise his imposing "delicious woman," even as he resolves to scale her heights and share her love. The song starts with another call from the chorus, which is gazing on this alluring woman:

Return, Return, O Shulamite,[60]
   Return, return, so that we may gaze on you. (7:1a)

Someone then replies indignantly to their longing. Since the man speaks next, he may well be the speaker here as well:

Why do you gaze on the perfect woman,
   As on the two battle-camp dance? (7:1b)

Having questioned their longing, the man then joins in it himself. This time, his song of praise moves up her body, from her dancing feet to her hair (7:2–6). He starts with images of finery, much like those in her praise of him: "the curves of your thighs are like ornaments, works of a master craftsman" (7:2). As he moves up her body, he uses imagery from the plant world for her navel and belly:

Your navel is a rounded bowl,
   May it not lack mixed wine!
Your belly is a mound of wheat,
   Encircled with lotus blooms.
Your two breasts are like two frisky fawns
   Lively gazelle twins. (7:3–4)

By the time he reaches her neck, the images have shifted to much larger things: towers, pools in Heshbon, the mountains of the Carmel range. Such powerful beauty is strong enough to capture a king:

> Your neck is like an ivory tower.
>   Your eyes are like the pools in Heshbon,
>   Next to the "daughter of nobles" gate.[61]
> Your nose is like the tower of Lebanon,
>   looking out over Damascus.
> Your head crowns you like the Carmel range.
>   And the hair on your head is like purple thread
>   A king is held fast in the tresses. (7:5–6)

The interchange ends not with distance, but with desire. The man concludes: "How beautiful you are, how lovely, oh, my love, delicious woman" (7:7).

So far, he has imaged her as formidable, a fortress city. Yet he next states his intention to overcome her inaccessibility:

> Your height once seemed like a palm tree,
>   And your breasts like date clusters.
> I said to myself, "let me climb the palm,
>   let me take hold of its branches."
> Let your breasts be now,
>   Like grape clusters on the vine,
>   And the fragrance of your breath like apricots.
> Your mouth is like the finest wine. (7:8–9)

Before he is finished with his poetic triplet, she completes it for him, speaking her openness to him:

> Flowing smoothly to my love,
> Moistening the lips of sleepers. (7:10)[62]

The poetic device of having her complete his words heightens their mutuality. This is not just male desire of a woman, nor female desire for a man, but mutual desire. A confirmation of this comes in the woman's next speech, in which she balances the divine pronouncement in the garden of Eden. There, God proclaimed to Eve that one consequence of the garden crime would be that "your desire will be for your husband and he will rule over you" (Gen. 3:16). Here in the Song, the woman uses the same words to describe her man's desire *for her*.

I am my love's,
   And his longing is for me. (7:11)⁶³

She still desires him too. The section concludes with her echo of his invitation to her at the outset of the Song. Just as he once invited her to join him outside in the springtime landscape (2:8–14), now she invites him to come out with her to the fields and vineyards (7:12–13a). She promises to give her love to him (7:13b–14), even as she wishes she could kiss him in public and bring him to her mother's home (8:1–2).

Then, just as at the beginning of the Song (2:6–7), she is in her lover's arms, calling on the daughters of Jerusalem not to ever awaken or arouse such a powerful and dangerous love before she is ready:

His left arm under my head,
   His right arm embraces me.
I make you swear,
   Oh daughters of Jerusalem,
To not ever awaken or arouse
   Love until she is ready. (8:3–4)

This picture of male and female desire is distinctive within the context of the Bible. Elsewhere in the Bible, passionate women are often caricatured as promiscuous and wild, unless their passion is for having sons who will ultimately become the ancestors of Israel and its kings. Powerful women like Delilah and Jezebel are images of danger. Yet the Song of Songs ultimately celebrates this powerful, passionate woman. It is her voice that is featured through more than two-thirds of the book, and, parallel to the praise of the "woman of power" in Proverbs 31, the man and others in the Song end up praising her incomparable worth.

Moreover, the often overpowering male of Israel's legal and prophetic texts is replaced here with a male passionately bound to the woman who loves him. He is captivated by but one of her glances, but one of the strands of her necklace (4:9). He stands in awe of her beauty, imaging her in ever more majestic ways as he continues his pursuit of her. Unlike many other Biblical male characters, he is not filled with anxiety about infidelity or promiscuity. This is clearest early on when the woman playfully asks the man:

Tell me, one who my whole being [*nephesh*] loves,
   Where do you pasture?
   Where do you lay down at noon?

>   Lest I be like a veiled woman [prostitute?][64]
>   among your friends' flocks. (1:7)

The man calls her bluff and tells her that if she is intent on playfully not knowing, she can go ahead and follow the flocks' tracks to the shepherds' tents:

>   If you will not know,[65]
>   oh most beautiful of women,
>   Take yourself out in the tracks of the flock,
>   And pasture your own goats
>   By the shepherds' tents. (1:8)

But this is not all. He recognizes that his bejeweled love drives other men wild. He next pictures her like a fertile mare sent among the stallions of the pharaoh's chariots (1:9). His recognition of others' appreciation of her beauty echoes her comment to him that "all the young women love you" (1:3–4).

Certainly, the lovers do not wish that their lover would pursue others or be pursued by them. After all, the woman "saved up" her lovemaking for her man (7:14) and asserted to the daughters of Jerusalem that "I am my love's and he is mine" (6:3). This bond, however, is not one of the male claiming power over his wife's reproduction. Instead, this is a mutual passion between a man and a woman who are as equal as they can be in their social context: "My love is mine, and I am his" (2:16), "I am my love's and he is mine" (6:3), "I am my love's, and his longing is for me" (7:11).

Song of Songs 8:5–14: Reverse Allegory

This final section of the Song picks up on many themes already mentioned. In the discussion of forbidden love we saw the brothers plotting to confine their nubile sister (8:8–9), and her intent to resist them (8:10). In the discussion of garden and world, we looked briefly at how the man compares Solomon's glorious vineyard unfavorably to the glory of his woman/vineyard (8:11–12). And we looked briefly at the concluding call for her love to flee (8:13–14) in the initial discussion of how the Song of Songs is a tease. There is one major text, however, that I have not yet discussed, a text that pulls together many of these themes and adds one of its own: the possibility of what I will term "*reverse allegory*," enriching human love with themes from divine-human love.

On the heels of the refrain in 8:4—"do not ever awaken or arouse love until she is ready"—we hear a question about a woman coming up out of the desert:

> Who is this woman, coming up from the desert,
>   Leaning on her lover? (8:5a)[66]

Within the flow of the Song, the mystery woman is the female lover. She speaks in the next section of how she "awakened" her lover under the shade of the apricot tree where he himself was conceived:[67]

> Under the apricot tree I awakened you,[68]
>   At the very place your mother conceived you,
>   There she conceived and there she bore you. (8:5b)

Having spoken of the beginning of the cycle of life, she then sings of the end—how love is as fierce as death, bitter as Sheol. It cannot be bought. She calls on her love to set her as a seal on his heart:

> Set me as a seal on your heart,
>   As a seal on your arm.
> For love is as fierce as death,
>   Severe as Sheol is jealousy.[69]
> Its tongues are tongues of flame,
>   An inferno.[70]
> Mighty waters cannot
>   extinguish love,
>   Nor can rivers drown it.
> If someone gave
>   All the wealth of his house for love,
>   He would be utterly ridiculed. (8:6–7)

This call is a major instance of a broader phenomenon in the Song, where language from other parts of the Bible is adapted to speak of the lovers' love. Wisdom instructions in the book of Proverbs tell students to "bind" the instructions of the teacher around their necks and write them on their hearts (Prov. 3:3).[71] The book of Deuteronomy, heavily influenced by such wisdom literature, adapts these sayings in speaking of how Israel should love God with all its heart, life strength, and might (Deut. 6:5). Right after giving this command, Moses goes on to tell Israel to "bind [these words] as a sign on your hand and be an emblem between your eyes" (Deut. 6:8).[72] Centuries of Jews have taken this to mean a requirement to bind this love

command on their arms and foreheads as phylacteries, reminding them always of God's call to be loved above and beyond all. Here, however, the
woman calls on her husband to do something else: to bind *her* as a seal on
his arm, as a seal on his heart.

This is an example of what I mean by reverse allegory, the application of
religious motifs to seemingly nonreligious realities. In traditional allegories,
everyday images are taken as symbols of an ultimate reality. But here, images
of ultimate reality are used to enrich discourse about everyday life. Already,
the Song of Songs resonates with Deuteronomy's call to love God with "all
your life strength" (Deut. 6:5) in having the woman describe her man as
"the one my life strength loves" (1:7).[73] When she says, "My love is mine
and I am his" (2:16), she echoes God's proclamations elsewhere in the Bible
that "I will be your God and you will be my people" (for example, Lev.
26:12).[74] Now, in chapter 8, this same female lover uses images of such
ultimate devotion to God as pointers to the kind of devotion she wants
from her love: she asks him to set her like a seal on his heart.[75]

This then might be a key to understanding other ways in which the Song
echoes the rest of the Bible. Many have observed how parts of the Song
pick up motifs from Biblical stories about God and Israel. The processions
out of the wilderness (3:6; 8:5) can be read as parallels to the Israelites' trek
through the wilderness.[76] The detailed description of Solomon's glorious
litter (3:7–10) resembles descriptions of the wilderness tabernacle and the
temple.[77] The man's descriptions of his female love often echo Biblical descriptions of the promised land,[78] and she, like the land, is associated with
milk and honey (4:11).[79] Her lament that she "sought and did not find" her
lover (for example, 3:1) echoes the prediction in Deuteronomy that if the
people seek God with all their heart and life strength, they will find God
(Deut. 4:29).[80] When she calls for her lost love and he does not answer (5:6),
this links with Biblical passages in which the Israelites call and God does
not answer them (for example, 1 Sam. 8:18). The list goes on.[81]

Many have seen such texts as clues that the Song is really an encoded
description of God's relationship with Israel. Such an approach, however,
violates too many other aspects of the text.[82] Instead, it is more likely that
the Song uses motifs from Israel's sacred story to enrich its picture of an
erotic relationship between human beings. The woman retraces Israel's steps
on her way to her beloved. Solomon's litter inlaid with love scenes (3:10)
is an echo of the wilderness tabernacle. Her cry of despair at the loss of
her love is like the cry of one abandoned by God. Her call on her love for
devotion is like God's call on Israel for passionate devotion.

An Ambiguous Conclusion

The song concludes with one final dialogue. The man now stands amidst his companions, the same companions she had once threatened to wander among (1:7), and he had playfully suggested she go ahead and do so (1:8). Like he did in the beginning (2:14), once more he calls to hear her voice:

> Oh woman sitting in the garden
>> My companions are listening.
> Let me hear your voice! (8:13)

She replies ambiguously. First, she tells him to "flee." Then, she echoes her earlier call for him to be her "stag" and to mount the spice mountains (2:17). Could she be calling once again for him to join her?

> Flee, my love,
>> Make yourself like a frisky gazelle
> Or like a vital young stag
>> On the mountains of spices! (8:14)[83]

So the Song ends, without any clear resolution. An American movie would have the lovers riding into the sunset. A more tragic approach would have them separated forever. But the Song teases us with a relationship in limbo. The love is still clandestine, the lovers not yet together. They remain in the garden, merged with the wild world around them ("gazelle," "stag," "mountain of spices"). The gazelle and stag, signs of the goddess, recall other shimmers of the divine seen throughout the song. Mutual desire, risk, joining, separation—all of these mix in this ambiguous ending to an elusive song.

The ancient Israelite audience would have been left with this picture as they turned back to their banquet and as the performers receded into the background. We turn now to look more specifically at how this magnificent poem might help us join sexuality and spirituality.

10
The Erotic and the Mystical

BRINGING SEXUALITY AND SPIRITUALITY
TOGETHER IN READING THE SONG OF SONGS

There is something seductive about the Song of Songs. As Cheryl Exum observes, "Something about the Song turns even the most hardened of feminist critics into a bubbling romantic."[1] The poem purports to let us eavesdrop on a private conversation, though in actuality, the text is quite public. It pretends to present raw lovers' voices unmediated by any narrator, though in fact these voices are artistic creations. The anonymity of the lovers makes it easier to identify ourselves with one of them. Insofar as we have felt similar desires, the poem invites us to identify with their speech. It lures us to climb into the dialogue and see their speech as the real speech of lovers, perhaps even the real speech of our love.[2] We imagine ourselves longing for a kiss like the woman when she says, "Let him kiss me with the kiss of his mouth" (Song 1:2).

To be sure, the picture of love here is not universal, nor is it perfect. The lovers in the tradition passed down to us are male and female;[3] young, not old; beautiful (at least in each other's eyes), not plain. Moreover, the man enjoys freedoms that the woman does not, while the woman must run risks that the man does not. This is no utopia. There are still hostile male groups, the woman's brothers and the guards, who would control and restrict the woman's sexuality.[4] And these hostile men are not entirely unsuccessful in the world of the poem. There is never any explicit description of the man and woman fulfilling their desire. The woman never even gets the kiss on the mouth that she desires at the outset (1:2). We can only read fulfillment of desire between the lines, in double entendres and fadeouts.[5]

Even if we acknowledge these facts, it is still clear that the Song of Songs imagines the world quite differently from most other Biblical texts. Where the dangerous foreign woman in Proverbs tempts the student toward death with kisses and a bed of spices, here the prominent female voice of the

Song of Songs yearns for the kisses of her lover's mouth and they speak frequently of their spiced bed. Where a proactive, rule-breaking woman is the image of a disobedient, adulterous community in Hosea, the Song of Songs features a woman who faces down the disapproval of her audience for her dark skin, seeks her lover at night, and revels in her love for him. To be sure, this otherwise atypical woman of the Song of Songs is not married, and so the Song does not celebrate extramarital sexuality. Yet it nevertheless presents an unusual view of premarital sexuality and non-reproductively focused female sexual initiative. Moreover, the jealous, over-powering male of many other Biblical texts is replaced here with a male lover willing to be vulnerable to love, to yield to it, and to be captivated by a powerful, incredible woman.[6]

Little wonder then that the Song has enjoyed such popularity in recent times. In a context where many women have achieved relative economic independence and have struggled against patriarchal restraints, the Song presents an unusually assertive woman, likewise struggling against the re-strictions of her brothers, the guards, and the culture as a whole. In a con-temporary context where sex is increasingly separate from reproduction, the Song of Songs presents an ancient fantasy of sexuality devoid of a focus on having children. Indeed, scholar Athalya Brenner has pointed out that many of the herbs and spices mentioned in the Song were used in Egypt and ancient Greece for birth control.[7] There are yet other ways in which the poetic world of the Song connects with modern trends in sexuality. Its picture of youthful, premarital sexuality resonates with the modern reality that many young people are sexually mature or active long before they are ready for marriage. And its focus on sexuality outside the context of mar-riage corresponds to the increase in nonmarital sexualities and their visibility in contemporary culture.

But how did ancient readers receive this perspective? Were they similarly attracted to it? It contrasts sharply with most other texts passed down through the Biblical tradition. Were ancient Israelites scandalized by the Song? Might it have functioned for them as "erotic literature that verges on soft pornography," as one scholar has proposed?[8]

We do not have enough early readings of the Song to answer these ques-tions.[9] Nevertheless, if there is one thing that has characterized most read-ings of the Song of Songs, it is their tendency to identify the Song as sexual *or* spiritual, not both.

As we will see, most ancient readings take the Song of Songs as spiritually erotic literature. In doing so, they testify to the dynamism of the Song itself and the tendencies of many world religious traditions to both join and oppose the erotic and the spiritual. Let us look at some spiritual and sexual interpretations of the Song before considering how these two dimensions can be connected.

The Song as Spiritual, Not Sexual

Most early interpreters understood the Song to be spiritual, *not* sexual. The same Rabbi Akiba who pronounced the Song to be "the holy of holies amidst the Writings" is also the one who said that "one who sings the Song of Songs like just one of the songs" has no place in heaven. Depending on the context, Akiba and other rabbis identify the woman of the Song as the Jewish house of study,[10] the Jewish court,[11] a group of the righteous,[12] or many other things. One early rabbinic tradition even likens the bulges produced by the poles of the tent sanctuary in Exodus to the woman of the Song's breasts pushing against her garment.[13]

Most often, however, the early rabbis understood the Song of Songs to be an expression of the love relationship we saw in the Prophets: the man of the Song of Songs is God, and the woman is Israel.[14] After all, Biblical texts present divine-human love as male-female love governed by much the same principles as male-female love on the human level. Given this, it was natural for the rabbis to understand the depiction of male-female love in the Song of Songs to be relevant to the divine-human marriage discussed elsewhere in the Bible.[15] Just as Hosea, the Deuteronomists, Isaiah, and Ezekiel apply human gender categories to divine-human love, it is but a small step to take the radically different picture of love in the Song of Songs and use it to depict that same divine-human love relationship differently. What may seem like a big jump to us was a much smaller leap to ancient ones.

Early Christians also interpreted the Song on a theological/mystical level. The church father Origen sets the tone for almost all subsequent interpretations of the Song with his commentary on the first portion (1:1–3:6).[16] In it, he argues for three levels in the Song, much like there are three levels of a human individual (body, soul, spirit): (1) the literal level of a marriage drama between Solomon and the pharaoh's daughter; (2) an allegorical level in which the book is the song of love between Christ and the church; and (3) a spiritual (or "tropological") level in which the book is the love song between God and individual souls (in the church). Origen was prompted in part by dialogue with Jewish contemporaries,[17] but his analysis was more systematic and erotic than contemporary Jewish comments about the Song of Songs. He tried verse by verse, chapter by chapter, to show how the first part of the Song of Songs could help fallen humans reclaim their nature as hot God-lovers and leave cold earth-love behind.

Many have supposed that such interpretations were just efforts to tame the wild sexuality of the Song, but they have not recognized that Origen and others believed that the hottest desire one can have is for God. Origen believed that God made the world through an immense erotic outpouring at the beginning of time. Though created to love God back, the world was turned so that creatures in it sometimes mistakenly love the creation rather than the Creator. As a result, human souls now are caught in a drama where they can choose either the original love of God for which they were created or the fallen love of the world. Thus, according to Origen, the rich language of the song—if read properly—can rekindle the soul's true spiritual senses, so that each person can see, taste, and feel Christ and be fully pierced by the arrow of God's love.[18] Consider Origen's commentary on Song of Songs 2:5, which Origen understands to read "for I am wounded by love":

> If there is anyone who has been pierced with the loveworthy spear of [Christ's] knowledge, so that he yearns and longs for him by day and night, can speak of naught but him, would hear of naught but him, can think of nothing else, and is disposed to no desire nor longing nor yet hope, except for him alone—if such there be, that soul then says in truth: "I have been wounded by love."[19]

Such erotically charged spiritual interpretation of the Song was hardly limited to Origen or to Christianity. Mystical Jewish Kabbala was built in large part around passionate commentary on the Song of Songs,[20] and Christians like Bernhard of Clairvaux and Mechthild of Magdeburg took interpretation of the Song of Songs to new levels when they joined the tradition of courtly love with Christian mysticism.[21]

During the late medieval period, we begin to see more interpreters read the woman of the Song of Songs as divine. As we have seen, there was already precedent for this reading in the Song itself, where the man describes his love as a semidivine goddess figure. Meanwhile, older commentaries had already given divine overtones to the woman of the Song as the church or as divinized Mary. Nevertheless, this took a new turn in the twelfth and thirteenth centuries, a time when troubadours across Europe were singing courtly love poems in praise of their pure "ladies" and feminine "Love" in general. Hildegard of Bingen suggested that the Song of Songs is the love song written by Solomon when he received divine (female) wisdom, to whom "he spoke . . . as to a woman in the familiar language of love."[22] The mystic Hadewijch of Brabent drew extensively on the Song of Songs and courtly love poetry in writing love poems to a divinely feminine Love.

Meanwhile, some Jewish mystical works likewise used the Song of Songs to image the believer's passionate attachment to various feminine principles: the divine Torah, the in-dwelling Shekinah, and so on. In these and other ways, the Song has been a way of imagining a love relationship with a feminine divinity, and not just a way of being a woman in love with a male god.

The Song of Songs has proven through history to be the kind of text that can help communities imagine themselves in love with God. Its depiction of love is not pure or painfree. The depiction of the lovers' relationship is not purely egalitarian. Nevertheless, this picture is evocative enough that believers can imagine themselves either as the lover in the Song, whether female or male, or as in love with God or a part of God, whether male or female. If there is any text in the Bible that might help us ground our eros in a deep love of God, this is that text.

Though we know that ancient communities had different views of gender from our own, it is still true that the Song's relatively egalitarian picture of mutually passionate love became the lens through which Jewish and Christian communities read the rest of the Bible. In the end, it was the Song of Songs, read theologically, and not Hosea that was preached on more often than any other Old Testament book in the thirteenth century. It was the Song of Songs and not Jeremiah or Ezekiel that was one of the most often copied manuscripts of the Middle Ages.[23] It was the Song of Songs and not Proverbs that Rabbi Akiba is reported to have described as the "holy of holies" among the Writings (m.Yad. 3:5).

Meanwhile, most early interpreters who read the Song sexually also denied that it was scriptural and were brutally persecuted. A major church father from ancient Antioch, Theodore of Mopsuestia, was condemned as a heretic, and his writings were burned; we only get fragments of his perspective through the quotes of his opponents. Sebastian Castellio, a contemporary of the Protestant founder John Calvin, was expelled from Geneva for insisting that the Song was primarily about human love. Others who advocated similar readings—Julian of Eclanum, Ishodad of Hedatta, Landri of Waben, an anonymous rabbi of the twelfth century—are distinguished by their almost total obscurity and small numbers amidst the mass of spiritual/theological commentaries, poems, and sermons based on the Song of Songs.

The Song as Sexual, Not Spiritual

Both the spiritual reading of the Song of Songs and its popularity did not persist. Grotius in 1644 compared the Song to Greek love lyrics; Bossuet

(1693) read it as a marriage text; and a host of authors in the eighteenth century interpreted it as a drama.[24] By the time Karl Budde wrote in March 1894, he could assert, "The age of allegorical explanation of the Song of Solomon has passed."[25] To be sure, Catholic scholars did not join in a historical-critical reading until the mid–1950s, when they were freed by church decisions to pursue a more historical approach. Soon they too began treating the Song as poems about human love.[26] In commentary after commentary, writers vigorously rejected the theological approach of earlier eras, ridiculing it as a grotesque twisting of the beautiful language of love in the Song. For example, Marvin Pope wrote in the introduction to his commentary:

> The flexibility and adaptability of the allegorical method, the ingenuity and imagination with which it could be, and was, applied, the difficulty and virtual impossibility of imposing objective controls, the astounding and bewildering results of almost two millennia of application to the Canticle, have all contributed to its progressive discredit and almost complete desertion.[27]

This comment is typical. Most recent treatments of the Song have insisted on reading it exclusively as poems about human love, *not* divine-human love.[28]

So, the sexuality-spirituality dichotomy continues. Before, we had readings that denied a sexual meaning to the Song and endorsed a spiritual reading. Now, we have interpretations that endorse a sexual reading and deny a spiritual meaning. Is it any wonder that this latter shift corresponded to a decrease in how frequently the Song was used by spiritual communities? As Protestants and then Catholics and some Jews began to apply a critical approach to the Song, it was used less and less in religious contexts. Academics might write about it, but pastors rarely preach about it. The Song is sometimes read at weddings or used in marriage counseling, and it appears once in the three-year cycle of readings used by many churches. But its usage—at least in Christian contexts—hardly compares with its prominence in earlier eras.[29]

Crossing Over the Sexual-Spiritual Divide

Toward the end of the twentieth century, however, many questioned this opposition between sexuality and spirituality. In the introduction to this book, I discussed Audre Lorde's influential essay on erotic power in women's lives. Her work sparked some Christian and Jewish thinkers to envision eros as a category that might join sexuality and spirituality.

Exactly these sorts of insights have led a minority of recent interpreters of the Song of Songs to question the sexuality-spirituality dichotomy that so dominates earlier readings of the Song. In 1986, the noted Catholic Biblical scholar Roland Murphy raised questions about the opposition of sexuality and spirituality in his commentary on the Song.[30] Soon several short articles for preachers appeared that argued for an interpretation of the Song of Songs on both sexual and spiritual levels.[31] The Jewish Biblical interpreter Adin Steinsaltz argued for a joining of the sexual and spiritual in interpretation of the Song of Songs.[32] By the end of the 1990s, a tide of scholarly readers had joined the chorus rejecting the past opposition of sexuality and spirituality in interpreting the Song, including myself,[33] Larry Lyke,[34] Alicia Ostriker,[35] Othmar Keel,[36] and Carey Ellen Walsh.[37]

Such interpretations are "in the air" now, but they correspond to a phenomenon that I will term *cross-over*, in which ancient poets use motifs from human love to describe divine-human love or vice versa. This phenomenon is as widespread as the different world traditions that, like Judaism and Christianity, have imaged the divine-human relationship in sexual terms: Hindu devotional traditions surrounding Krishna and Shiva, Tibetan Tantric meditation on the female escorts of the celestial Buddha, and the spectacular mystical visions of Muslim Sufi poets like Jalladin Rumi. Consider, for example, the twelfth-century Bengali poet Jayadeva, who wrote an Indian "Song of Songs." Before he wrote, Hindu tradition already had a series of legends about how the god Krishna seduced and made love to a group of cowgirls, including his main love, Radha. Drawing on Sanskrit human love poetry, Jayaveda developed a series of love poems about Krishna and Radha. In contrast to the Song of Songs, however, he added frequent reminders to the reader of his spiritual aims: "to you who hear this poem may welfare be given by the arm of Kamsa's destroyer [Krishna], . . . that arm a long while kissed by the herd-girls beloved, in their joy."[38] Later he says, "Let us worship for sin's destruction Sri Govinda's [Krishna] foot, . . . bowing in deep devotion."[39] Two hundred years later, another Bengali poet, Vidyapati, uses the spiritual love imagery of the Gita Govinda to describe the ideal human love of his courtly patrons. Thus, cross-over happened in the reverse direction. Whereas Jayaveda uses human love motifs in his spiritual love poem, Vidyapati uses spiritual love motifs in his praise of human love.[40] Such shifts back and forth across the divine-human divide indicate how fluid the boundaries can be between theological and nontheological uses of erotic imagery.

Indeed, we have seen the same cross-over in ancient love poetry and the Song of Songs itself. Mesopotamian poets use motifs from sacred marriage texts in songs about human love, and they often use the characters of the sacred marriage framework for strikingly playful, noncultic depictions of desire. Hathor is frequently invoked in Egyptian love poems, and the man is sometimes praised as a human reflection of the sun god, Re. And, as we saw, the divine shimmers below the surface of even the Song of Songs itself. Though the book is focused on the drama of human love, the poet draws on varied ancient cultic elements to enrich the picture of the lovers' passion: signs of the goddess in invocations not to awaken love before she is ready, ancient songs of praise of cult statues, and so on. The poet alludes more and less explicitly to the Biblical sacred story, reapplying specifically theological and legal motifs to the lovers' passion in a form of reverse allegory. Even the form of the book as a whole—as a set of dialogues and related monologues between lovers—is closest to the Mesopotamian sacred marriage texts than to other extant poetry.

These sorts of prompts within the Song itself help explain why so many interpreters understand the Song on its deepest level to be about God's love for God's people. Not only did the prophets of ancient Israel and the church already image God married to the people. Not only was the Song of Songs itself built with genres and motifs taken from poetry about divine love. But love poetry itself is so metaphorical that its motifs are easily reapplied. Within the Song, the man can be an apricot tree (2:3) or a gazelle (2:9, 17). The woman is a prancing mare (1:9), a lotus (2:1–2), a dove (2:14; 4:1), and especially a garden (4:12–15; 6:2–3) or vineyard (8:11–12). Little wonder, then, that later interpreters took such already elusive language and reapplied it to Israel, the church, the soul, and other possible love partners of God. And little wonder that those same interpreters were worried that their passionate poetry could just as easily be interpreted in the reverse direction.

Putting Sexuality and
Spirituality Together

So far, we have looked at how love language crossed over the divine-human divide. I and others have affirmed the importance of reading the Song on multiple levels. Let us now look at how one might join those levels.

Here, more than anywhere else, I have been taught by the students with whom I have worked. For several years, I have taught several graduate seminars on the Song of Songs in which we focus on the issue of divine and human eros in the Song and its readings. One student, Lynda Mc-Clanahan, powerfully stated the problem when she wrote:

When reality is divided up between sacred and profane, all experience inevitably gets labeled one way or the other. We live in a world where sex is literally everywhere, relatively easy to get and not much more important than the central nervous system's response to particularly interesting stimuli. The fact that we should also regard the eroticism in SoS [the Song] as being functionally profane is just one of the many oddities of our culture.

Thank God another oddity guarantees we are culturally prohibited from taking out our ecclesiastical Exacto knives and getting rid of it. Something apparently very nasty is lodged deep in the heart of the bible. As part of the "Good Book," we are forced to see it as holy. Yet SoS is so obviously "unholy" within the sacred/profane dichotomy which we unconsciously use to measure these things (spiritual-disembodied love yes/carnal-embodied love no) that we haven't the faintest idea of how to preach it, let alone figure out why we should even try. SoS sits in the middle of scripture like a sexy evening dress at an afternoon tea party, but it is also a holy riddle disguised as a pair of lace panties. It has the same power to dissolve the brain into the heart as a Zen koan and deftly wears down nearly every boundary we can think of. Because the poem has this effect, it blurs the edges between the lovers, between God and the individual soul, between Yahweh and Israel, and even between culture and whatever it is we would be without it.[41]

McClanahan, like Kellogg at the outset of this book, pushes us to think about what it might mean to join sexuality and spirituality, not just compare or contrast them.

Another approach is to return to the topic of animal sexuality with which we began in the introduction. Sex for animals is often a dangerous thing. Not only must they often traverse new territory and expend time finding a mate, but they are unusually vulnerable to predators for the moments they couple, exposed and preoccupied. The powerful sex drive of animals impels them to become vulnerable despite their other instincts, even to risk their lives so they can reproduce. Within humans, it is broader. Eros is a fundamental spiritual impulse to reach out from ourselves for connection, to become vulnerable, often against our other instincts. Our sexual eros impels us to seek out bodily connection with others, risking suffering in the process. Mystical writers experience a similar erotic impulse toward God, one that often impels them to persevere in their faith and to endure persecution. Human eros, on whatever level, pushes us out from safe limits and makes us risk ourselves with others.

To be sure, in our post-Freudian age, it is all too easy to dismiss writings about spiritual eros as the sublimations of sexually frustrated mystics. We are prone to understand such imagery as a sexualization of fundamentally nonsexual realities. Yet we need to reexamine our own assumptions. Why is it that we so easily assume that sex is a purely bodily function? As mentioned in the introduction, Freud and others argued that humans are born with highly fluid sexual desire, feeling sexlike erotic passion for all sorts of people and things.

Meanwhile, much of the Biblical tradition embraces passion on multiple levels, while reserving a special place for our desire for God. The passionate humans who were created in the garden are "very good." God made them for erotic connection to each other and the earth. God's own passionate breath enlivens them. The Bible emphatically calls on Israel to love God with all its heart, life breath, and strength (Deut. 6:5). It is these words Israel is to bind on its hand and head. These different forms of passion are not the same, nor are they contradictory. Humans were made to love God *and* others. We are first and foremost erotic creatures. We are made to be grounded in love of God above all, but we are impelled by our love of God toward erotic connection with others as well.

How do we find language that gets beyond the sexual-spiritual divide? Even the terms *sexuality* and *spirituality* separate at the very point where we need to connect categories. One way to image unified passion is suggested by another former student, Kathleen Richards, who writes about how the poetic language of the Song enables us to move from one level to the other and back. Building on recent theories of metaphor, she starts by talking of how poetry is a "violation of reality" in which its transgressions of language invite the listener to journey to a "world not their own." Moreover, once the author has begun this process of having one thing stand for another, "the door is swung wide open for others to do the same." As a result, the Song itself can be read as working on multiple levels, a series of potential metaphorical "transparencies" where one level need not eliminate another:

> This [the Song] is a text about lovers; but *beneath* these humans, and *with* these humans, there is the presence of the Divine. Why would one want to keep that presence out of this garden? That would simply create another hide and seek scene, like the Garden of Eden, between human and God. . . .
>
> The sensuous celebration of the body, both human and Divine, is laid over this scene like a series of transparencies. This is the celebration of love. This is the poem. This is the Divine. This is the Church. This is the Christ. As a man loves a woman, so God loves them both. As a man loves a woman so Christ loves the Church. As each transparency is lifted there is always the Song of Songs, but as one drops them back into place, the scene in this garden of lovers'

delights begins to fill with all the combinations and possibilities of love.[42]

Taking Richards's image further, perhaps the Song and its readings can invite us to reread our world as an erotic one overlaid with a series of transparencies. On one level are our attachments to loved ones, nature, and other things. It is easy to be caught up in that level alone, and become addictive and destructive. Yet there is also the possibility of seeing our world through another transparency, where our beloved, our world, shimmers with the reality of God. On one level, eros opens us to sensuous connection with another person, a poem, a piece of nature, the world. Yet on another level, our eros opens us to experiencing God loving us in and through those things. As Susan Griffin suggests, "For this is the meaning of desire, that wanting leads us to the sacred."[43]

Does this mean that we must love the world as if it were God? Not necessarily. On the one hand, reading the world/the Song through multiple transparencies, we can see our erotic connections as tastes of the very best God has to offer us. Our most positive experiences of the erotic—insofar as we have them—can be powerful signs of God's presence in our lives, a divine beauty that attracts us, a divine reality that loves us back.

On the other hand, we can also acknowledge that God always lies beyond even our best erotic connections. The most we experience in life are partial tastes of ultimate fulfillment, brief hints of the greater good for which we long. To forget this is to risk loving things as if they were God.

Here again, the Song of Songs is helpful. For as we saw, it is a tease. Though it occasionally implies consummation, the Song, like its Egyptian counterparts, says little about fulfillment of desire. Instead, it emphasizes each lover's longing for a beloved who is just out of reach. The lovers praise each other, call out to each other to come to the garden, wish to be together, remember, and yet, as we saw, the Song ends not with the lovers together, but with them apart, still inviting connection:

Flee, my love,
> Make yourself like a [frisky] gazelle
> Or like a [vital] young stag
> > On the mountains of spices! (Song 8:14)

Yes, earlier in the Song, lovemaking appears imminent or just past, as when the woman describes the man holding her, "his left arm under my head, his right arm embraces me." Yes, there are points of the Song where it obliquely implies lovemaking, but only through double entendres. The emphasis on passionate longing rather than explicit lovemaking is one element that makes the Song erotic, indeed spiritual, rather than merely pornographic.

Earlier, I mentioned other world traditions that testify to the connection of eroticism and spirituality. I end this chapter with a poem from the Sufi tradition by the great mystic Rumi as translated by Coleman Barks. This poem, speaking of love of God/the world, evokes better than any prose words of mine could the experience of reading life through multiple transparencies:[44]

There is a community of the spirit.
Join it, and feel the delight
of walking in the noisy street,
and *being* the noise.

Drink *all* your passion
and be a disgrace.

Close both eyes
to see with the other eye.
Open your hands,
if you want to be held.

Sit down in this circle.

Quit acting like a wolf, and feel
the shepherd's love filling you.

At night your beloved wanders.
Don't accept consolations.

Close your mouth against food.
Taste the lover's mouth in yours.

You moan, "She left me." "He left me."
Twenty more will come.

Be empty of worrying.
Think of who created thought!

Why do you stay in prison
when the door is so wide open?

Move outside the tangle of fear-thinking.
Live in silence.

Flow down and down in always
widening rings of being.

There's a strange frenzy in my head,
of birds flying,

each particle circulating on its own.
Is the one I love *everywhere*?[44]

This lovely rendering of a Sufi poem joins individual and community, world and lover, call and promise. Like the Song of Songs read on multiple levels, this work by Rumi is a call to a broadly erotic life. The passion it depicts is rooted in God, but expands outward. The world is not God. No human lover is God. Yet reality is infused with the frenzy of the divine lover. The poem starts, "There is a community of the spirit./Join it, and feel the delight." We turn now to a different community of spirit, the body of Christ, and echoes of Old Testament gardens in the New Testament.

IV
Concluding Reflections

11
The Word Made Flesh

ECHOES OF OLD TESTAMENT GARDENS
IN THE NEW TESTAMENT

Gardens do not disappear in the New Testament, but they are changed. Sexuality and eros are almost never explicitly affirmed. Yet a closer look reveals a set of eros-affirming Christian garden texts amidst the broader Christian tradition. In the introduction to this book I summarized ways in which the New Testament contributed to the sexual-spiritual split that has characterized much of Western culture. This legacy makes it all the more important to show that the erotic vision of the Old Testament was not lost in the New Testament.

As we will see, this vision is not just continued but developed in several key New Testament texts. Jesus in the Gospels of Matthew, Mark, and Luke uses the creation story of Genesis 1–2 to affirm the erotic bond between men and women. Jesus in the Gospel of John echoes Isaiah's vineyard love song, but identifies himself as the "true vine," to which believers connect by "loving" each other. Finally, a story later in the Gospel of John echoes the woman's nighttime search for her lover in the Song of Songs. Now, Mary Magdalene is the lover, and she seeks her beloved Jesus in the garden where he was crucified. Each of these texts echoes a different Old Testament garden text and adds its own twist to it. Taken together with ancient love poetry, these New Testament garden texts can prompt Christians to think in new ways about the interpenetration of the earthly and divine, not just in Jesus Christ, but in other lovers and elements of the world around them.

The Eden Garden and
the New Creation

There are two major sorts of reflections of the Eden garden in the New Testament: affirmations of splits between body and spirit and male and female in Pauline literature and affirmation of the erotic fleshly bond in a Jesus saying in the Gospels.

References to creation in the Pauline letters partake heavily of the post-garden ethos, where earthly humans are alienated from their desire and men rule over women. For Paul himself, "flesh and blood cannot inherit the kingdom of God." We will fully bear God/Christ's image only at the end of time when God replaces our bodies of dust with immortal, perfect bodies, free of desire (1 Cor. 15:20–56). This rejection of the body extends to restrictions on women in later Christian literature. A letter attributed to Paul, 1 Timothy, forbids women from teaching in churches because Eve was to blame for the garden crime:

> I permit no woman to teach or to have authority over a man; she is to keep silent. For Adam was formed first, then Eve; and Adam was not deceived, but the woman was deceived and became a transgressor. Yet she will be saved through childbearing, provided they continue in faith and love and holiness, with modesty. (1 Tim. 2:12–15)

We have already seen how Genesis itself does not support such exclusive condemnation of Eve nor affirmation of sexual hierarchy. Moreover, most scholars think this letter's claim to be from Paul is false.[1] Nevertheless, this passage has exercised enormous influence. It was one of the first texts to blame Eve for the garden fall, and churches today still use it to justify their ongoing refusal to ordain women and their insistence on women's destiny to raise children and submit to their husbands' authority.

But this is not the whole story of New Testament readings of the Eden garden. There is another other text that focuses explicitly on the issue of erotic connectedness in Genesis 1–2. It occurs in a story about Jesus found in the Gospels of Mark and Matthew (Mark 10:2–9; Matt. 19:3–9).[2] In it, Jesus contrasts the law of the Eden garden to the law of Moses. Here is the version of the story in Mark:

> Some Pharisees came, and to test him they asked, "Is it lawful for a man to divorce his wife?" . . . He answered them, "What did Moses command you?" They said, "Moses allowed a man to write a certificate of dismissal and to divorce her." But Jesus said to them, "Because of your hardness of heart he wrote this commandment for you. But from the beginning of creation, 'God made them male and female.' For this reason a man shall leave his father and mother and be joined to his wife, and the two shall become one flesh.' So they

are no longer two, but one flesh. Therefore what God has joined together, let no one separate." (Mark 10:2–9)

Paul records a similar opposition of Jesus to divorce (1 Cor. 7:10–11) and there were other gospel traditions that Jesus opposed remarriage (Mark 10: 10–12; Matt. 5:31–32; Luke 16:18).[3] This story, however, is unique in linking Jesus' opposition to divorce to God's creation intention that men and women become "one flesh."

Most people use this saying to judge those who divorce, but it is as remarkable for what it affirms in terms of marriage as for what it forbids in terms of divorce. Its celebration of marriage clashes with the ambivalence toward marriage seen elsewhere in Jesus traditions and in Paul. Paul frames his Jesus-based admonition to stay in marriage (1 Cor. 7:12–24) with admonitions before and after to avoid marriage, or at least to avoid sex in marriage (1 Cor. 7:1–11, 25–40). In contrast, the Jesus of this saying combines Genesis 1 and Genesis 2 to celebrate God's creation of humanity as sexed beings—"male and female."

Jesus affirms and reaffirms the human destiny to become one flesh: "they are no longer two, but one flesh." This is a strikingly sensual description of marriage. The Jesus of this story stresses the fleshly, embodied character of the bond between partners. He does not talk at all about any "original" sin in Eden, Eve's sin, female destiny to bear children, or male rule over women. Genesis 3 is not in view. Instead, he contrasts God's creative intention with "the law of Moses." Where his opponents try to derive a ruling about divorce from a law about remarriage (Mark 10:2), Jesus focuses instead on God's creation of humans as erotically joined beings. It is this prefall reality of fleshly bondedness that Jesus wants us to emulate. He looks to Genesis 1–2 and not the later part of the Torah for revelation of God's erotic will for humanity.

I have heard it said that people are more often right in what they affirm than in what they deny. The same could be said about this story from Mark. On the plus side, the text affirms the sacredness of intimate committed relationships. Contemporary media culture celebrates the almost druglike rush of new love and passing sexuality. This text, however, affirms the holiness of day-in, day-out bondedness. And this need not mean just sexual bondedness, though that is clearly in view in both Genesis 2 and Mark 10. For many who have undergone divorce have found that such sexual bondedness is only part of the one flesh that is torn when committed people part. Instead, the one flesh that is created through long-term physical intimacy also includes the fabric of shared memories, a network of in-laws and friends, a dwelling and shared belongings, and (often) shared children.

This is the one flesh that hurts so much when one divorces, the "one flesh" created through years of intimate, day-to-day life together and shared history. This Markan Jesus recognizes the existence of this deep bond, says God willed it from the beginning, and urges people not to separate what God has joined together. This can be an important message.

That said, we must also acknowledge how the unqualified denial of divorce in this text has deeply hurt people over the centuries. For the reality of human marriage does not always match the Eden vision that the Markan Jesus emphasizes. What about cases where men "rule" over women and physically abuse them? What about cases where one or the other parent sexually abuses the children? Then there are cases where one spouse abandons the other, whether physically or in spirit; cases where one spouse descends into alcoholism or drug addiction; cases where a spouse is sexually unfaithful to the other or ends the sexual relationship with the other. The Jesus presented in Mark ignores these and other ways in which marriages fall short of the Eden garden.[4] He sovereignly dictates that no one should ever divorce, and the already sex-negative church has taken this saying and used it to imprison men and (particularly) women trapped in life-damaging marriages. This unnuanced Jesus saying has become a harsh Christian "law," which has been life-denying in ways that Jewish divorce law is not.

One way to deal with this would be to deny that Jesus ever said this thing. Scholars already doubt that the story's picture of conflict with the Pharisees is historical. Rather, the story's depiction of Jesus' critique of the Pharisees tells us more about the later church's conflict with the Pharisaic movement than it does about anything that happened with Jesus himself.[5] Could it be that his rejection of divorce is likewise a creation of the early church? This is possible, but the widespread occurrence of Jesus' antidivorce saying throughout Paul and the Gospels suggests otherwise. Though we cannot be sure that Jesus prohibited all divorce, we certainly cannot be sure he did not prohibit it either.

Another response is to recognize how Jesus' words reflect their time and place. People lived, on average, less than half as long as they do now. As a result, lifelong commitment would have meant a marriage of ten to fifteen years in Jesus' time. Moreover, the Jesus saying may reflect a belief that God would soon end the world as it is and restore it to how God had originally intended it.[6] Given this imminent transformation, the Jesus of this saying urges believers to live out that Eden reality now and not subject themselves to the compromises of the law of Moses.

Certainly, we confront this story in a quite different world. In place of short life expectancy, we have long life expectancy and major cultural and personal changes (job, home, and so on) throughout the span of a marriage. Where early Christians expected that God would soon return the world to its primeval state, now people have to contend with a world of lasting imperfections, including lifeless, dishonest, or violent marriages. Where people of that time were focused on sex within heterosexual marriage, we now recognize other ways in which people can be one flesh in many life-affirming ways. People still connect with each other as erotic men and as erotic women: "God made them male and female" (Mark 10:6; cf. Gen. 1:27). But the old fears and imperatives that drove homophobia and criticism of nonmarital sexuality need no longer rule our lives.

Once we acknowledge the ways this text has hurt and still hurts people, we can see how it might contain a surplus of experience that can inform our lives. I suggest that this surplus lies in the text's decisive affirmation of the erotic connection envisioned in Genesis 1–2. For the picture in Genesis 2 already stretches beyond the ancient focus on reproduction in its emphasis on sexual connectedness as a good in itself, rather than just as a means of having children. Whereas the urge to protect gender hierarchy stands behind ancient homophobic prohibitions against men having sex with other men, Genesis 2 strongly stresses the mutuality of the first man and woman. The author of Genesis 2 certainly did not envision it as an affirmation of erotic relationships more generally. But the story still emphasizes the embodied connection between male and female equals, rather than the hierarchical elements of the traditional family structure. And it is this emphasis on the fleshly connection between peers that the Jesus of Mark 10 affirms.

Insofar as we extend that connection to other erotic relationships, we might hear the Jesus of Mark 10 affirming their goodness too: "what God has joined together, let no one separate" (Mark 10:9). Insofar as Genesis 2 affirms the equality of the partners in that relationship, so also Mark 10 could be understood as an affirmation of relationships that achieve such mutuality and equality, a bondedness of partners formed into one flesh, the goodness of a relationship between equals who "correspond to each other" (Gen. 2:18, 20, 22–23). Read in light of Genesis 2, the Jesus of Mark 10 is not endorsing violent, abusive, alienated marriages. Rather, in citing the Genesis 2 vision of erotic connectedness between equals, this Jesus affirms the inherent, God-created goodness of enduring erotic connections between peers—not just male-female but also female-female and male-male. This affirmation is an implicit critique of relationships that starkly contrast with that vision, including marriages.

Taken this way, the story in Mark 10:2–9 and Matthew 19:3–9 stands as a profound confirmation of God's erotic intention for humanity and an implicit critique of antisexual tendencies both within the Bible and elsewhere. Within Mark 10, Genesis 1–2 stands as a Bible within the Bible. The picture of humanity made in God's image in Genesis 1 and God's affirmation of erotic connectedness in Genesis 2 constitute a norm against which to judge later attempts to destroy erotic connections that God has created: man to woman, man to man, woman to woman. When certain Christians assert that they can offer Christian "love" to a "homosexual" person, while insisting that such "homosexual" people not be in the erotic relationships to which they are drawn, when moralists try to separate people involved in mutual, loving relationships based on their interpretations of Mosaic law or later Pauline equivalents, we can see the Jesus of this story responding by affirming that the two "have become one flesh" and by asserting that "what God has joined together, let no one separate" (Mark 10:8–9).

Sharing Jesus' Passion: Jesus Christ as Garden Vine

We turn next to Isaiah's vineyard love song (Isa. 5:1–7). As in the case of the Eden garden, there are multiple echoes of this text in the New Testament. Again, there are two major alternatives.

The first major reflection of Isaiah's vineyard is in a vineyard parable found in Matthew, Mark, Luke, and even the noncanonical Gospel of Thomas. Particularly in the version found in Mark, Jesus uses motifs from Isaiah's vineyard song to describe the care that a man lavished on his vineyard.[7] He begins by saying, "A man planted a vineyard, put a fence around it, dug a pit for the wine press, and built a watchtower" (Mark 12:1). But here the similarity to Isaiah's song ends. This is just a prelude to a story in which the man leases the vineyard to tenants, who then reject and kill the landlord's messengers, including his son, when they come to collect the landlord's rent (Mark 12:1–9).[8] Jesus' vineyard parable has obvious connections to the later account of his crucifixion, but no links to erotic passion. The vineyard is no woman, it bears no grapes or berries, and the landlord has no feelings for the vineyard itself. There is not one trace of betrayed love.

We do see hints of such eros however, in the other New Testament allusion to Isaiah's vineyard, John 15:1–6. But there are some crucial changes from the Isaiah text, already evident in Jesus' claim at the outset that he himself is the "true vine":

> I am the true vine, and my Father is the vinegrower. He removes
> every branch that bears no fruit. Every branch that bears fruit he
> prunes to make it bear more fruit. You have already been cleansed
> by the word that I have spoken to you. Abide in me as I abide in
> you. Just as the branch cannot bear fruit by itself unless it abides in
> the vine, neither can you unless you abide in me. I am the vine, you

are the branches. Those who abide in me and I in them bear much
fruit, because apart from me you can do nothing. Whoever does not
abide in me is thrown away like a branch and withers; such branches
are gathered, thrown into the fire, and burned. (John 15:1–6)

In both Isaiah and John, God is the vintner. But whereas Isaiah's vineyard
poem implies that the vineyard is an unfaithful woman, Jesus' speech identifies him as the "true vine."

Still, images of women lie submerged beneath the focus on Jesus. Wisdom
texts from around Jesus' time identify the fruitful vine featured here with
both female Wisdom and the fruitful tree of life. Take for example, the
following poem from the Wisdom of Ben Sira, where a female Wisdom
figure echoes ancient love poetry in describing herself as "sweeter than
honey":

> Like a [great tree] I spread out my branches,
>   and my branches are glorious and graceful.
> Like the vine I bud forth delights,
>   and my blossoms become glorious and abundant fruit.
> Come to me, you who desire me,
>   and eat your fill of my fruits.
> For the memory of me is sweeter than honey,
>   and the possession of me sweeter than the honeycomb.
> Those who eat of me will hunger for more,
>   and those who drink of me will thirst for more.
> (24:16–21, NRSV adapted)

This poem describes female Wisdom as a vine whose taste makes one hun-
ger for more: "memory of me is sweeter than honey, and the possession of
me sweeter than the honeycomb." But in John 15, Jesus claims that he, not
Wisdom, is the "true vine." It is he, not Wisdom, who bears fruit. Moreover, the image works differently. In Ben Sira, Wisdom herself bore fruit
through her branches, but in John 15, the vine's branches are those followers
of Jesus who "abide" in him. They are the ones who must "bear fruit."

We see more links to Isaiah 5 in Jesus' discussion of those followers who
fail to "bear fruit." In Isaiah, God proclaims judgment on the vineyard
because it yielded rotten berries instead of good grapes (Isa. 5:2). As a
consequence, God proclaims God's plan to strip the vineyard and remove
protection from it. In contrast, Jesus in John 15 proclaims judgment on
branches that fail to yield fruit (John 15:2). They will be gathered and burned
in fire (15:6). Thus, as in the Mark story of the vineyard and tenants, we
see echoes in John 15 of the emphasis on God's wrath in Isaiah 5:1–7, even
though the vineyard symbol is used so differently.

So far we have seen little emphasis on love in either Isaiah 5:1–7 or in John 15:1–6. But John 15 defines Jesus' law as one of extending God's love: "As the Father has loved me, so I have loved you; abide in my love" (John 15:9). This means keeping Jesus' commandments, and his commandment is "to love one another as I have loved you" (John 15:12).[9] This must be the sort of intense love that Jesus will show to them in the crucifixion: "laying down his life for those he loves" (John 15:13).[10] Jesus goes on to emphasize his intimacy with his disciples: "No longer do I call you servants, . . . rather, I have called you my beloved" (John 15:15). The section concludes with a repetition of Jesus' call for the disciples to "love one another."

This entire love program revolves around Jesus' intent to share his "joy" with his disciples and "fulfill" their own joy (John 15:11).[11] In what does this joy consist? *Joy* is a frequent word in the Gospel of John, starting with the joy of John the Baptist at hearing the voice of Jesus, the bridegroom (John 3:29). But the most extended and vivid description of joy connects with female bodily experience in the description of childbirth:

> Very truly, I tell you, you will weep and mourn, but the world will
> rejoice; you will have pain, but your pain will turn into joy. When a
> woman is in labor, she has pain, because her hour has come. But
> when her child is born, she no longer remembers the anguish
> because of the joy of having brought a human being into the world.
> So you have pain now; but I will see you again, and your hearts will
> rejoice, and no one will take your joy from you. (John 16:20–22)

In this way Jesus depicts an intense love for others and motherlike joy that is stronger than death or any pain. His followers are given one main commandment to attain such ecstasy, and that is to love one another intensely. This is not a sexually erotic love. Rather it is a broader and yet still intense eros love, which might bind a community together.

In this way John 15 balances elements of Isaiah 5:1–7, while maintaining some of its harsh edge. On the one hand, the gender dichotomy of Isaiah 5:1–7 and related texts is gone. No longer are the unfaithful typified as a female vineyard. Jesus is now the vine. No longer do we have a wrathful husband and an unfaithful spouse. Instead we have branches, which succeed or do not succeed in keeping Jesus' commandment of love and so abide in him. On the other hand, these branches have different destinies, and here is where the harshness of the passage sets in. Those who love so intensely that they lay down their lives for each other are those who bear fruit, while those who do not so love are discarded. John's Gospel presents its readers with a clear choice between a life of love and a life without. There is no middle ground.

Mary Magdalene's Passion in a Garden

Finally, we turn to one more New Testament garden text: the account in John 20 of Mary Magdalene's encounter with Jesus at the garden tomb. Only the Gospel of John places Jesus' crucifixion and burial near such a garden (John 19:41).[12] Given the associations with gardens that we have seen elsewhere, this is significant. Therefore, it should not be a complete surprise that John's account of a garden crucifixion is linked to the most likely New Testament allusion to the Song of Songs.[13]

Earlier in John's Gospel we see possible echoes of the Song of Songs. In John 12, just prior to Jesus' betrayal and crucifixion, Mary of Bethany uses her hair (cf. Song 7:6) to anoint Jesus with fragrances reminiscent of the Song of Songs (Song 1:12–14; 4:10–14). After Jesus' crucifixion, John says that Jesus' body is anointed with "myrrh and aloes." As Raymond Brown notes, this is an unusual combination of spices. Aloe is not typically used in burials. The same combination, however, myrrh and aloe, does occur in Song of Songs 4:14. They are the last two spices mentioned in the man's description of his lover as a garden of spices.[14] Soon, Jesus' fragrant body is laid in a tomb in a garden (John 19:40–42).

The most striking links to the Song of Songs come immediately after this burial, in two night scenes with Mary Magdalene that echo the female lover's search for her love in Song of Songs 3:1–4. At the outset of John 20:

Early on the first day of the week, while it was still dark, Mary Magdalene came to the tomb and saw that the stone had been removed from the tomb. So she ran and went to Simon Peter and the other disciple, the one whom Jesus loved, and said to them, "They have taken the Lord out of the tomb, and we do not know where they have laid him."

[She comes back with the disciples, and they find the tomb empty.]

Then the disciples returned to their homes. But Mary stood weeping outside the tomb. As she wept, she bent over to look into the tomb; and she saw two angels in white, sitting where the body of Jesus had been lying, one at the head and the other at the feet. They said to her, "Woman, why are you weeping?" She said to them, "They have taken away my Lord, and I do not know where they have laid him." When she had said this, she turned around and saw Jesus standing there, but she did not know that it was Jesus. Jesus said to her, "Woman, why are you weeping? Whom are you looking for?" Supposing him to be the gardener, she said to him, "Sir, if you have carried him away, tell me where you have laid him, and I will take him away." Jesus said to her, "Mary!" She turned and said to him in Hebrew, "Rabbouni" [Teacher]. Jesus said to her, "Do not hold on to me, because I have not yet ascended to the Father. But go to my brothers and say to them, 'I am ascending to my Father and your Father, to my God and your God.' " (John 20:1–2, 10–17)

This story parallels Song of Songs 3:1–4 only to diverge at the end. Both John 20 and Song of Songs 3:1–4 occur at night. Mary's repeated cry in John—"they have taken away the Lord/my lord, and we/I do not know where they have laid him"—echoes the repeated statement of the woman of the Song when she "sought him . . . and did not find him." Mary's implicit query to the angels at the tomb about where Jesus is recalls the woman of the Song of Songs asking if the guards of the city have seen her love. Yet at this crucial point, the texts part ways. When the woman finds her man, different things happen. The woman of the Song of Songs finds and seizes her true love, not letting him go until she takes him to her mother's house. In contrast, when Mary finds Jesus, he says, "Do not hold on to me, because I have not yet ascended to the Father."[15] Whereas the man in the Song of Songs is brought to the chamber of her mother's house, Jesus must leave this tomb/chamber on his way to his father's house.

Understood as an allusion to the Song of Songs, John 20 straddles the divine-human divide we have been discussing. On the one hand, Mary Magdalene loves a human Jesus. Indeed, his statement "do not hold on to me" suggests that Mary has touched him (John 20:17).[16] Moreover, she is apparently special to him. He calls her "Mary" (John 20:16). This is the only instance in the entire Gospel of John where Jesus calls a woman by name (cf. John 10:3). On the other hand, the text wants to stress his heavenly origins and destiny. This passage is placed on the border of Jesus' resurrection, just after he dies (John 19) and before his appearances to the disciples in Jerusalem (John 20:19–29) and Galilee (John 21). Indeed, his call not to hold him in John 20:17 indicates that he is on his way from one plane to another.[17]

Such a blended treatment is unprecedented in early interpretations of the Song of Songs. Indeed, we have no other clear interpretations of the Song that are this early. The few rabbinic references to the Song occur in documents that were edited more than a century later. Moreover, early Jewish and Christian interpretations of the Song are either sexual or theological, never both. There are a few oblique rabbinic comments that suggest that some people still used the Song of Songs as a source of human love poetry. That may be the origin of the usage in John 20. At the same time, the bulk of Jewish and early Christian interpretations take the Song to be about love between God and God's people. In contrast, John 20, if it is indeed an allusion to the Song of Songs, blends both approaches. It depicts the longing of Mary to find her Lord's human body, but it is clear that this Lord is also a heavenly figure.

This depiction of longing, like the Song of Songs, is a tease. It describes a Jesus who is longed for and present, yet also unreachable. The Song of Songs ends with the call to the lover to "Flee, my love, make yourself like a gazelle, or like a young stag on the mountains of spices!" (Song 8:14). Here in John 20, a Jesus fragrant with spices pulls himself away from Mary Magdalene. The rest of the Gospel of John includes more scenes that work with the same dynamic of bodily presence and absence. Jesus shows his disciples his pierced hand and side (John 20:20) and allows Thomas to touch him (John 20:27). Nevertheless, the gospel also seems to recognize the difficulty of belief for others without such a sensuous connection to the risen Jesus. Toward the end, the narrator has Jesus say to Thomas, "Have you believed because you have seen me? Blessed are those who have not seen and yet have come to believe" (John 20:29). The readers are those who have not had a chance to "hold," "see," or "touch" Jesus' body.

This text focuses on intense longing, though not specifically sexual desire. Given the gospel's focus on Jesus' divinity, this story has more in common with divine-human love texts than with purely human love poetry. Nevertheless, contrary to popular interpretations, the text does not judge Mary for her passion to see and touch Jesus. Past commentators on John 20 have been quick to criticize Mary for trying to "cling" to Jesus and hold him back from his heavenly destiny. Yet the gospel appears to have a much more positive take on her character. After all, she and not any of the disciples is the first to come looking for Jesus. She and not the disciples stays by the tomb when it appears that Jesus is gone. She is the one who gets to see and touch Jesus first. And when Jesus tells her that she cannot keep holding him, it is only to emphasize that Jesus is in a liminal space that does not allow a lasting embrace.[18] It is Mary and Mary alone who weeps and mourns after Jesus dies (John 20:11, 15). Though Jesus had predicted that the disciples would weep before feeling the joy that he brought (John 16:20), it is only Mary who acts this out—first weeping and later holding Jesus (John 20:15, 17). Just as Jesus uses the example of a woman giving birth as an image of pain followed by joy, so Mary-as-woman exemplifies this process in this first resurrection experience.[19]

Church tradition has transformed this Mary Magdalene of John 20 into a prostitute who loved Jesus. Soon after Jesus' death, the Mary of this story was identified with the sinful woman who anointed and kissed Jesus' feet in Luke (Luke 7:39) and the Mary from whom seven demons had been cast out (Luke 8:2). This mixture of different figures became a single "saint" to whom a feast day was dedicated.[20] In this way, the church created a Mary figure, who fell easily into half of the old gender dichotomy: woman as whore or virgin. The only difference from the prophetic texts we examined is that this supposed whore, Mary, is not the people or the city. This did not keep believers, however, from seeing this saint, Mary, as a model of the sinful church in relation to Jesus. Other New Testament texts envision the church as Christ's pure bride (2 Cor. 11:2; Eph. 5:23–32) or a purified Jerusalem as Christ's pure bride (Rev. 21:2, 9),[21] much like Israel was God's pure bride on the other side of the painful exile (Isa. 54:4–8; 62:4–5). These traditions regarding sinful Mary Magdalene, however, exploit the other side of the gender dichotomy. They use the stereotype of a promiscuous, rule-breaking woman to characterize the sinful community.

Yet the resonances of John 20 to the Song of Songs suggest a way to reread this text without such stereotypes from our postgarden existence. After all, we have seen how texts like the Song of Songs resist the dichotomies of so much of the rest of the Bible and later Christian tradition. Though other laws and narratives may vilify sexually proactive women, the Song of Songs celebrates female sexual passion. Church tradition may have wanted to find in the Mary of these texts a prostitute on which to model its own infidelity to an angry God, but John 20 simply depicts a woman desperately seeking the Lord she loves, willing to go to any lengths to find him, asking everyone she meets if they know where he is. She is no model of inappropriate eros. Her passionate longing is her greatest strength in this story. In it, she models the love that the Johannine Jesus calls on all of his disciples to exhibit (John 13:34; 15:12, 17).

This should not just lead us to affirm female passion. It should help us affirm passionate love in all human beings. One of the things that drives the whore-virgin dichotomy is the ancient belief that women—at least, "bad women"—are more passionate than men, indeed dangerously passionate. As long as erotic desire is located primarily in women, then men will deal with their own passion in oblique ways—both living it out in destructive ways and projecting their fear of their desire onto women.

Thus both John 20 and the Song of Songs can be dangerous if they are used to reinforce the image of women as symbols of passion. Despite some enculturated and biological differences, men and women are as similar erotically as we are different: both are driven toward erotic connection with others, embracing (often imperfectly) long-term relationships, sometimes jealous and fearful of competitors, cherishing children, and so on. These similarities are already implied in the idea that God created both men and women in the bodily image of the one God. And this principle must be remembered as we relate Biblical women's passion to our own.

That said, Mary's passion here models the interpenetration of human and divine elements in eros. Yes, Mary seeks the human, touchable man whom she calls "my teacher." Yet this man stands just on the other side of death and is already on his way back to his and her father, God. As orthodox Christian theology has affirmed, this Jesus whom she loves is both human and divine at the same time. And the text nicely depicts the elusiveness of their encounter. Mary does find her Jesus, unlike the others who came with her, and she succeeds in touching, even holding him. Yet he is on his way somewhere else, like the lover of the Song of Songs.

Just as many seek and taste God in the midst of their erotic experience of another person, so Mary temporarily sees and touches God in the person of Jesus. Yet just as spiritually erotic experiences only last for a time, so also her experience of Jesus is limited. It can be no more without sliding into idolatry. We must open ourselves to experiencing God in our intimate encounters with others. We were made for this. Yet we risk self-destruction when we identify our erotic experience of others with God, becoming addicted to getting the same, repetitive erotic fix from other human beings. The interpenetration of erotic and spiritual experiences is ephemeral and elusive, much like the interpenetration of human and divine in this story of Jesus.

Concluding Reflections

So the New Testament, like the Old Testament, has *multiple* perspectives on eros and divine-human connectedness. For example, we have many texts from Paul and elsewhere that deny the body and are ambivalent (or negative) about deep human connectedness. Yet, we have seen a strain of garden texts—Jesus' affirmation of the eros of Genesis 1–2, Jesus proclaiming himself to be a vine of love corresponding to the vineyard of Isaiah's love song, and Mary Magdalene's passionate searching for and finding of Jesus just on the other side of the resurrection—that emphasize passion. None is as clearly focused on eros as their Old Testament counterparts. Yet each preserves and develops the Old Testament picture of eros in ways distinct from much of the New Testament and early Christian tradition.

Put together, these New Testament garden texts create an evocative picture of a Christian community that is built on God's tangible love as seen in Jesus, a community called to extend that love to each member. This picture links in turn with Rita Nakashima Brock's proposal of an erotic Christology in her book *Journeys by Heart*.[22] Building on various strains of feminist erotic theory and theology, Brock proposes refocusing Christology on the healing and transformative power of "Christa community." Brock contrasts this approach with traditional "heroic Christology," that is, a Christology that focuses on the individual Jesus and an abusive God's need to crucify him. Instead, she rereads the Gospel of Mark as a story of the healing community that grew up around Jesus, a community that was empowered to persevere on the other side of his tragic death. Brock's rereading of Mark links well with the rereading of texts from John proposed here. The John texts present Jesus as the true vine and call on the disciples to love one another in order to abide in him. Moreover, the Gospel of John uses women as models for this process—a woman persevering through the pain of childbirth to the joy afterward, Mary Magdalene weeping, searching, and then finding Jesus. As in the Prophets, believers are imaged as women in John. But unlike many of the prophetic texts, the passion of the women in these New Testament garden texts is good.

Of course, there are other ways to read these texts. Moreover, there is much more in these texts that one might lift up and criticize. Why should Christians only love "one another" as suggested in John? Why not take more seriously the prohibition of divorce and the exclusive focus on heterosexuality of Jesus in Mark (10:2–9)? Is not the "love" envisioned in John nonembodied and otherworldly? After all, the first letter of John easily combines the command to "love one another" with a call not to "love the world or things in the world" and to deny the "desire of the flesh" (1 John 2:15–17).

I choose to understand this "desire of the flesh" to be addictive love, an idolatry of things or people. Nevertheless, I have had to make many such choices throughout these and preceding chapters, just like anyone who tries to use such ancient texts to inform contemporary life. We must always choose to take certain aspects of a text as helpful, and helpful in particular ways. We must ask, "Is there a surplus of experience?" and "Where?" The difference is not whether or not one does this, but whether or not one is honest about doing so. This reading, at least, is open to the diversity of the New Testament and clear about its presuppositions.

The end of the New Testament highlights the problem. The last six chapters of Revelation present a dichotomy that should be familiar to the reader by now: God's destruction of the "whore" Babylon (Rev. 17:1–19: 6) versus Christ's marriage to the pure "bride," the new Jerusalem (Rev. 19:7–22:21). Over there stands the whore, "holding in her hand a golden cup full of abominations and the impurities of her fornication" (Rev. 19: 5). Like so many female communities in the Old Testament she will be made "desolate and naked," before being "burned with fire" (Rev. 17:16). Over here, the angels proclaim the coming of the lamb's bride:

> For the marriage of the Lamb has come,
>   and his bride has made herself ready;

to her it has been granted to be clothed
  with fine linen, bright and pure. (Rev. 19:7–8, NRSV)

This pure woman, this "new Jerusalem," is the group of righteous people
in the church, and "the fine linen is the righteous deeds of the saints" (Rev.
19:8). Toward the end, the book calls on its readers in words reminiscent
of the female lover's call to her lover in the Song of Songs. There she says,
"Come my love, let us go out in the field" (Song 7:12). In Revelation, a
similar desire appears as the longing for the second coming of Jesus. This
is a yearning of the female community/female Spirit for Jesus: "The Spirit
and the bride say, 'Come.' And let everyone who hears say, 'Come' " (Rev.
22:17). At the end of the book, Jesus is quoted as saying, "Surely I am
coming soon," and the author adds, "Come, Lord Jesus!" (Rev. 22:20).[23]
The calls of the Song of Songs are answered—or are they?

The reader of the New Testament has a choice about how to take such
texts. Many will continue to vilify "whore Babylon" and focus on the
proper eros of a femalelike church for its male Lord, Jesus. That is certainly
how the majority of ancient readers took it. Yet this approach must partake
of the vicious divine-human gender continuum, the whore-virgin dichotomy, and the feminization of passion that was characteristic of postgarden
rules.

We can also choose to seek another message in the New Testament. We
can seek a life-giving reading with the same intensity that Mary Magdalene
searched for her lost Lord. There is Jesus' affirmation of Genesis 1–2 rather
than the postgarden rules. There is a community called to love each other
with such intensity that its members will lay down their lives for each other.
There is a tomb garden where two human beings touch (Mary and Jesus),
one recognizing the divine in the other.

Perhaps this tangible Jesus as a sign of God's love can be a model of God's
tangible presence in others we love. So much of the tradition emphasizes
how God "became flesh" in Jesus. The church is often called "Christ's
body" (for example, 1 Cor. 12). Christian theology emphasizes that God's
love was made real through the bodily presence, crucifixion, and resurrection of this earthy human man who grew up in first-century Galilee. And
this tangible presence is regularly celebrated in Christian communion, where
bread and wine are eaten and drunk as Christ's body and blood.

Yet if we focus too exclusively on God's revelation through this earthy
man, we may miss ways in which he might be a paradigm of how God is
equally present in others. Yes, this tangible Jesus, a "word made flesh,"
embodies God's love in a radical way. Yet this is not necessarily a "no" to
God being tangibly present in others. Within the Song of Songs, the lovers

experience tastes of the divine in each other. The church has sometimes recognized marriage as a sacrament through which believers can sensuously experience the divine, and sacraments in general are sensuous rituals that can make God's presence tangibly real to believers.[24] Traditions like these can be prompts to recognize more broadly how God is not present just in Jesus Christ. Instead, "Jesus Christ" can be a sign for Christians of God's ephemeral, teasing presence in others whom we love and in the world in general.

12
Epilogue

THE EROTIC WORD

Looking Back

At the outset of this volume, we saw how the Bible has been used to
suppress sexuality, but by now we have seen how the Bible—read through
the lens of its garden texts—can be read to evoke eros, including sexual
eros. From the garden of Eden story to the Song of Songs, the Bible can
be used to cultivate a passionate life, one infused with eros for God, others,
and the world. Where the Bible has separated sex and spirit, these garden
texts can join them. Where advertising aims to warp human desire, these
texts can root our diverse passions in love of God. Amidst the massive sexual
shifts in our culture, the Eden and Song of Songs garden texts envision a
sexuality grounded in intimacy and mutual desire. They neither endorse all
forms of sexual exchange nor do they conform to the Victorian rules that
have been used to police many nonmarital relationships.

We started with the garden of Eden, the creation of erotic male and
female humanity by an erotic God; we were made in that God's image,
inflamed by that God's breath. We were made for intimate connection with
each other and the earth. Although we do not always live in a sensuous
garden of intimate connection, the Bible judges other realities—for example, marriage and reproduction—by that standard. Later, we saw Mark's
Jesus judge contemporary rules about marriage by the garden ideal of intimacy.

We moved on to Isaiah's vineyard garden, an example of how ancient
Israel saw itself as the "woman" vulnerable to and loved by her husband,
God, who punished her for her failure to be faithful to him. This picture
of God in love with an entire people is unique among world religions. It
testifies to the importance of passion for God and it critiques ultimate at-

tachment to anything else. Yet this picture is infected with the male-focused gender rules of life outside the garden. In focusing on God's violent punishment of God's promiscuous "wife," the texts image the worst in love, not its best. This is true of New Testament reflections of Isaiah's garden as well. Mark's Jesus presents the garden as an image of divine destruction, and John's Jesus juxtaposes the picture of him as the true vine for those who love each other with the threat to cut off and burn unproductive branches that fail to do so.

But there is another Biblical garden. The Song of Songs celebrates a couple's attempts to resist post-Eden rules and taste love in a garden themselves. The poetry of the Song elegantly depicts their desire and teasingly implies its consummation. Traditional male-female, divine-human gender roles are undermined as the male and female roles evolve over the course of the poem. Meanwhile, the boundaries of the characters blur. They, particularly the woman, merge with the world around them. And, as in other love poetry, the divine sometimes shimmers through them.

In this way, the Song of Songs evokes multiple dimensions of love. Its depiction of the man and woman as partially merged with the landscape around them offers one way of joining love of a person and love of the earth. Just as the Eden story describes the creation of humans from the earth to work and protect it, so the Song offers a vision of the joining of love of a person with love of the world around them. Meanwhile, the Song joins the sexual and spiritual dimensions of love, depicting the divine as shimmering through the lovers. Both dimensions are present in the most likely New Testament reflection of the Song of Songs—the story of Mary Magdalene's seeking and finding of Jesus at the garden tomb.

These texts are cultural resources as we confront some of the contemporary challenges discussed at the outset of this book. Where our society tends to separate sex from spirituality, crucial texts in the Bible join them. Where the Bible has been used to alienate people from their sexuality, we can look to texts like Genesis 1–2 to affirm that this is how God made us. Where the Bible has been cited as the authority for modern forms of family and marriage, we can point to the fact that few seriously affirm the full range of Biblical commands about sex, whether in the Old or New Testaments. Moreover, the broader principles behind these rules are depicted in the garden of Eden story as aspects of postgarden life that God did not originally intend for God's creation. Finally, where the Bible has been used to link sexuality to reproduction, texts like Genesis 2, Mark 10, and the Song of Songs depict intimacy as the central aspect of sexual eros. Together with the Eden story, they envision humanity as created from the earth, infused with God's breath, reflecting God's divinity in our earthly forms, and called to a life of caring for the earth from which we came and loving each other and God.

In this way, the Bible offers a vision of sexuality that goes beyond the moralism and sexual exchange that characterizes much of our culture. The Bible does not just tell people to do whatever feels good, nor to just avoid what is bad. Nor does the Bible offer any single norm for sexuality, however much modern readers strive to create such a norm out of a mix of Victorian images of the family, Old Testament honor laws, and early Christian texts generally ambivalent about sexuality and family. Yet this closer look at the Bible has revealed texts like the Eden creation story and the Song of Songs that evoke a sexuality joined with spirituality, an eros that involves the whole person. Taken as a whole, the Bible does not endorse any one cultural model of sexuality or eros. Yet crucial parts of it deeply affirm divine and human passion, a passion that joins humans to one another, the earth, and to God.

Monogamy and the Erotic God

That said, we need to recognize that the Hebrew Bible affirms God's special passion for a particular people, Israel. Though God starts with humanity as a whole, most of the Hebrew Bible is focused on God's choice of Israel out of the peoples of the world and the story of God's covenant with Israel. Indeed, a closer look at the Bible reveals many implicitly erotic aspects to God and Israel's relationship. We already saw how the book of Deuteronomy describes God's love for Israel using the same word, *ḥashaq*, that is used elsewhere for a man's intense desire for a woman. And God is jealous throughout much of the Torah. Much divine law focuses on keeping God's partner separate from the other nations of the world.[1] Yet, as in the Song of Songs, the relationship is not fully consummated. Though the relationship between Israel and God sometimes reaches a high of direct encounter (Exod. 19, 24), the Torah ends with Israel still outside the land, and the broader Biblical history sees Israel go off into exile. No wonder then that the rabbis could so easily intertwine the Song's tantalizing depiction of love gained and lost with the Torah picture of the ups and downs of God's relationship with Israel.[2]

Yet what about the others, non-Jews, like myself? Is there something here for me too? The broader Christian Bible would say "yes," at least for those who are Christian. It takes God's love for Israel as a paradigm of God's love for the church. Where the Old Testament envisions God's passion for Israel, Paul and his heirs envision the church as "a chaste virgin to Christ" (2 Cor.

11:2). This perspective then dominates much Christian interpretation of the Song of Songs and other Biblical texts.

One major problem with this view is that it often involves a simultaneous assertion that God has rejected Israel. It is not enough that God married the church, but God must have rejected the synagogue in the process, a sort of divine serial monogamy. Indeed, some ancient illustrations of the Song of Songs even depict an enthroned Christ embracing the newly wed-ded church while pushing a divorced synagogue away. Figure 12.1 is an illumination in the initial O of a medieval Song of Songs manuscript. Christ is embracing the church to his right, while he pushes away a rejected (yet still crowned) synagogue on his left. This image illustrates how jealousy was transmitted to the divine realm with anti-Semitic results. Christians did not see enough room in God's heart for both them and the people of Israel. As a result, much Christian theology has insisted that God somehow gave up God's passion for Israel and replaced it with love for the church. This idea has not only resulted in the killing of millions of Jews over the centuries, but it has also produced a Christian picture of God as someone whose love cannot be trusted.

Yet there is another way. Perhaps here we could take seriously the Biblical idea of humanity made in God's image and see the mix of human sexualities as testifying to God's pluriform eros. Perhaps we could affirm that, though human love may be limited, God is capable of passionate love for many. Just as some world religious traditions affirm God's ability to be passionately in love with multiple individuals (for example, Sufism and Bhakti Hindu-ism), we could affirm God's ability to be intimately and passionately in-volved with multiple religious communities. Robert Williams, a gay man who studied with Carter Heyward, put it this way:

> The urge to come out, to overcome oppression and self-loathing, to celebrate who I am, is the siren call of God, the Divine Lover—the most promiscuous of all lovers.[3]

This need not be an indiscriminate promiscuity, especially if it were imaged through the lens of the Song of Songs. It might be better articulated as the abiding, intimate bonds of God to different people and communities. This would be a polygamous, polyandrous God, involved in faithful and highly particular relationships with multiple partners.

Though made in God's image, most humans cannot invest deeply in such multiple relationships. Almost always we privilege certain ones over others, and the search for newness can hurt our lovers, children, and friends. Though it is not possible to say how capable humans might be in sustaining life-giving erotic relationships with multiple partners, it is safe to say that

Fig. 12.1. Dijon Biblical Manuscript 14, f. 60. Collection Bibliothèque municipale de Dijon, Ms.14f°60, cliché F. Perrodin.

such multiple relationships do not work for many, possibly most people. Yet, even if not acted on, perhaps our longing for connection to multiple others reflects God's broad passions. Even human uneasiness with monogamy, our restless passion, might be a way that our erotic selves testify to God's fire moving through us.

The Human Erotic Calling

When asked what the greatest commandment of them all was, the Gospels testify that Jesus answered with the ancient Israelite Shema: "You shall love the lord your God with all your heart, and with all your soul and with all your mind and with all your strength" (Mark 12:28–30; Matt. 22:34–38; Luke 10:25–27). Notably, this is the commandment that faithful Jews throughout the ages have bound on themselves, like a seal of a love stronger than death. And many Jews have been called upon to live out that love over time, crying out as they were killed the first words of this great commandment, "Hear oh Israel, the Lord our God is one."

Like them, we do not have infinite time to choose in which world we will live. Our time is running out; we must answer this invitation from God, the divine love and lover, and choose God's somewhat mad world.

So many of us live our lives as if there is still so much time to love, and yet I am reminded of the following poem from Rainer Marie Rilke's early notebooks:

I cannot believe, that puny death,
over whose head we daily gaze,
remains such a worry to us and a care.

I cannot believe, that he truly threatens;
I'm still living, I have time to build:
My blood will be red long past the red of the rose.

My grasp of things is deeper than the clever game
with our fear which Death likes to play.
I am the world,
from which he slipped and fell.

    Death is like
those circling monks who walk around so;
One fears their return,
One never knows: is it the same one every time,
are there two, are there ten, are there a thousand or even more?
One only knows this strange, yellow hand,
which is reaching out so naked and so near—
There, there:
as if it came out of your own clothes.[4]

Like the speaker in the poem, I sometimes find myself pretending that death has no purchase on my world. Sometimes I write obscure scholarly articles as if I had forever. Yet there is that yellow hand, the hand that I know one day will reach out, so naked and so near, as if it came from my own clothes.

What will define my life then? Years from now, no one will have heard of me. My books and articles, at best, will be of merely historical interest. Yet, to some extent or another, I will have passionately loved, however imperfectly, sending that love out into the world.

Of course I, like all others, have and will drift into loving some things compulsively, turning things into God. Yet that is not the love to which the garden texts of Scripture call us. Read as Scripture, a text like the Song of Songs is not a call to hedonism or addictive seeking.

Instead, read through the lens of its garden texts, the Bible invites us to that deeper eros. This is not an eros that pursues every sexual urge. It is not a flitting to and fro in search of the things that advertising and media tell us we should want. It is identifying and answering God's deepest call to us through the goodness of creation. It is listening to that part of ourselves that was created for deep connection to others. It is risking vulnerability to God and others in intimacy. Taken on this level, eros for God and God's creation is not an either-or choice. Our yearning for connection with God can be expressed through seeking connection with each other and creation. The Song helps us here. Against the dualistic theology of ancient and modern interpretations of the text, I have argued that it images a love in which the lovers merge with their world and shimmer with the divine, a love that is sexually erotic and exquisitely spiritual at the same time, indeed, a love that is all the more exquisitely spiritual for being sexually erotic.

Finally, this call to erotic love could be extended more broadly to encompass humanity as a whole. All too often we live our lives as if humankind were forever, that the United States, that our religious community (the church, for example) will go on existing indefinitely, that the ecosystem on earth will still be functioning billions of years from now. Yet it is far more likely that through one or another catastrophe, our stay in the cosmos will be ended. Our books and learning will be buried. Our cities will be dust as winds howl over the ruins of what once was humanity.

What will many of our accomplishments mean in that endtime? What will define our stay in this cosmos? I would argue that it is this: how deeply, how fully, how broadly we loved. Many generations before us have loved and created us, and they have worked and died to create the institutions and contexts in which we too could love, even as we too work to create the conditions for future generations to live and love as well.

So now we are here, gifted with the gardens of the Bible, reading traditions like the Song of Songs, which call us to love not only God, but also God's creation and each other in that broader eros/love to which the garden texts call us. With what time is left to us, we are called to settle for nothing less than a passionate love affair with God and with life, embracing God and the creation through which God shimmers, living madly in the fantasy that this universe is not purposeless, but that we are called toward the drama and pain of life and love lived to the fullest.

In this way might we discover a love fierce as death, with tongues of flame, an inferno,

a love which mighty waters cannot overcome,
   nor rivers drown it,

a love so much more precious than jewels,
   that someone trying to buy it with everything they had would be
     mocked
to love with all our heart, all our life strength,
   and all our might . . .
until we die with our love on our lips.[5]

Notes

The notes to this book only partially reveal the extent to which this work is built on my colleagues' research. I have tried to acknowledge major intellectual debts but did not want to create a huge scholarly apparatus. My debt to a given work often goes far beyond its appearance in a note here or there.

CHAPTER I

1. For a broader overview of this history of interpretation and reflection, see David Carr, "The Song of Songs as a Microcosm of the Canonization and Decanonization Process," in *Canonization and Decanonization*, ed. A. van der Kooij and Karel van der Toorn (Leiden: Brill, 1998), 173–89. Carr's subsequent article-length studies pursuing this question include "The Song of Songs and Falling in Love with God," *Bible Today* 36 (1998): 153–58; "Rethinking Sex and Spirituality: The Song of Songs and Its Readings," *Soundings: An Interdisciplinary Journal* 81 (1999): 418–35; "Gender and the Shaping of Desire in the Song of Songs and Its Interpretations," *Journal of Biblical Literature* 119 (2000): 233–48; "Ancient Sexuality and Divine Eros: Rereading the Bible through the Lens of the Song of Songs," *Union Seminary Quarterly Review* 54 (2001): 1–18; and "Passion for God: A Center in Biblical Theology," *Horizons in Biblical Theology* 23 (2001): 1–24.

2. Daniel H. Garrison, *Sexual Culture in Ancient Greece* (Norman: University of Oklahoma Press, 2000), 246–69.

3. Also see Matt. 22:30; Luke 20:35.

4. Also see Matt. 12:46–50; Luke 8:19–21.

5. For arguments that Paul was highly ambivalent about the institution of the family, see Dale Martin, *The Corinthian Body* (New Haven, Conn.: Yale University Press, 1995), 198–212; and Martin, "Paul without Passion: On Paul's Rejection of Desire in Sex and Marriage," in *Constructing Early Christian Families: Family as Social Reality and Metaphor*, ed. Halvor Moxnes (New York: Routledge, 1997), 201–15, esp. 201–4. Mark Jordan points out the ambiguity and lack of precision of many passages from Paul that are often used for more specific rules about sexuality in *The Ethics of Sex* (Oxford: Blackwell, 2002), 24–29.

6. 1 Thess. 4:3–8; 1 Cor. 6:9–20; Gal. 5:19–21; and Rom. 1:24–27; cf. 1 Cor. 5:1–13. See Bernadette Brooten, *Love between Women: Early Christian Responses to Female Homoeroticism* (Chicago: University of Chicago Press, 1996), 189–362, for the state of the art regarding Paul's view of sex between women. As for Paul's view of sex between men, his pairing of terms for sex between men in texts like 1 Cor. 6:9—*malakoi* and *arsenokoitai*—suggest that he, like contemporary non-Christian moral philosophers, was thinking particularly of the practice of older males maintaining youthful male lovers. See Robin Scroggs, *The New Testament and Homosexuality: Contextual Background for Contemporary Debate* (Philadelphia, Pa.: Fortress, 1983), esp. 99–122. Nevertheless, there is no evidence that he would have been more friendly toward other forms of male-male sex.

Also, Acts, an early history of the emergence of the church, ascribes to James and the early leaders of the Jerusalem church the stipulation that avoidance of "fornication" (nonreproductive sexuality) was one of the minimum requirements for gentile converts to become Jesus followers (Acts 15:20, 29; 21:25; cf. James 2:11). It is difficult to determine whether this truly happened, or whether the historian who wrote Acts was influenced by thinkers like Paul on this point.

7. This and other translations of the New Testament are taken from the New Revised Standard Version (NRSV).

8. Oration 18, "On the Death of His Father," in *A Select Library of the Nicene and Post-Nicene Fathers of the Christian Church*, vol. 7, 2d ser. (New York: Christian Literature, 1894), 257.

9. E.g., Augustine, *The City of God: Books VIII–XVI*, trans. Gerald G. Walsh and Grace Monahan (New York: Fathers of the Church, 1952), bk. 14:21–26, pp. 395–407; *On Forgiveness of Sins and Baptism* 21,35–24,38, in *Answer to the Pelagians I*, Works of Saint Augustine I/23, trans. Roland J. Teske (Hyde Park, N.Y.: New City, 1997), 103–5; *Against Julian* 6,15, in *Answer to the Pelagians II*, Works of Saint Augustine I/24, trans. Roland J. Teske (Hyde Park, N.Y.: New City, 1998), 317; *On Marriage and Desire* 6,7–7,8 in *Answer to the Pelagians II*, 32–33; and *Answer to the Two Letters of the Pelagians* 17,34–35 in *Answer to the Pelagians II*, 133–134.

10. For more detailed study of the development of Christian views about sexuality and celibacy, see Peter Brown, *The Body and Society: Men, Women, and Sexual Renunciation in Early Christianity* (New York: Columbia University Press, 1988).

11. I am indebted for this term and the analysis of its importance to Philip Sheldrake, "Spirituality and Sexuality," in *Embracing Sexuality: Authority and Experience in the Catholic Church*, ed. Joseph Selling (Aldershot, England: Ashgate, 2001), 25–27.

12. For a good brief survey of Christianity and sexuality, see Jack Dominian, "Sexuality and Interpersonal Relationships," in Selling, *Embracing Sexuality*, 5–8.

13. A point made well in R. Tannahill, *Sex in History*, rev. ed. (Chelsea, Mich.: Scarborough House, 1992), 160–61.

14. For a more nuanced survey of various Jewish views of sexuality, see David Biale, *Eros and the Jews: From Biblical Israel to Contemporary America* (New York: Basic, 1992), esp. 33–190.

15. Derrick Sherwin Bailey, *Sexual Relation in Christian Thought* (New York: Harper, 1959), 133–34.

16. E.g., T. G. Tappert, ed. and trans., *Letters of Spiritual Counsel* (London: SCM, 1955), 274.

17. Jordan, *Ethics of Sex*, 57–62, cf. 117–25.

18. Kathy Rudy provides a helpful discussion of how this ideal has been appropriated by recent conservative Christian movements in *Sex and the Church: Gender, Homosexuality, and the Transformation of Christian Ethics* (Boston: Beacon, 1997), 15–44.

19. For an excellent detailed survey of sexuality in American history, see John D'Emilio and Estelle B. Freedman, *Intimate Matters: A History of Sexuality in America* (New York: Harper and Row, 1988).

20. For a sensitive survey of the balance of romantic and exchangelike forces in recent American culture, see Steven Seidman, *Embattled Eros: Sexual Politics and Ethics in Contemporary America* (New York: Routledge, 1992).

21. Jordan, *Ethics of Sex*, 131–35 argues persuasively that the earlier loss of regulative power over sex was more fundamental than the changes often associated with the "sexual revolution."

22. D. Sölle and Shirley Cloyes, *To Work and to Love: A Theology of Creation* (Philadelphia, Pa.: Fortress, 1984), 116–26.

23. Audre Lorde, "The Uses of the Erotic: The Erotic as Power," in her *Sister Outsider: Essays and Speeches* (Freedom, Calif.: Crossing, 1984), 56.

24. Carter Heyward, "Love and Sexuality," in her *The Redemption of God: A Theology of Mutual Relation* (Washington, D.C.: University Press of America, 1982), 217–25, reprinted in revised form as "Sexuality, Love, and Justice," in her *Our Passion for Justice: Images of Power, Sexuality and Liberation* (New York: Pilgrim, 1984), 83–93; Heyward, *Touching Our Strength: The Erotic as Power and the Love of God* (San Francisco: Harper and Row, 1989); Sölle and Cloyes, *To Work and to Love*; Beverly Harrison, "The Power of Anger in the Work of Love," in *Making the Connections: Essays in Feminist Social Ethics*, ed. Carol S. Robb (Boston: Beacon, 1985), 3–21; and Rita Nakashima Brock, *Journeys by Heart: A Christology of Erotic Power* (New York: Crossroad, 1988). Note as well Alexander C. Irwin, *Eros towards the World: Paul Tillich and the Theology of the Erotic* (Minneapolis, Minn.: Fortress, 1991).

25. Plaskow, *Standing Again at Sinai: Judaism from a Feminist Perspective* (New York: Harper and Row, 1990), 170–210.

26. Larry J. Uhrig, *Sex Positive: A Gay Contribution to Sexual and Spiritual Union* (Boston: Alyson, 1986); J. Michael Clark, *A Lavender Cosmic Pilgrim: Further Ruminations on Gay Spirituality, Theology and Sexuality* (Garland, Tex.: Tangelwild, 1990); Marvin Ellison, *Erotic Justice: A Liberating Ethic of Sexuality* (Louisville, Ky.: Westminster John Knox, 1996); and Daniel Spencer, *Gay and Gaia: Ethics, Ecology and the Erotic* (Cleveland, Ohio: Pilgrim, 1996).

27. Quoted from the beginning of tape 3a. Terry Kellogg, "The Importance of Healthy Sexuality and Spirituality in Relationships," in *Return to Intimacy: Relationships, Spirituality, Sexuality and Workaholism* (Minneapolis, Minn.: Lifeworks Communications, 1990).

28. For more nuanced discussion of this phenomenon among primates, see J. Diamond, *Why Is Sex Fun? The Evolution of Human Sexuality* (New York: Basic, 1997), 63–88.

29. For helpful overviews, see Donald Marshall and Robert Suggs, eds., *Human Sexual Behavior: Variations in the Ethnographic Spectrum* (Englewood Cliffs, N.J.: Prentice-Hall, 1971).

30. This point, among others, is made well in Judith Plaskow, "Decentering Sex: Rethinking Jewish Sexual Ethics," in *God Forbid: Religion and Sex in American Public Life*, ed. Kathleen Sands (New York: Oxford University Press, 2000), 30–38.

31. Some have suggested that early Christianity embraced a form of altruistic love that was opposed to the desires of the self. The Greek term for such love is *agape*, and it was taken as the superior Christian form of love, replacing selfish eros love. A. Nygren's *Agape and Eros*, trans. Philip Watson (Philadelphia, Pa.: Westminster, 1953) is the classic statement, often picked up by others. More recent studies, however, have questioned this interpretation. See in particular, Mary Blye Howe, "Passionate Love," *Mars Hill Review* 11 (1998): 53–62, for discussion and citation of earlier studies.

Moreover, eros and agape forms of love are not opposed when they are at their best. As Paul Ricouer points out, an eros without agape love can be a brutal, selfish, chaotic force ("Wonder, Eroticism, and Enigma," in *Sexuality and Identity*, ed. Hendrik M. Ruitenbeek [New York: Dell, 1970], 16). But eros also impels us to open up to others (Sölle and Cloyes, *To Work and to Love*, 141–55), and eros can keep an agape love for others from being disinvolved and moralistic (Irwin, *Eros towards the World*, 1–22). Therefore, this book articulates a Biblical vision of erotic love in which both components are important.

32. This latter example is from Howard Thurman, *Jesus and the Disinherited* (Nashville, Tenn.: Abingdon, 1949), 30–31.

33. I am indebted to Phyllis Trible, *God and the Rhetoric of Sexuality* (Philadelphia, Pa.: Fortress, 1978), for the initial observation of the link between the Eden garden and the Song of Songs.

34. Here I build on Carey Ellen Walsh's observations in *Exquisite Desire: Religion, the Erotic and the Song of Songs* (Minneapolis, Minn.: Fortress, 2000), 87–90.

35. Sheila Briggs, "Sexual Justice and the 'Righteousness of God,' " in *Sex and God: Some Varieties of Women's Religious Experience*, ed. Linda Hurcombe (New York: Routledge and Kegan Paul, 1987), 274.

CHAPTER 2

1. For a survey of the history of interpretation of the "image of God" with a focus on the last century, see Gunnlaugur A. Jónsson, *The Image of God: Genesis 1:26–28 in a Century of Old Testament Research*, trans. Lorraine Svendsen (Lund, Sweden: Almqvist and Wiksell, 1988).

2. Christoph Uehlinger, "Anthropomorphic Cult Statuary in Iron Age Palestine and the Search for Yahweh's Cult Images," in *The Image and the Book: Iconic Cults, Aniconism, and the Rise of Book Religion in Israel and the Ancient Near East*, ed. Karel van der Toorn (Leuven, Belgium: Peeters, 1997), 97–155.

3. This use of the Hadadyisi statue in relation to Gen. 1:26–27 is not new. See, for example, C. Dohmen, "Die Statue von Tell Fecherije und die Gottesebenbildlichkeit des Menschen: Beitrag zur Bilderterminologie," *Biblische Notizen* 22 (1983): 91–106.

4. The most prominent proponent of this view was Paul Humbert, *Etudes sur le récit du paradis et de la chute dans la Genèsis* (Neuchatel, France: Université de Neuchatel, 1940), 153–75. He was preceded by Theodore Nöldeke [Review of Friedr. Delitzsch's Hebrew-Aramaic Dictionary], *Zeitschrift der deutschen mor-*

genländischen Gesellschaft 40 (1886): 733–34; Nöldeke, "*selem* und *salmawet*," *Zeitschrift für die alttestamentliche Wissenschaft* 17 (1897): 183–87; and Herman Gunkel, *Schöpfung und Chaos in Urzeit und Endzeit* (Göttingen: Vandenhoeck and Ruprecht, 1895), 11.

5. This was argued in a article by W. Gross, "Die Gottebenbildlichkeit des Menschen im Kontext der Priesterschrift," *Theologische Quartalschrift* 161 (1981): 259–61, esp. n. 61 on 259.

6. R. H. Pfeiffer, *State Letters of Assyria: A Transliteration and Translation of 355 Official Assyrian Letters Dating from the Sargonid Period (722–625 B.C.)* (New Haven, Conn.: American Oriental Society, 1935), 120.

7. From Boyo Ockinga, *Die Gottebenbildlichkeit im alten Ägypten und im Alten Testament* (Wiesbaden, Germany: Harrassowitz, 1984), 21–22.

8. Ockinga helpfully surveys and puts in perspective some Egyptian texts that border on asserting a general similarity of humans to God in *Gottebenbildlichkeit*, esp. 139–41.

9. See Isa. 14:6; Ezek. 34:4; Pss. 72:8; 110:2.

10. See Frank Moore Cross, *Canaanite Myth and Hebrew Epic: Essays in the History of the Religion of Israel* (Cambridge, Mass.: Harvard University Press, 1972), 186–90, for a still-classic survey of the Biblical evidence in the northwestern Semitic context.

11. Job 1:1–2:6. See also 1 Kings 22:19–23; Isa. 40:1–8; Pss. 89:7–8.

12. To the best of my knowledge, this idea was first proposed by O. Loretz, *Die Gottebenbildlichkeit des Menschen* (München, Germany: Kösel, 1967), 67–68. Phyllis Bird, " 'Male and Female He Created Them': Gen. 1:27b in the Context of the Priestly Account of Creation," *Harvard Theological Review* 74 (1981): 148, argues against Loretz that the plural is only meant here to set up a distance between God (singular) and humans (plural). She asserts that the idea that humans have a godlike, sexed body would have been utterly foreign and repugnant to the priestly author. This seems to attribute body-denying attitudes to this Israelite writer that are more at home in the Greco-Roman world.

13. Howard Eilberg-Schwartz, *God's Phallus and Other Problems for Men and Monotheism* (Boston: Beacon, 1994), 107–8, notes how the Bible generally portrays Yahweh in a desexualized way.

14. The gender of the word *eretz*/earth in Hebrew is female, and so the Hebrew verbs in this section are feminine.

15. For persuasive arguments regarding the role of the earth and waters in the most ancient versions of Genesis 1 (reflected in the old Greek translation), see esp. William P. Brown, *Structure, Role and Ideology in the Hebrew and Greek Texts of Genesis 1:1–2:3* (Atlanta, Ga.: Scholars, 1993), 42–45, 128–36.

16. See Stephen Moore, *Poststructuralism and the New Testament* (Minneapolis, Minn.: Fortress, 1994), 74–81, for discussion of scholarship on the general lack of coherence in texts.

CHAPTER 3

1. See D. Carr, *Reading the Fractures of Genesis: Historical and Literary Approaches* (Louisville, Ky.: Westminster John Knox, 1996), 15–22, for a brief overview of examples and a summary of the differences between ancient and modern assumptions about authorship.

2. For a summary of the arguments for these two texts being by different

authors, see Carr, *Reading the Fractures*, 62–68. A significant minority of scholars would argue that Genesis 1:1–2:3 was not originally separate from Genesis 2:4–3:24, but was conceived from the outset by its (later) authors as an editorial prelude to that story.

3. I have argued in another context that the core of this chapter itself once existed prior to its incorporation in the broader Eden story. At one point, the story would have ended with the man's song of joy at seeing his wife and the explanation of marriage (Gen. 2:23–24). See D. Carr, "The Politics of Textual Subversion: A Diachronic Perspective on the Garden of Eden Story," *Journal of Biblical Literature* 112 (1993): 577–583.

4. For more associations, see Carr, *Reading the Fractures*, 246–47.

5. This contrasts with the proposal of P. Trible, *God and the Rhetoric of Sexuality* (Minneapolis, Minn.: Fortress, 1978), 80–81, 100–101, that, at the beginning, *haadam* has no gender. There is no evidence that *haadam* suddenly gains gender at the end of the chapter. Rather, his song in Gen. 2:23 presupposes that woman was taken from him when he was already a "man." For more detailed arguments against Trible's proposal, see S. Lanser, "Feminist Criticism in the Garden: Inferring Genesis 2–3," *Semeia* 41 (1988): 70–72. Still, in other ways, Trible and others have effectively shown the wrongness of interpretations that assert a woman's subordinate status on the basis of the sequence of creation in Genesis 2. More recently, Ken Stone has argued that the text displays the contradictions of heterosexual ideology in positing an original "man/human" prior to the presence of a "woman" with whom he could be a "man." See his "The Garden of Eden and the Heterosexual Contract," in *Take Back the Word*, ed. Robert Goss and Mona West (Cleveland, Ohio: Pilgrim, 2000), 64–67.

6. Notably, this text is unique in the Hebrew Bible in envisioning the male as departing his household to live with his wife. Other Biblical texts depict the wife leaving her household to live with her husband. The other possible exception are texts in the Song of Songs (e.g., 3:5), which envision the woman bringing the man to her home.

7. Plato, *Symposium* 189A–193A.

8. André Guindon, *The Sexual Language* (Ottawa: University of Ottawa Press, 1977), 68.

9. Audre Lorde, "The Uses of the Erotic: The Erotic as Power," in her *Sister Outsider: Essays and Speeches* (Freedom, Calif.: Crossing, 1984), 58.

10. Sölle and Cloyes, *To Work and to Love*, 129–39.

11. David Biale, *Eros and the Jews: From Biblical Israel to Contemporary America* (New York: Basic, 1992), esp. 48–57, details a general affirmation of marriage within the rabbinic tradition combined with an ambivalence about desire originating from Greco-Roman culture.

CHAPTER 4

1. For a convenient summary of some major proponents of this view, see Jean M. Higgins, "The Myth of Eve the Temptress," *Journal of the American Academy of Religion* 44 (1976): 639–44.

2. K. R. Joines, "The Serpent in Gen. 3," *Zeitschrift für die alttestamentlich Wissenschaft* 87 (1975): 4–9.

3. Carol Meyers, *Discovering Eve: Ancient Israelite Women in Context* (New York: Oxford University Press, 1988), 95–121.

4. Martha Nussbaum, *Fragility of Goodness: Luck and Ethics in Greek Tragedy and Philosophy* (Cambridge: Cambridge University Press, 1986), 25–50.

5. A. Gardner, "Genesis 2:4b–3: A Mythological Paradigm of Sexual Equality or of the Religious History of Pre-Exilic Israel?" *Scandinavian Journal of Theology* 43 (1990): 14.

6. For more background on these arguments and translations, see David Carr, "The Politics of Textual Subversion: A Diachronic Perspective on the Garden of Eden Story," *Journal of Biblical Literature* 112 (1993): 588–90.

7. The language used here is characteristic of death penalty law.

8. Frank Rich, "Naked Capitalists," *New York Times Magazine*, May 20, 2001, p. 51.

9. For a sensitive discussion of how the wisdom traditions of the Bible might be a resource for this process, see Choon-Leong Seow, "A Heterosexual Perspective," in *Homosexuality and Christian Community*, ed. Choon-Leong Seow (Louisville, Ky.: Westminster John Knox, 1996), 19–25.

CHAPTER 5

1. For a survey of the relevant studies and discussion, see Carol Meyers, *Discovering Eve: Ancient Israelite Women in Context* (New York: Oxford University Press, 1988), 47–71; Athalya Brenner, *The Intercourse of Knowledge: On Gendering Desire and "Sexuality" in the Hebrew Bible* (Leiden: Brill, 1997), 61–69.

2. The latter parallels widespread imagery in modern Mediterranean societies. See Carol Delaney, "Seeds of Honor, Fields of Shame," in *Honor and Shame and the Unity of the Mediterranean*, ed. David Gilmore (Washington, D.C.: American Anthropological Association, 1987), 35–48; and Raymond Jamous, "From the Death of Men to the Peace of God: Violence and Peace-making in the Rif," in *Honor and Grace in Anthropology*, eds. J. G. Peristiany and J. Pitt-Rivers (Cambridge: Cambridge University Press, 1992), 168–69.

3. See also Prov. 2:16–19; 5:3–6; 6:24–35; 22:14; 23:27–28.

4. This point was made by Carol Meyers in a lecture in Heidelberg, October 21, 2001, at a symposium honoring Gerhard von Rad, Das Alte Testament und die Kultur der Moderne. The proceedings of the symposium had not appeared by the time of this writing. One could add to her reflections, however, that the risk of AIDS and other sexually transmitted diseases has added a new level of threat to both partners in the present context, which was not present before.

5. The wife is listed in the last of the Ten Commandments as one of the various types of property belonging to a neighbor that a man should not covet (Exod. 20:17, Deut. 5:21).

6. For an excellent discussion of both Biblical and ancient Near Eastern adultery laws, see Raymond Westbrook, "Adultery in Ancient Near Eastern Law," *Revue Biblique* 97 (1990): 542–580. Westbrook's points about the focus on women in the ancient Near East could be extended to many other cultures. See, for example, the more recent discussion of sexual mores in Egypt in Lynn Meskell, *Private Life in New Kingdom Egypt* (Princeton, N.J.: Princeton University Press, 2002), esp. 94–102. In the course of a nuanced survey of sexual norms operative in New Kingdom Egypt—norms that were not enforced publicly through legal pronouncements, but embodied in wisdom texts and divorce documents—she likewise notes that male sex with unmarried women was not treated as problematic.

7. Holiness laws in Lev. 21 add extra regulations for priests, forbidding them from marrying any woman (prostitute, widow, or divorced) who had sex with another man (Lev. 21:7, 14).

8. See Westbrook, "Adultery," 562–66, on the various punishments for adultery. Prov. 6:33–35 argues against the idea that payment would sometimes appease the wronged husband, but the text presumes that some people believed it did. For a stimulating survey of other ways Biblical texts work at cross-purposes with themselves on sexual issues, see David Biale, *Eros and the Jews: From Biblical Israel to Contemporary America* (New York: Basic, 1992), 15–32.

9. Examples of men lying with women include the story of Jacob's wives bargaining for bed privileges with him (Gen. 30:14–16), laws about intercourse (Exod. 22:15, 18; Lev. 15:33; Deut. 22:22–29; 27:20–23), stories revolving around David and Bathsheba (2 Sam. 11:4, 11; 12:11, 24), and Amnon's rape of Tamar (2 Sam. 13:11).

10. Saul Olyan, " 'And with a Male You Shall Not Lie the Lying Down of a Woman," *Journal of the History of Sexuality* 5, no. 2, (1994): 179–206. As he shows, the issue is primarily one of honor, not of bodies per se. Thus, there would not necessarily be a primal Israelite fear of the homoerotic implications of the man-God relationship as Howard Eilberg-Schwartz presupposes throughout his book, *God's Phallus and Other Problems for Men and Monotheism* (Boston: Beacon, 1994). Eilberg-Schwartz works with intensely body-focused constructions of both gender and sexual relations, which are at home in his initial Freudian framework but somewhat alien to the Biblical context. In contrast, as we will see in our look at the prophets, both sexual relations and gender were constructed as much around relations of power as they were around differences in body parts. Certainly, Israel and especially its neighbors were quite conscious of bodies, but they did not use them to define gender or sexual relations in the same way we do. For a history of the development of modern body-focused constructions of gender, see Thomas Laqueur, *Making Sex: Body and Gender from the Greeks to Freud* (Cambridge, Mass.: Harvard University Press, 1990).

11. See references to this in divine imitations of divorce speeches in Hos. 2:3 (Hebrew 2:5), 9–10 (Hebrew 11–12); Jer. 3:1–3; 13:22; Ezek. 16:37–39, (16:56–57), 23:26, 29.

12. In this case, Tamar is a widow, but she is committed by the law of Levirate marriage (Deut. 25:5–10) to Shelah, Judah's youngest son (Gen. 38:11). Note that God's wife is likewise threatened with burning in Ezek. 16:41 for sexual infidelity.

13. This may have been by stoning. God's wife is threatened with being stoned for sexual infidelity in Ezek. 16:40 and 23:47, and the story of the accused adulteress in the New Testament presupposes stoning as the penalty for adultery (John 8:2–11).

14. An additional law specifies death by burning for any priest's daughter who becomes a prostitute (Lev. 21:9). Some have understood Deut. 23:18 to prohibit prostitution in general, but it only specifies that *Israelite* daughters not be prostitutes. Many translations of the verse understand it to refer to sacred prostitution (e.g., NRSV "temple prostitute"), but recent scholarship has shown that there probably was no such thing in ancient Israel. For a helpful discussion of the passage and summary of the relevant research, see Jeffrey Tigay, *Deuteronomy* (Philadelphia, Pa.: Jewish Publication Society, 1996), 215–16, 480–81.

Stories such as Genesis 19 and Judges 19 indicate that men in extreme circumstances might choose to allow their daughter or concubine to be raped in order to avoid the rape of a guest under their protection. Though these texts show an unbelievable disregard for the welfare of the women involved, they are meant to emphasize the exemplary hospitality of the hosts.

15. Lev. 20:15–16; cf. Deut. 27:21.

16. Deut. 27:20, 22–23; Lev. 20:11–12, 14, 17, 19–21; cf. Lev. 18:6–18.

17. Lev. 20:18; cf. 18:19. Indeed, as Debra Haffner points out, the Bible devotes seven times as much space to prohibition of sex during a woman's period as it does to condemnation of male-male intercourse. See her paper "The Really Good News about Sex in the Bible," at www.siecus.org.

18. In addition, an isolated law in Deuteronomy proclaims that those who wear clothes of the other sex are "abhorrent to the Lord your God" (Deut. 22:5).

19. Lev. 21:7 sets an even higher standard for priests: they may not marry any woman who has had sexual relations with another man.

20. See Brenner, *Intercourse of Knowledge*, 136–39, for a review and discussion of the relevant literature.

21. Examples include Gen. 29:1–30; Exod. 21:5. Note also Gen. 2:24 and Eccles. 9:9. In addition, the Song of Songs envisions an ideal of mutual desire (e.g., Song 2:16, 6:3).

22. Compare the alternative approaches to Mal. 2:10–16 of David Petersen, *Zechariah 9–14 and Malachi* (Louisville, Ky.: Westminster John Knox, 1995), 194, 198–200, and Julia O'Brien, "Judith as Wife and Husband: Deconstructing Gender in Malachi," *Journal of Biblical Literature* 115 (1996): 241–50. Petersen understands the text to be condemning the people's marriage to the goddess Asherah, but he can only support this reading by significantly altering the Hebrew text. O'Brien argues that the "wife of youth" in Mal. 2:14–16 is Yahweh. Her approach, however, does not account for the emphasis on tears and weeping in 2:13, nor does it explain how Yahweh could be both the "wife of youth" and the witness to marriage with her in 2:14. As O'Brien suggests, Mal. 2:10–16 echoes earlier prophetic texts, but the language appears to be reapplied to human relationships.

Two other prophetic texts, Hos. 4:10–19 and Jer. 5:7–9, may condemn Israelite men for sex outside of marriage. On Hosea, see in particular Mayer Gruber, "Marital Fidelity and Intimacy: A View from Hosea 4," in *A Feminist Companion to the Latter Prophets*, ed. Athalya Brenner (Sheffield, England: Sheffield Academic Press, 1995), 169–79. On Jeremiah, see Athalya Brenner, "On Prophetic Propaganda and the Politics of 'Love': The Case of Jeremiah," in Brenner, *Feminist Companion to the Latter Prophets*, 260. Both of these texts also condemn worship of other gods, and it is not clear whether the sexual images are metaphors for cultic infidelity or descriptions of sexual infidelity. In addition, both of these prophets seem to be condemning practices that were accepted elsewhere in the society. They are not summarizing a societal moral consensus.

23. Prov. 18:22; 19:14; 31:10–31.

24. Prov. 5:15–23; Sir. 9:1–9.

25. Prov. 23:26–28; 29:3; Sir. 19:2–3; cf. Prov. 22:14 on an adulterous woman. These values are summarized in a late addition to the book of Ben Sira (Sir. 26:19–27 in the Greek and Syriac translations), which praises the good wife, criticizes the bad wife, and urges the male hearer to sow his own "field" and avoid prostitutes and adultery with other men's wives.

26. P. Trible, *God and the Rhetoric of Sexuality* (Philadelphia: Fortress, 1978), 123.

CHAPTER 6

1. Carey Ellen Walsh, *Exquisite Desire: Religion, the Erotic and the Song of Songs* (Minneapolis, Minn.: Fortress, 2000), 87–90 builds on her more extensive discussion of vitriculture in her *The Fruit of the Vine: Vitriculture in Ancient Israel* (Winona Lake, Ind.: Eisenbrauns, 2000).

2. Papyrus Harris 500, group C, no. 18. The translation is from Michael V. Fox, *The Song of Songs and Ancient Egyptian Love Songs* (Madison: University of Wisconsin Press, 1985), 26.

3. Translation by S. N. Kramer in J. Pritchard, *Ancient Near Eastern Texts Relating to the Old Testament*, 3d ed. (Princeton, N.J.: Princeton University Press, 1969), 643.

4. E.g., Song 2:15; 7:12–13 (cf. 6:2, 8:12).

5. Song 2:17; see also 4:6; 8:14.

6. The expression translated here as "stripped bare" can also be rendered "burned." Though it fits with a common punishment for adultery, this alternative translation does not fit the immediate context of Isa. 5:5 as well and makes the rest of the pronouncement of judgment senseless.

7. See also Mic. 1:4. For a broader survey of ancient Israelite everyday life, see Carol Meyers, *Discovering Eve: Ancient Israelite Women in Context* (New York: Oxford University Press, 1988), 47–71.

8. H. W. F. Saggs, *The Might that Was Assyria* (London: Sidgwick and Jackson, 1984), 261.

9. Saggs, *The Might that Was Assyria*, 262.

10. On the possible connections, see A. Van Selms, "Hosea and Canticles," in *Studies on the Books of Hosea and Amos: Papers Read at 7th and 8th Meetings of Die Oud Testamentiese Werkgemeinskap in Suid-Afrika (1964–1965)*, ed. A. H. van Zyl (Potchefstroom: Pro Rege-Perse Beoerk, 1966), 85–88; Fokkelien van Dijk-Hemmes, "The Imagination of Power and the Power of Imagination: An Intertextual Analysis of Two Biblical Love Songs: The Song of Songs and Hosea 2," *Journal for the Study of the Old Testament* 44 (1989): 79–82. For some additional observations of potential connections between Hosea and the Song of Songs, see F. Landy, *Hosea* (Sheffield, England Sheffield Academic Press, 2000), 35–37, 79, 138, 160, 164, 167, 170, 173; and E. Davis, *Proverbs, Ecclesiastes, and Song of Songs* (Louisville, Ky.: Westminster, 2000), 250.

11. This "blame the victim" dynamic has been noted by others in other contexts, e.g., Angela Bauer, *Gender in the Book of Jeremiah: A Feminist-Literary Reading* (New York: Lang, 1999), 50–51.

12. The most eloquent exploration of this remains Gracia Fay Ellwood, *Batter My Heart* (Wallingford, Pa.: Pendle Hill, 1988).

13. Other possible spurs may have included the close association of cities with women in the ancient Near East and the possible previous marriage between Yahweh and the goddess Asherah, a relationship replaced in Hosea by the marriage of Yahweh with Israel or the land. Neither of these precursors, however, focus on the themes of exclusivity and punishment so prominent in Hosea's poetry. I plan to devote a separate study to looking at the complex, interrelated factors behind this marriage imagery. In the meantime, see my com-

ments regarding this issue in David Carr, "Gender and the Shaping of Desire in the Song of Songs and Its Interpretations," *Journal of Biblical Literature* 119 (2000): 239–240.

14. William Moran, "The Ancient Near Eastern Background of the Love of God in Deuteronomy," *Catholic Biblical Quarterly* 25 (1963): 77–87, esp. 78–80; see also Moshe Weinfeld, *Deuteronomy and the Deuteronomic School* (Oxford: Clarendon, 1972), 82–83.

15. See R. Yaron, "Matrimonial Mishaps at Eshnunna," *Journal of Semitic Studies* 8 (1963): 1–16, for a translation and discussion of earlier proposals. In this respect, these ancient Near Eastern texts, including the Bible, are drawing more on male-female images of devotion than on parent-child images. For helpful discussion of kinship language in ancient Near Eastern treaties, see Frank Moore Cross, "Kinship and Covenant in Ancient Israel," in Cross, *From Epic to Canon* (Baltimore, Md.: John Hopkins University Press, 1998), esp. 5–11.

16. R. Koschaker, *Journal of Cuneiform Studies* 5 (1951): 108 and nn. 12–13, lists political uses of this phrase.

17. Delbert Hillers, *Treaty-Curses and the Old Testament Prophets* (Rome: Pontifical Institute, 1964), 58.

18. See also Isa. 19:16; Nah. 3:13.

19. Isa. 3:17–26; 47:1–4; Jer. 13:22–27; Ezek. 16:35–39, 23:9–10, 26–29; Hos. 2:9–10 (Hebrew 2:11–12); Nah. 2:10 (Hebrew 2:11), 3:5; Zech. 14:2. This list is adapted from F. Rachel Magdalene, "Ancient Near Eastern Treaty-Curses and the Ultimate Texts of Terror: A Study of the Language of Divine Sexual Abuse in the Prophetic Corpus," in *A Feminist Companion to the Latter Prophets*, ed. Athalya Brenner (Sheffield, England: Sheffield Academic Press, 1995), 327. See 328–34 for discussion of these examples.

20. Pamela Gordon and Harold Washington, "Rape as a Military Metaphor," in *Brenner, Feminist Companion to the Latter Prophets*, 317–18, suggest that the overall feminization of cities and nations can be attributed to this dynamic. Magdalene, "Ultimate Texts of Terror," 335, concurs. As Tikva Frymer-Kensky points out, however, the metaphor also expresses how the city contains, protects, and nurtures its inhabitants and the palace with in its walls. See Frymer-Kensky, *In the Wake of the Goddesses: Women, Culture, and the Biblical Transformation of Pagan Myth* (New York: Macmillan, 1992), 172. This link of sex and gender to power is a helpful balance to modern body-centered concepts of gender.

21. For a thorough argument along these lines, see Alice A. Keefe, "The Female Body, the Body Politic and the Land: A Sociopolitical Reading of Hosea 1–2," in *Brenner, Feminist Companion to the Latter Prophets*, 70–100. This approach meshes well with the treaty material discussed in the previous chapter.

22. See also Deut. 10:12, 20; 11:1, 13, 22; 19:9; 30:6, 16, 20; Josh. 22:5; 23:8, 11 (cf. 23:12–13).

23. E.g., Deut. 6:14; 8:19; 11:28; 13:3; 28:14; 32:16–18; Jer. 7:6, 9; 11:10; 13:10; 16:11; 25:6; 35:15.

24. Cf. the use of the same word to describe desire in Gen. 34:8 and Deut. 21:11. This point comes from Jon Levenson, "The Universal Horizon of Biblical Particularism," in *Ethnicity and the Bible*, ed. Mark G. Brett (Leiden: Brill, 1996), 156.

25. This is a counterpart to Egyptian and Mesopotamian expressions in which a woman describes a man she herself chooses, as opposed to one chosen for

her. The phrase "man of my heart" appears repeatedly in Mesopotamian love songs (see B. Alster, "Sumerian Love Songs," *Revue d'assyriologie* 79 [1985]: 155–58; and Thorkild Jacobsen, *The Harps that Once . . . : Sumerian Poetry in Translation* [New Haven, Conn.: Yale University Press, 1987], 88), while the female lover in Egyptian love songs frequently speaks of one whose heart is "in balance" with hers (Fox, *Song of Songs*, text numbers 11 [p. 20], 17 [p. 26], 20a [p. 31]).

Ellen Davis suggests that this expression in the Song may be an allusion to Deut. 6:4–5 (*Proverbs, Ecclesiastes, and Song of Songs*, 245, 255). Yet unlike actual allusions to Deut. 6:4–5 in later Biblical history (esp. 2 Kings 23:25), the Song of Songs does not include the other parts of Deut. 6:4–5 ("heart" and "might") nor does it refer to the "law of Moses." Now standing as part of a Bible that includes Deuteronomy, the Song resonates with it, but it does not show signs of being intended as an explicit allusion to that book.

26. E.g., Deut. 28:15–68 (Hebrew 28:1–69). Note, in addition, the way the conclusion to Leviticus (Lev. 26:12) echoes the formal pronouncement of marriage that a man would proclaim over his new wife in describing God's attachment of Israel to him: "I will be your God and you will be my people" (cf. the reverse of the pronouncement in Hos 2:2 [Hebrew 2:4]).

27. See also Jer. 2:2–3, 20–25, 33–37.

28. On Jeremiah's feminine imagery, see in particular M. Shields, "Circumcision of the Prostitute: Gender, Sexuality, and the Call to Repentance in Jeremiah 3:1–4:4," *Biblical Interpretation* 3 (1995): 61–74; A. R. Pete Diamond and Kathleen M. O'Connor, "Unfaithful Passions: Coding Women, Coding Men in Jeremiah 2–3 (4.2)," *Biblical Interpretation* 4 (1996): 288–310; and Bauer, *Gender in the Book of Jeremiah*.

29. Ezek. 16:53–63 is the main exception, but it is quite a contrast to Hosea's reconciliation speech.

30. On Ezekiel's feminine imagery, see in particular J. Galambush, *Jerusalem in the Book of Ezekiel: The City as Yahweh's Wife* (Atlanta, Ga.: Scholars Press, 1992).

31. H. Wildberger, *Isaiah 1–12*, trans. Thomas Trapp (Minneapolis, Minn.: Augsburg, 1991), 178.

32. For the most thorough exploration of the antecedents of this passage see John M. Berridge, *Prophet, People and the Word of Yahweh: An Examination of Form and Content in the Proclamation of the Prophet Jeremiah* (Zürich: EVZ Verlag, 1970), 151–55. For engagement with more recent treatments, see Bauer, *Gender in the Book of Jeremiah*, 114–117.

CHAPTER 7

The epigraph to the chapter is from a case study in Alyce D. LaViolette and Ola W. Barnett, *It Could Happen to Anyone: Why Battered Women Stay*, 2d ed. (London: Sage, 2000), 101.

1. Bernard Anderson, *Understanding the Old Testament* (Englewood Cliffs, N.J.: Prentice Hall, 1986), 312. The 1998 revised edition of this text reads "so that the 'wife' Israel could no longer pursue her 'lovers' " (p. 281) where the

earlier edition reads "so that the 'wife' Israel, may stand naked and humiliated in the presence of her lovers."

2. Gracia Fay Ellwood, "Rape and Judgment," *Daughters of Sarah* 11, no. 4 (1985): 9–13, and *Batter My Heart* (Wallingford, Pa.: Pendle Hill, 1988).

3. Drorah Setel, *Prophets and Pornography: Female Sexual Imagery in Hosea*, in *Feminist Interpretation of the Bible*, ed. L. Russell (Philadelphia, Pa.: Westminster Press, 1985), 86–95.

4. See especially J. C. Exum, "Prophetic Pornography," in her *Plotted, Shot and Painted: Cultural Representations of Biblical Women* (Sheffield, England: Sheffield Academic Press, 1996), 101–28. See also the essays in A. Brenner and C. Fontaine, eds., *A Feminist Companion to the Latter Prophets* (Sheffield, England: Sheffield Academic Press, 1995); Renita Weems, *Battered Love* (Minneapolis, Minn.: Fortress, 1995); R. Abma, *Bonds of Love: Methodic Studies of Prophetic Texts with Marriage Imagery* (Assen, Netherlands: Van Gorcum, 1999); and Gerlinde Baumann, *Liebe und Gewalt: Die Ehe als Metapher für das Verhältnis JHWH—Israel in den Prophetenbüchern* (Stuttgart, Germany: Katholisches Bibelwerk, 2000).

5. I am indebted to Colleen Conway for development of much of this thought about the conjunction of divinity and maleness. Her more extensive work on this topic in the first century c.e. will appear shortly.

6. The extreme power differential between God and humanity means that God-human relations are considered in these prophetic texts as a subset of male-female relations. There is no apparent anxiety whatsoever about a homoerotic implication in these texts, contra Howard Eilberg-Schwartz, *God's Phallus and Other Problems for Men and Monotheism* (Boston: Beacon, 1994), 97–102, 110–13, 127–30.

7. See Matt Ridley, *The Red Queen: Sex and the Evolution of Human Nature* (New York: Macmillan, 1994), 203–30, for a survey and references to relevant studies.

8. M. Sherif et al., *Intergroup Cooperation and Competition: The Robbers Cave Experiment* (Norman, Okla.: University Book Exchange, 1961). See Gene Harris, *The Nurture Assumption: Why Children Turn Out the Way They Do* (New York: Free Press, 1998), 123–45, for an accessible survey of other studies relevant to group formation.

9. K. Mori, *Stone Field, True Arrow* (New York: Holt, 2000), 111.

10. Psychotherapist Anne Wilson Schaef discusses some provocative analogies between addiction on an individual and on a community level in her book *When Society Becomes an Addict* (San Francisco: Harper and Row, 1987).

11. The parallels in Matthew and Luke are Matt. 22:34–40 and Luke 10:25–27.

CHAPTER 8

1. Lila Abu-Lughod, *Veiled Sentiments: Honor and Poetry in a Bedouin Society* (Berkeley: University of California Press, 1986), 171–77.

2. See Abu-Lughod, *Veiled Sentiments*, 171–232, for detailed discussions of these topics.

3. Elizabeth Fernea, *Guests of the Sheik: An Ethnography of an Iraqi Village* (Garden City, N.Y.: Anchor, 1969).

4. For an overview of literature on Middle Eastern women, see Elizabeth Warnock Fernea, "Research in Middle Eastern Women: State of the Art," in *Understanding Women: The Challenge of Cross-Cultural Perspectives*, ed. Marilyn Robinson Waldman et al. (Columbus: Ohio State University Press, 1992).

5. Unni Wikan, "Shame and Honour: A Contestable Pair," *Man*, n.s. 19 (1984): 635–52.

6. Kaveh Safa-Isfahani, "Female-Centered World Views in Iranian Culture: Symbolic Representations of Sexuality in Dramatic Games," *Signs* 6 (1981): 33–53.

7. Teri Joseph, "Poetry as a Strategy of Power: The Case of Riffian Berber Women," *Signs* 5 (1980): 418–34.

8. John Winkler, *The Constraints of Desire: The Anthropology of Sex and Gender in Ancient Greece* (New York: Routledge, 1990).

9. Jerrold S. Cooper, "Sacred Marriage and the Popular Cult in Early Mesopotamia," in *Official Cult and Popular Religion in the Ancient Near East*, ed. Eiko Matsushima (Heidelberg, Germany: Universitätsverlag C. Winter, 1993), 90–94; Martti Nissinen, "Akkadian Rituals and Poetry of Divine Love," in *Mythology and Mythologies: Melammu Symposia II*, ed. R. M. Whiting (Helsinki, Finland: Neo-Assyrian Text-Corpus Project, 2001), 93–94.

10. B. Alster, "Sumerian Love Songs," *Revue d'assyriologie* 79 (1985): 132–34.

11. The translation is from B. Alster, "The Manchester Tammuz," *Acta Sumerologica* 14 (1992): 19.

12. For discussion of the time range of these and likely precursor texts, see G. Leick, *Sex and Eroticism in Mesopotamian Literature* (New York: Routledge, 1994), 102–10.

13. For a superb overview of the relevant texts, see Nissinen, "Akkadian Rituals and Poetry of Divine Love," 95–125.

14. This text appears to be a sacred marriage ritual imported to Egypt by immigrants from Babylon who had lived in Samaria prior to moving to Egypt. For the text, see Richard C. Steiner, "The Aramaic Text in Demotic Script," in *The Context of Scripture*, ed. W. Hallo and K. Lawson Younger (New York: Brill, 1996), 1:309–27.

15. For an overview of a variety of rituals and helpful cross-cultural comparisons, see Leick, *Sex and Eroticism*, 130–38.

16. For discussion of two instances where the king does seem to be present, see Nissinen, "Akkadian Rituals and Poetry of Divine Love," 96, 108–9.

17. M. Nissinen, "Love Lyrics of Nabû and Tashmetu: An Assyrian Song of Songs?" in *Und Mose schrieb dieses Lied auf: Studien zum Alten Testament und zum Alten Orient*, ed. Manfried Dietrich and Ingo Kottsieper (Münster, Germany: Ugarit, 1998), 596–97. For an overview of the wealth of texts referring to later sacred marriage rites, see Nissinen, "Akkadian Rituals and Poetry of Divine Love," 95–125.

18. Translations in the preceding section are from Nissinen, "Love Lyrics," 588–90.

19. Thorkild Jacobsen, *The Harps that Once . . . : Sumerian Poetry in Translation* (New Haven, Conn.: Yale University Press, 1987), 93.

20. The clearest examples can be found above and in Jacobsen, *Harps*, 94. Note also Jacobsen, *Harps*, 88–89, which includes a brief reference to marriage. These texts are discussed in Leick, *Sex and Eroticism*, 111–29. Leick also assigns

two "tapstress" poems to this group (113–16, regarding Jacobsen, *Harps*, 95–96), but they end with the typical blessing of the divine marriage texts.

21. M. Held, "A Faithful Lover in an Old Babylonian Dialogue," *Journal of Cuneiform Studies* 15 (1961): 6–9; J. Westenholz, "A Forgotten Love Song," in *Language, Literature, and History: Philological and Historical Studies Presented to Erica Reiner*, ed. F. Rochberg (New Haven, Conn.: American Oriental Society, 1987), 423–24. A catalog of love songs indicates that there were probably many more such secular love songs but most have been lost (J. Black, "Babylonian Ballads: A New Genre," *Journal of the American Oriental Society* 103 [1983]: 27–29).

22. The texts are found in Jacobsen, *Harps*, 3–9, 13–15.

23. A. Brenner and F. Van Dijk-Hemmes, *On Gendering Texts: Female and Male Voices in the Hebrew Bible* (Leiden: Brill, 1992), 6, suggest redirecting the focus away from establishing female authorship for various individual texts and toward ways that certain texts present a distinctively women's voice.

24. Ake W. Sjöberg, "In-Nin-Sha-Gur-Ra: A Hymn to the Goddess Inanna by the En-Priestess Enheduanna," *Zeitschrift für Assyriologie* 65 (1976): 163–253.

25. Jacobsen, *Harps*, 11.

26. Jerrold S. Cooper, "Gendered Sexuality in Sumerian Love Poetry," in *Sumerian Gods and Their Representations*, ed. I. L. Finkel and M. J. Geller (Groningen, Netherlands: Styx, 1997), 85–97. The following argument is a summary of Cooper's position. The following translations are from his article as well. On this topic, see also Cooper, "Enki's Member: Eros and Irrigation in Sumerian Literature," in *Dumu-e2-Dub-Ba-A: Studies in Honor of Ake W. Sjöberg*, ed. H. Behrens et al. (Philadelphia, Pa.: University Museum, 1989), 87–89.

27. For example, Leick, *Sex and Eroticism*, 21, 58 follows Cooper's basic division.

28. See S. Morenz, *Egyptian Religion*, trans. Ann E. Keep (Ithaca, N.Y.: Cornell University Press, 1973), 162–63, for discussion.

29. The best attested version can be found in Miriam Lichtheim, *Ancient Egyptian Literature: A Book of Readings*, vol. 2, *The New Kingdom* (Berkeley: University of California Press, 1976), 214–23 (see esp. 217, 219–20). Cf. Papyrus Jumilhac III, 1–6, in which Seth transforms himself into a bull to capture Isis (translated in L. Manniche, *Sexual Life in Ancient Egypt* [London: Kegan Paul, 1987], 54). The relevant episode from Papyrus Kahun is translated in J. G. Griffiths, *The Conflict of Horus and Seth from Egyptian and Classical Sources* (Liverpool, England: Liverpool University Press, 1960), 42.

30. For an excellent edition and discussion of these texts, see Michael V. Fox, *The Song of Songs and Ancient Egyptian Love Songs* (Madison: University of Wisconsin Press, 1985). His translations and notes on the poems themselves are on 3–81. For more recent literature and a theoretically sophisticated placement of these poems in broader social context see Lynn Meskell, *Private Life in New Kingdom Egypt* (Princeton, N.J.: Princeton University Press, 2002), especially 128–34.

31. Musicians at a banquet, from the Tomb of Nakht, mid–fifteenth century B.C.E. Photograph courtesy of the Metropolitan Museum of Art (15.5.19d).

32. For discussion of the motif of naked young women, see Gay Robins, "Dress, Undress, and the Representation of Fertility and Potency in New Kingdom Egyptian Art," in *Sexuality in Ancient Art: Near East, Egypt, Greece and Italy*, ed. Natalie Boymel Kampen (Cambridge: Cambridge University Press, 1996), 30–34.

33. Translations and arguments for the preceding half of the paragraph come from Fox, *Song of Songs*, 244–45.

34. Robins, "Dress," 33–34.

35. The quote is based on excellent translations by Lichtheim, *Ancient Egyptian Literature*, 2:182, and Fox, *Song of Songs*, 52.

36. This rendering is based on both Lichtheim, *Ancient Egyptian Literature*, 2: 182–83 (esp. for the first part), and Fox, *Song of Songs*, 52–53 (for the last six lines).

37. Such echoes were first pointed out by Franz R. Schröder, "Sakrale Grundlagen der altägyptischen Lyrik," *Deutsche Vierteljahrsschrift für Literaturwissenschaft und Geistesgeschichte* 25 (1951): 273–93, and expanded in several articles by Philippe Derchain: "Le Lotus, la mandragore et le perséa," *Chronique d'Égypte* 50 (1975): 65–86; "La perruqe et le cristal," *Studien zur altegyptischen Kultur* 2 (1975): 55–74; and "Symbols and Metaphors in Literature and Representatives of Private Life," *Royal Anthropological Institute News* 15 (1976): 7–10. Fox, *Song of Songs*, 235–36, adds some observations and puts these studies in perspective, and Meskell, *Private Life*, pp. 114–15, 143, and passim, argues that sexuality was not a category separate from religion and other aspects of life in New Kingdom Egypt.

38. Carol Meyers, "The Drum-Dance-Song Ensemble: Women's Performance in Biblical Israel," in *Rediscovering the Muses: Women's Musical Traditions*, ed. Kimberly Marshall (Boston: Northeastern University Press, 1993), 49–67, 234–38.

39. Translation from Fox, *Song of Songs*, 248.

40. Robins, "Dress," 34–35.

41. See Fokkelien van Dijk-Hemmes, "Traces of Women's Texts in the Hebrew Bible," in van Dijk-Hemmes and Brenner, *On Gendering Texts*, 71–83, for a discussion of female authorship of love songs in the Bible and citations of earlier literature.

42. Translation here and in the following section comes from H. J. Kraus, *Psalms 1–59*, trans. Hilton C. Oswald (Minneapolis, Minn.: Augsburg, 1988), 450–51. The Hebrew verses for these citations are 45:3–4a and 7.

43. Kraus, *Psalms 1–59*, 453.

CHAPTER 9

1. For fuller discussion, see David Carr, "Passion for God: A Center in Biblical Theology," *Horizons in Biblical Theology* 23 (2001): 18–19.

2. The most compelling recent treatments to orient themselves around the refrains are J. C. Exum, "A Literary and Structural Analysis of the Song of Songs," *Zeitschrift für die alttestamentliche Wissenschaft* 85 (1973): 47–79; Trible, *God and the Rhetoric of Sexuality* (Philadelphia: Fortress, 1978), 146–52; and Timothea Elliot, *The Literary Unity of the Canticle* (Bern: Peter Lang, 1989). Already in the twelfth century Rupert of Deutz oriented his commentary around the refrains; see E. Ann Matter, *The Voice of My Beloved: The Song of Songs in Western Medieval Christianity* (Philadelphia: University of Pennsylvania Press, 1990), 159–63. Note that the semi-refrain in 5:8 (amidst 5:2–6:3) is usually understood in such treatments to be a play on the broader pattern in 2:7, 3:5, and 8:4, but not a mark of a major division.

3. Tosephta Sanhedrin 12:10. See Fox, *Song of Songs and the Ancient Egyptian Love Songs* (Madison, Wisc.: University of Wisconsin Press, 1985), 249, for use of this example and broader arguments for the original setting of the Song. He argues against setting the Song of Songs in an Israelite equivalent of the sacred marriage ceremony (for which there is no clear evidence).

4. For useful discussion of how the Song as a whole poetically engages the senses, see Robert Alter's afterword in Ariel A. Bloch and Chana Bloch, *The Song of Songs: A New Translation with an Introduction and Commentary* (New York: Random House, 1995), 122–27.

5. O. Keel, *Song of Songs* (Minneapolis, Minn.: Fortress, 1994), 69–71.

6. See Fox, *Song of Songs*, 107, on the translation of this line.

7. On the lotus, see M. Pope, *Song of Songs* (Garden City; N.Y.: Doubleday, 1977), 368, and Keel, *Song of Songs*, 78–80; cf. Fox, *Song of Songs*, 107.

8. Here I follow Fox, *Song of Songs*, 107, and Bloch and Bloch, *Song of Songs*, 55, 149, in translating *tapuaḥ* as "apricot." I add "trees" to the rendering because they represent the correlate to "young men" in the next line.

9. Fox, *Song of Songs*, 108–9.

10. Fox, *Song of Songs*, 110 (following Gordis and others) points out that the Hebrew verb root used here (*ᶜvr*) is not used elsewhere to refer to sexual arousal, but merely for awakening a sleeper. Therefore, he proposes that what is meant here is that the daughters are not to disturb the lovers until they are ready, an oath designed to suggestively leave the audience hanging about what actually transpires afterward. Nevertheless, this makes interpretation of the next line difficult, since love is rarely "ready" to be disturbed. Moreover, why would the daughters be involved in such disturbing? Finally, in this case and others, the woman is experiencing some distress connected with her love, in this case, lovesickness. So the oath more probably relates to the frustration of lovemaking, rather than to its consummation.

11. Keel, *Song of Songs*, 92–94.

12. Fox, *Song of Songs*, 195–226, provides an excellent overview of both unifying elements in the Song and the problems with proposing any one structure. Note as well J. Munro's exploration of some elements of a protoplot in *Spikenard and Saffron: The Imagery of the Song of Songs* (Sheffield, England: Sheffield Academic Press, 1995), 35–42, 110–14, 145–46.

13. Tremper Longman III, *Song of Songs* (Grand Rapids, Mich.: Eerdmans, 2001), 39–43, provides a helpful overview and critique of the major options.

14. Jack M. Sasson, "On M. H. Pope's Song of Songs," *Maarav* 1 (1979): 182; Fox, *Song of Songs*, 310–15; Benjamin J. Segal, "Double Meanings in the Song of Songs," *Dor le Dor* 16 (1987–1988): 249–55; Roland Murphy, *The Song of Songs* (Minneapolis, Minn.: Fortress, 1990), 102–3 and n. 395; Fiona Black, "What Is My Beloved? On Erotic Reading and the Song of Songs," in *The Labor of Reading: Desire, Alienation and Biblical Interpretation*, ed. Fiona Black et al. (Atlanta, Ga.: Society of Biblical Literature, 1999), 35–52; J. Cheryl Exum, "The Eye of the Beholder," in *The Labor of Reading*, 71–86; and Carey Ellen Walsh, *Exquisite Desire: Religion, the Erotic and the Song of Songs* (Minneapolis, Minn.: Fortress, 2000), esp. 25–45.

15. Paul Ricoeur, "Wonder, Eroticism, and Enigma," in *Sexuality and Identity*, ed. Hendrik M. Ruitenbeek (New York: Dell, 1970), 13–24.

16. The Hebrew can be read as either "and" or "but." Keel, *Song of Songs*,

47–49, argues that the "blackness" spoken of here is the numinous blackness of black goddesses seen in Greece. Thus he argues for the translation "and" in this context.

Fox, *Song of Songs*, 101, argues persuasively on the basis of the context that "but" is the more likely alternative. Later on, the woman will ask her companions not to stare at her blackness (1:6), thus implying that she is self-conscious about her skin color. Nevertheless, this self-consciousness has to do with tanning resulting from working in the sun, not any antiblack racism in Israelite society. The text's depiction of the woman's attitude toward her skin color only has racial implications for later readers interpreting it within a racially charged context. See also the excellent brief discussion by Longman, *Song of Songs*, 95–96.

17. These renderings of 1:6 depend on Bloch and Bloch, *Song of Songs*, 141.

18. The problem that many commentators have in understanding how one might speak of someone being "black" from having a tan may derive partly from their failure to realize that people with dark skin can also tan.

19. Christopher King, "A Love as Fierce as Death: Reclaiming the Song of Songs for Queer Lovers," in *Take Back the Word: A Queer Reading of the Bible*, ed. Robert Goss and Mona West (Cleveland, Ohio: Pilgrim, 2000), 128–30, highlights the way this poem can be used to affirm all who face societal disapproval for their sexual identity.

20. This is a free rendition of the Hebrew: "the blossoms have appeared in the land."

21. On the translation and this season, see Keel, *Song of Songs*, 101.

22. Bloch and Bloch, *Song of Songs*, 156.

23. Murphy, *Song of Songs*, 141, takes this as the woman's reply to the man's request. This would fit the sequence, but it has at least two problems: (1) it is spoken by a group, and (2) she is already quoting the man's speech (see 2:10), so this would be her quote of herself answering the man she is quoting.

24. Fox, *Song of Songs*, 114; Keel, *Song of Songs*, 108–10.

25. Fox, *Song of Songs*, 135; Keel, *Song of Songs*, 155.

26. This phrase is from Fox, *Song of Songs*, 118.

27. King, "Love as Fierce as Death," 136–37.

28. See Longman, *Song of Songs*, 60–62, who cites a student's dissertation on the topic: G. Schwab, "The Song of Songs' Cautionary Message concerning Human Love," Ph.D. diss., Westminster Theological Seminary, 1999.

29. This means "husband of a multitude" in Hebrew, perhaps an echo of Solomon's reputation for having a large harem (1 Kings 11:3).

30. Munro, *Spikenard and Saffron*, 99, argues that this is the woman. Many others maintain that it is the man, comparing his female vineyard to Solomon's.

31. Fox, *Song of Songs*, 186–90, provides an excellent, brief overview of dating discussions.

32. If there is any section of the Song that corresponds to the plot of the Mesopotamian sacred marriage, it is the wedding-to-garden pattern in Song of Songs 3:6–5:1. See Nissinen, "Akkadian Rituals and Poetry of Divine Love," in R. M. Whiting, ed., *Mythology and Mythologies: Melamu Symposia II* (Helsinki, Finland: Neo-Assyrian Text-Corpus Project, 2001), 95–125. The case for a sacred marriage background here in the Song would be stronger if we had direct evidence in this text or elsewhere for goddess worship in ancient Israel.

33. For excellent arguments for *ṣamah* as locks of hair rather than veil see Bloch and Bloch, *Song of Songs*, 166–68.

34. Here and elsewhere I have been informed by Robert Alter's description of the commingling of landscape and lovers in the Song. See his discussion in the afterword, of Bloch and Bloch, *Song of Songs*, 121–31, which is anticipated by his reflections in *The Art of Biblical Poetry* (New York: Basic, 1985), 194–203. On this, see also Landy, *Paradoxes of Paradise: Identity and Difference in the Song of Songs* (Sheffield, England: Almond, 1983), 75, 88–89 and Munro, *Spikenard and Saffron*, 51–52.

35. As Keel, *Song of Songs*, 147, points out, this may refer to the series of necklaces worn by rich women. Note how the image is continued with images of jewelry in the next couplet.

36. On associations with fawns and gazelles, see Keel, *Song of Songs*, 147–51.

37. Keel, *Song of Songs*, 155.

38. Here we see a continuation of the wedding image from 3:7–11 in the man's use of "bride" language to refer to his love. In what follows, he will call his love "my bride" or "my sister, my bride" four times. Is the singer playing Solomon on his wedding day, praising the woman, his bride? Perhaps. Or maybe the singers are presenting a series of vignettes, in which the male lover impersonates a shepherd one moment and King Solomon the next, playing out the erotic fantasies of ancient love. The poetry does not give us enough to construct any detailed picture of the players here. See Fox, *Song of Songs*, 292–294, for an evocative argument about how these roles function in the love poetry.

39. On translation of this verse, see Bloch and Bloch, *Song of Songs*, 179–80, who cite Prov. 7:18 for the idea of "drinking one's fill of love," and Isa. 29:9 and 49:26 for the use of the Hebrew verb *shakar* with object as "get drunk with." Alternatively, most of the major versions and subsequent interpreters have opted for translating *dodim* (translated here as "lovemaking") at the end of 5:1 as parallel to *re^cm* (friends) thus: "eat, friends"/"drink and get drunk, lovers." Though more subtle, this reading also implies that the lovers are getting drunk on love.

40. Alter, in Bloch and Bloch, *Song of Songs*, 130.

41. See the discussion of 3:1–5 and 5:6–7 earlier in this chapter.

42. Cf. Fox, *Song of Songs*, 146–47, who argues that this must be a call *not* to tell him of her embarrassing lovesickness. Note, however, how the daughters of Jerusalem respond in the next verse. Her request seems to presuppose not just general embarrassment at how people will see her behavior but to be a specific inquiry about why she is chasing him (which answer she gives).

43. Literally, "his appearance."

44. This translation of 6:2b–3 follows Keel, *Song of Songs*, 208, fairly closely.

45. Within the Bible, the closest analogy to this text is the story in Daniel about the creation of a huge idol with a head of gold, chest and arms of silver, iron legs, and feet made of clay and iron (Dan. 2:31–33).

46. This saying is attributed to Rabbi Akiba in the Mekhilta (on Exod. 15:2), but it is anonymous in *Sifre* (on Deut. 33:2), and its connection to Akiba in the *Mekhilta* may be an attempt to attribute a famous interpretation to a sage already linked to the Song in other writings. These texts in turn may be pointedly nonmystical replies to a yet earlier mystical commentary on the text, the Shiur Qomah. See Saul Liebermann, "Mishnat Shir ha-Shirim," appendix D in Gershom Scholem, *Jewish Gnosticism, Merkabah Mysticism and Talmudic Tradition* (New York: Jewish Theological Seminary of America, 1960), 118–26.

47. Susan Smith, "The Bride Stripped Bare: A Rare Type of the Disrobing of Christ," *Gesta* 34 (1995): 126–46.

48. At the end of this chapter, I will respond to those who see the Song as Biblical history encoded as a love story.

49. For example, in the dialogue of Nabu and Tashmetu, linked by Nissinen to the Song of Songs ("Love Lyrics of Nabû and Tašmetu: An Assyrian Song of Songs?" in Manfried Dietrich and Ingo Kottsieper, eds. *'Und Mose Schrieb dieses Lied auf'*: Studien *zum Alten Testament und zum Alten Orient* [Münster: Ugarit-Verlag, 1998], the gods are mentioned by name in lines 2–6, 11–12, 15, 17, and (recto) 9, 13, 15–16, 25.

50. See the next chapter for examples from the Hindu Gita Govinda.

51. Longmann, *Song of Songs*, 22–24, nicely contrasts the Song with texts that were written to be read as allegories.

52. Munro, *Spikenard and Saffron*, 35–39, points this out.

53. On the translation, see Fox, *Song of Songs*, 135–36; cf. Keel, *Song of Songs*, 162–63.

54. The meaning here and in 6:10 is fundamentally uncertain. Cf. Fox, *Song of Songs*, 152, and Bloch and Bloch, *Song of Songs*, 191–92.

55. On the trill, see Keel, *Song of Songs*, 219–20.

56. See Keel, *Song of Songs*, 220 for other occurrences of the Hebrew verb *shaqaph* (look down) with deities in Deut. 26:15; Pss. 14:2, 85:11 [Heb 85:12], 102:19 [Heb 102:20]; Lam. 3:50.

57. For links to sun imagery, see Murphy, *Song of Songs*, 176, who cites Isa. 24:23 and 30:26 on the poetic usage here.

58. This obscure verse has been variously interpreted and amended. I have just translated what is there.

59. This interpretation of historical intent contrasts with Fiona Black's suggestive, readerly reflections on resonances with the grotesque in the depiction of the woman's body in the Song of Songs and its readings. See Black, "Unlikely Bedfellows: Allegorical and Feminist Readings of Song of Songs 7.1–8," in *The Feminist Companion to the Song of Songs*, ed. Athalya Brenner and Carole R. Fontaine (Sheffield, England: Sheffield Academic Press, 2000), 115–29; and Black, "The Grotesque Body in the Song of Songs," Ph.D. diss., University of Sheffield, 1999.

60. See Fox, *Song of Songs*, 157–58, on the importance of the definite article in eliminating some options. The main remaining choices are to interpret this as a gentilic—Shulamite or Shunemite—possibly linking with Bathsheba, as a qal passive in the qutal pattern, or as an adjectival derivation from an unknown noun *shulam* (meaning: perfect one). Whatever the derivation, I think there is an implied wordplay on "peace" given the prominence of the root for peace (Hebrew *šlm*) in her name and the appearance of this name in such close connection with war imagery. This association with peace would also explain the question related to battle camps. Note Song 8:10, where the woman describes herself as appearing like one who brings out peace.

61. See Fox, *Song of Songs*, 160.

62. See Fox, *Song of Songs*, 163, and Murphy, *Song of Songs*, 187.

63. For more extensive comparison of the Song with Gen. 2–3, see in particular Landy, *Paradoxes of Paradise*, 183–265. He discusses this passage on 249–52.

64. The Hebrew word here, *ʿotyah*, means "wrapped." First-century textual traditions (Septuagint, Peshitta, Symmachus, Vulgate, and Targum) witness to a variant, easier reading of *ṭoʿayyah* or *ṭoʿyyah*, which would result in "lest I lose my way among the flocks of your companions" (Bloch and Bloch, *Song of Songs*, 49). This, however, appears to be a solution to a more difficult reading, and it does not explain the similitude in the Hebrew, *like* one who is wrapped/lost. See Pope, *Song of Songs*, 330–31, and Fox, *Song of Songs*, 103, for discussions of the associations of veiling with prostitution.

65. Fox, *Song of Songs*, 103.

66. We saw the same pattern of refrain and wilderness procession in chapter 3 (3:5, 3:6–11).

67. Murphy, *Song of Songs*, 191, points out that only the late vocalization of the Hebrew Bible indicates that the woman is speaking. Other elements, such as the reference to the one who bore the love (cf. 3:4; 8:2), indicate that the man might be speaking to the woman.

68. Fox, *Song of Songs*, 168, argues at length that this means "simply to wake one from sleep." Sex is only implied (according to Fox) by the waking up from a night's sleep together. There is probably, however, a double entendre at work here, especially given the emphasis that this awakening occurs at the same place that the man's mother conceived him.

69. See Fox, *Song of Songs*, 169–70, on the proper translation of *qinʾah* (jealousy).

70. See Fox, *Song of Songs*, 170, on the divergent Hebrew readings.

71. See also Prov. 6:21 and 7:3 for slightly different formulations.

72. The same sequence of love command and the command to bind words appears again in Deut. 11:13 and 18.

73. Also in Song 3:1, 2, 3, 4.

74. This formula occurs also in the Song at 6:3 and (in different form) at 7:11. Other similar Biblical texts include Jer. 7:23, 11:4 and Ezek. 34:30, among others. On interpretation of these formulas, cf. A. Feuillet, "La formule d'appartenance mutuelle (ii, 16) et les interpretations divergentes du Cantique des Cantiques," *Revue Biblique* 68 (1961): 5–38. This is one of the most probable examples of a place where other texts apply the language of human love to the divine-human relationship, while the Song of Songs (re)applies that language in the way it was generally used. The formula of belonging may have been the legally binding part of an ancient Israelite marriage.

75. Davis, *Proverbs, Ecclesiastes, and Song of Songs*, (Louisville, Ky.: Westminster John Knox, 2000), 298, argues that the following comment on jealousy echoes the praise of divine jealousy elsewhere in the Bible. This connection is more tenuous because it is not clear just how positive the description of jealousy in the Song of Songs is ("bitter [Hebrew *qasheh*] as Sheol is jealousy").

76. A. Robert, *Le Cantique des Cantiques: Traduction et commentaire* (Paris: Gabalda, 1963), 140–44; Ellen Davis, "Romance of the Land in the Song of Songs," *Anglican Theological Review* 80 (1998): 543–44; Davis, *Proverbs, Ecclesiastes, and Song of Songs*, 260–62.

77. Robert, *Cantique des Cantiques*, 155–58; Exod. 25–31, 35–40; 1 Kings 6–7.

78. Davis, *Proverbs, Ecclesiastes, and Song of Songs*, esp. 264, 269, 285–286.

79. Walsh, *Exquisite Desire*, 90–91.

80. Davis, *Proverbs, Ecclesiastes, and Song of Songs*, 255, who also notes resonances with Jer. 29:13 and Isa. 9:13, 31:1.

81. See, for example, Alicia Ostriker's proposal that the woman's refusal to let her man go (Song 3:4) resonates with the story of Jacob's refusal to let God go at the Jabbok, in "A Holy of Holies: The Song of Songs as Countertext," in *Brenner and Fontaine, Feminist Companion to the Bible*, 45–46.

82. On this, see the earlier discussion of the interpenetration of divine and human in the Song despite the focus on the human level.

83. See Keel, *Song of Songs*, 285, on the multivalence of this final call.

CHAPTER 10

1. J. Cheryl Exum, "Ten Things Every Feminist Should Know about the Song of Songs," in *The Feminist Companion to the Song of Songs (Second Series)*, ed. Athalya Brenner and Carole R. Fontaine (Sheffield, England: Sheffield Academic Press, 2000), 25.

2. Exum, "Ten Things Every Feminist Should Know," 25–27; and J. Cheryl Exum, "How Does the Song of Songs Mean? On Reading the Poetry of Desire," *Svensk Exegetisk Årsbok* 64 (1999): 48–51.

3. In most cases, the masculine or feminine gender of the speaker is only present in the vowels of the Hebrew text. These vowel marks were added several hundred years ago, long after the consonantal text had become fixed, though the marks do reflect a reading tradition that was often much older. One might argue that the distribution of vowels reflects a particular construction of gender and sexuality that is not shared by the older, consonantal text. Still, however the love poems are assigned, it is likely that they are meant to image love between a man and a woman.

4. For broader discussion of the limitations of the Song of Songs, see Ilona Pardes, *Countertraditions in the Bible: A Feminist Approach* (Cambridge, Mass.: Harvard University Press, 1992), 118–43; Daphne Merkin, "The Women in the Balcony: On Rereading the Song of Songs," in *Out of the Garden: Women Writers on the Bible*, ed. Christina Buchmann and Celina Spiegel (New York: Fawcett Columbine, 1994), 238–51; D. Clines, "Why Is There a Song of Songs and What Does It Do to You If You Read It?" in Clines, *Interested Parties: The Ideology of Writers and Readers of the Hebrew Bible* (Sheffield, England: Sheffield Academic Press, 1995), 94–121; Donald C. Polaski, " 'What Will Ye See in the Shulamite': Women, Power and Panopticism in the Song of Songs," *Biblical Interpretation* 5 (1997): 64–81; Exum, "Ten Things Every Feminist Should Know"; and Black, "The Grotesque Body in the Song of Songs" (Ph.D. diss., University of Sheffield, 1999).

5. See especially J. Cheryl Exum, "The Eye of the Beholder," in *The Labour of Reading: Desire, Alienation and Biblical Interpretation*, ed. Fiona Back et al. (Atlanta, Ga.: Society of Biblical Literature, 1999), 71–86.

6. For additional contrasts of the female in the Song of Songs with other Biblical texts, see Fokkelien van Dijk-Hemmes, "The Imagination of Power and the Power of Imagination," in *A Feminist Companion to the Song of Songs*, ed. A. Brenner (Sheffield, England: Sheffield Academic Press, 1993), 156–70; and Ilona Pardes, " 'I Am a Wall, and My Breasts Like Towers': The Song of Songs and the Question of Canonization," in Pardes, *Countertraditions in the Bible*, 118–43.

7. A. Brenner, *Intercourse of Knowledge: On Gendering Desire and 'Sexuality' in the Hebrew Bible* (Leiden: Brill, 1997), 69–89, esp. 87–89.

8. The latter is suggested by Clines, "Why Is There a Song of Songs?" 101. For discussion, see 100–106. See also Polaski, 'What Will Ye See?' 71–80, who argues that the powerful woman of the Song is only constructed as such by the assumed values of an all-powerful male gaze.

9. I will discuss a possible interpretation of the Song of Songs in the New Testament in the next chapter. Otherwise, we are limited to sources from the second century and later, along with some early rabbinic traditions that may obliquely testify to the ongoing secular use of the Song of Songs: a tradition attributed to Gamaliel about the use of Song 3:10–11 as a love song sung in the fall on Yom Kippur, The Day of Atonement (Mishnah Taanit 4:8), and a tradition attributed to Akiba that criticizes use of the Song of Songs in wine houses (Tosephta Sanhedrin 12:10). Note also the Testament of Solomon 26:1–5, which attributes Solomon's loss of his magic powers to his falling in love with the Shulamite (Song 7:1).

10. b. ᶜErub. 21b; b. B.Bat. 7b.

11. b. Sanh. 14b, 36b; b. Yebam. 101a: b. Qidd. 76b; cf. b. Yebam. 109b; b. Soṭa 45a.

12. Sifre ᵓllh hdbrym 10.

13. Tosephta Kippurim 2:5.

14. m. Taᶜan. 4:8; t. Soṭa 9:8; b. Šabb. 88; b. Yoma 75a; b. Sukk. 49b; b. ᶜErub. 21b; b. Taᶜan. 4a; Mek. bšlh šrh 3. See also the stimulating survey of the feminization of male rabbis by Eilberg-Schwartz, *God's Phallus and Other Problems for Men and Monotheism* (Boston: Beacon, 1994), 163–96, and Stephen D. Moore's analysis of a similar group of texts from the perspective of queer theory, *God's Beauty Parlor and Other Queer Spaces in and around the Bible* (Stamford, Calif.: Stamford University Press, 2001), 29–39.

15. For a more detailed argument and the linking of this to recent gender theory, see David Carr, "Gender and the Shaping of Desire in the Song of Songs and Its Interpretations," *Journal of Biblical Literature* 119 (2000): 235–40.

16. Origen was preceded slightly by the theologian Hippolytus, with whom he was in conversation. Hippolytus's work, however, does not appear to have been as influential as Origen's and was not as completely preserved.

17. For the variety of views on the direction of the influence, compare Y. Baer, "Israel, the Christian Church, and the Roman Empire, from the Time of Septimus Severus to the Edict of Toleration of A.D. 313," in *Studies in History*, ed. A. Fuks and I. Halpern (Jerusalem: Magnes/Hebrew University, 1961), 99–106; E. E. Urbach, "The Homiletical Interpretations of the Sages and the Expositions of Origen on Canticles, and the Jewish-Christian Disputation," in *Studies in Aggadah and Folk Literature*, ed. J. Heinemann and D. Noy (Jerusalem: Magnes, 1971), 247–75; and R. Kimelman, "Rabbi Yohanan and Origen on the Song of Songs: A Third-Century Jewish-Christian Disputation," *Harvard Theological Review* 73 (1980): 567–95. Kimmelman argues persuasively that at least some of Origen's polemics prompted the interpretations of his Jewish contemporaries, rather than the other way around.

18. Brown, *The Body and Society: Men, Women and Sexual Renunciation in Early Christianity* (New York: Columbia University Press, 1988), 162–76; B. McGinn, *The Foundations of Mysticism*, vol. 1 of *The Presence of God: A History of Western Christian Mysticism* (New York: Crossroad, 1990), 108–30, esp. 117–

24. Compare Moore, *God's Beauty Parlor*, particularly 27–28, who takes Origen's allegory to be a way for him to escape an encounter with the Song of Song's female protagonist. Later, on pp. 48–49, he reads Bernard of Clairvaux's interpretation as a reflection of his avoidance of "the sexual, the sensual, the fleshly, the female." Though such elements of avoidance are certainly present in Origen and those who followed him, I am suggesting that it is a mistake to read the popularity of theological-mystical interpretations of the Song of Songs primarily in relation to what they negate. Moreover, in contrast to Moore's presentation of Origen and others as involved in homoerotic relations with the divine (see especially p. 27 and note 9 on pp. 213–14), here I am arguing that Origen and others saw themselves as women relating to God, not men masquerading as women in an essentially homoerotic relationship.

19. Origen, *The Song of Songs: Commentary and Homilies*, trans. R. P. Lawson (Westminster, Md.: Newman, 1957), 198.

20. Liebermann, "Mishnat Shir ha-Shirim," Appendix D in Gershom Scholem, *Jewish Gnosticism, Merkabah Mysticism and Talmudic Tradition* (New York: Jewish Theological Seminary of America, 1960), 118–26. Arthur Green, "The Song of Songs in Early Jewish Mysticism," *Orim: A Jewish Journal at Yale* 2 (1987): 49–63; and Biale, *Eros and the Jews: From Biblical Israel to Contemporary America* (New York: Basic, 1992), 141–144 (on Hasidism).

21. U. Müller, "Mechthild von Magdeburg and Dantes Vita Nuova oder orotische Religiosität und religiöse Erotik," in *Liebe als Literatur: Aufsätze zur erotischen Dichtung in Deutschland*, ed. Rudiger Krohn (Munich: Beck, 1983), 163–76; H. Kunisch, "Die mittelalterliche Mystik und die deutsche Sprache," in Kunisch, *Kleine Schriften* (Berlin: Kuncker and Humbolt, 1968), 21–78; Tony Hunt, "The Song of Songs and Courtly Literature," in *Court and Poet: Selected Proceedings of the Third Congress of the International Courtly Literature Society*, ed. Glyn S. Burgess et al. (Liverpool, England: Cairns, 1981), 189–96; and E. Wainwright-deKadt, "Courtly Literature and Mysticism: Some Aspects of Their Interaction," *Acta Germanica* 12 (1980): 41–60.

22. *Book of Divine Works*, vol. 39, translation from B. Newman, *Sister of Wisdom: St. Hildegard's Theology of the Feminine* (Berkeley: University of California Press, 1987), 65.

23. Statistics are from Wilfred Cantwell Smith, *What Is Scripture?: A Comparative Approach* (Minneapolis, Minn.: Augsburg, 1993), 22–23, 248–49 n. 4.

24. Biale, *Eros and the Jews*, 161–62, notes one instance in which a Jewish enlightenment writer, Judah Leib Ben-Ze'ev (1764–1811) transformed the Song into a pornographic tract.

25. Karl Budde, "The Song of Solomon," *The New World* 3 (1894): 56.

26. Note, however, that Catholic scholars such as Roland Murphy have proven much more sympathetic toward the earlier theological approach than their Protestant counterparts. See, for example, Murphy, "History of Exegesis as a Hermeneutical Tool: The Song of Songs," *Biblical Theology Bulletin* 16 (1986): 87–91.

27. Marvin Pope, *The Song of Songs: A New Translation with Introduction and Commentary* (Garden City, N.Y.: Doubleday 1977), 90.

28. Some examples of work from the 1990s are Diane Bergant, *Song of Songs: The Love Poetry of Scripture* (New York: New City Press, 1998), 7–11; Ariel Bloch and Chana Bloch, *The Song of Songs: A New Translation with an Introduction*

and Commentary (Berkeley: University of California Press, 1988); Clines, "Why Is There a Song of Songs?" 100–121 (though Clines argues that modern readings also fail to be sufficiently critical); André LaCocque, *Romance She Wrote: A Hermeneutical Essay on Song of Songs* (Harrisburg, Pa.: Trinity, 1998), esp. 1–68; John Snaith, *Song of Songs* (Grand Rapids, Mich.: Eerdmans, 1993), 3–6; and Renita Weems, "The Song of Songs," in *The New Interpreter's Bible: A Commentary in Twelve Volumes*, vol. 5, *Introduction to Wisdom Literature, Proverbs, Ecclesiastes, Song of Songs, Wisdom, Sirach,* ed. Leander Keck et al. (Nashville, Tenn.: Abingdon, 1997), 370–71. See also Diane Burgant, *The Song of Songs* (Collegeville, Minn.: Liturgical Press, 2002).

29. I have received some anecdotal reports from Jewish colleagues that the situation is roughly similar in many Jewish contexts, but it depends substantially on the level to which such contexts are open to a historical-critical reading of the Bible.

30. Murphy, "History of Exegesis as a Hermeneutical Tool," 87–91; and Roland Murphy, *The Song of Songs* (Minneapolis, Minn.: Fortress, 1990), 91–105. Note similar comments along these lines in Helmut Gollwitzer, *Song of Love: A Biblical Understanding of Sex*, trans. Keith Crim (Philadelphia, Pa.: Fortress, 1979), esp. 23–24.

31. Jerry Moye, "Song of Songs—Back to Allegory? Some Hermeneutical Considerations," *Asia Journal of Theology* 4, no. 1 (1990): 120–24; Robin Payne, "The Song of Songs: Song of Woman, Song of Man, Song of God," *Expository Times* 107 (1996): 329–33; and John Richardson, "Preaching from the Song of Songs: Allegory Revisited," *Evangelical Review of Theology* 21 (1997): 250–257.

32. Adin Steinsaltz, *On Being Free* (Northvale, N.J.: Aronson, 1995), 133–144.

33. David Carr, "Rethinking Sex and Spirituality: The Song of Songs and Its Readings," *Soundings: An Interdisciplinary Journal* 81 (1999): 418–35; and Carr, "Gender and the Shaping of Desire in the Song of Songs and Its Interpretations," *Journal of Biblical Literature* 119 (2000): 233–48.

34. Larry Lyke, "The Song of Songs, Proverbs and the Theology of Love," in *Theological Exegesis: Essays in Honor of Brevard S. Childs,* ed. Christopher Seitz and Kathryn Greene-MacCreight (Grand Rapids, Mich.: Eerdmans, 1999), 208–23. Note also the critical retrieval of an allegorical approach to the Song by Ellen Davis, which likewise is done in the tradition of Childs's canonical approach. Davis, however, generally emphasizes an allegorical interpretation of the Song over a sexual one, especially in her "Romance of the Land in the Song of Songs," *Anglican Theological Review* 80 (1998), 533–46. She appears to advocate a more mixed position in *Proverbs, Ecclesiastes, and Song of Songs* (Louisville, Ky.: Westminster John Knox, 2000), esp. 233 and 269. Cf. Nicholas Ayo, *Sacred Marriage: The Wisdom of the Song of Songs* (New York: Continuum, 1997).

35. Ostriker, "A Holy of Holies: The Song of Songs as Countertext," in the *Feminist Companion to the Song of Songs,* 37–42.

36. Othmar Keel, "Erotisches im Ersten Testament," *Meditation* 26, no. 2 (2000): 7–9.

37. Carey Ellen Walsh, *Exquisite Desire: Religion, the Erotic and the Song of Songs* (Minneapolis, Minn.: Fortress, 2000).

38. George Keyt, *Srī Jayadeva's Gīta-Govinda: The Loves of Krṣṇa and Radha* (Bombay, India: Kutub-Popular, 1940), 47.

39. Keyt, *Gita-Govinda*, 80.

40. W. G. Archer, *Love Songs of Vidyāpati* (London: George Allen and Unwin, 1963), 23–36.

41. Lynda McClanahan, "Song of Songs 2:8–14," p. 14. Unpublished seminar paper quoted with permission.

42. Kathleen Richards, "Song of Songs 2:8–14," pp. 10–11. Unpublished seminar paper quoted with permission.

43. Susan Griffin, *Pornography and Silence: Culture's Revenge against Nature* (New York: Harper & Row, 1981), 262.

44. Rendering of Rumi by Coleman Barks with John Moyne, A. J. Arberry, and Reynold Nicholson, "A Community of the Spirit," in *The Essential Rumi* (San Francisco: HarperSanFrancisco, 1995), 2–3. Quoted with permission.

CHAPTER 11

1. For a judicious recent overview of the scholarly discussion, see Raymond Brown, *Introduction to the New Testament* (Garden City, N.Y.: Doubleday, 1997), 662–68.

2. J. Fitzmeyer argues that Luke likewise had this tradition, but omitted it because it resembled the Jesus saying against remarriage, which Luke had preserved from the sayings source Q (Luke 16:18; Matt. 5:31–32; Mark 10:10–12), *The Gospel according to Luke* (Garden City, N.Y.: Doubleday, 1981), 81–82, 1119–20.

3. These probably come from the sayings source Q. Notably, they are exclusively male-oriented, corresponding to the fact that men and not women had the legal right to divorce their spouses in Palestinian Judaism. In contrast, Paul adapts the tradition to his Hellenistic context when he forbids both men and women from divorce. There women could divorce their husbands as well.

4. Notably, the Gospel of Matthew adds the provision that divorce is allowable in cases of adultery (Matt. 5:32; 19:9). Nevertheless, the widespread presence of the same saying without this condition in other traditions (Mark 10:9; Luke 16:18; 1 Cor. 7:10–11) suggests that this is a specifically Matthean addition.

5. See, for example, Eduard Schweizer, *The Good News according to Mark*, trans. Donald H. Madvig (Atlanta, Ga.: John Knox, 1970), 202–3. He is one of many who point out that the question the Pharisees ask in this story is not one they actually would have asked. Such portrayals are part of a more general phenomenon in the New Testament in which early Christian writers make Jesus look good by making the Pharisees look bad.

6. That this saying would reflect such a belief in the end of the world does not entail that Jesus himself believed such an end of the world was coming soon. That would depend on whether or not this saying actually originated with Jesus. As for Jesus himself, Marcus Borg (among others) has argued at length that Jesus did not believe in an impending cosmic apocalypse. See Borg, *Jesus in Contemporary Scholarship* (Valley Forge, Pa.: Trinity, 1994), 47–96. Some others have not been persuaded. For one example, see Bart D. Ehrman, *Jesus: Apocalyptic Prophet of the New Millennium* (New York: Oxford University Press, 1999), esp. 125–39.

7. The author of Mark is probably responsible for the addition of imagery from Isa. 5:1–2. The version preserved in the Gospel of Thomas 65 lacks the

Isa. 5:1–2 material and shows that an earlier form of the parable probably focused exclusively on the horror of vineyard tenants killing the landlord's messengers and son. Only later did Mark, and those who used Mark (Matthew and Luke) add motifs from Isaiah's vineyard song.

8. The parallels are Matt. 21:33–41 and Luke 20:9–16.

9. Similar commands appear elsewhere in Johannine literature. See John 13: 34; 15:17; 1 John 2:7–11; 3:11–24; 4:7–21.

10. This and the following renderings follow Raymond Brown's translation, *The Gospel according to John* (Garden City, N.Y.: Doubleday, 1970), 659, 664, where Greek *philoi* is rendered as "beloved/those he loves" rather than the more innocuous "friends" of standard translations.

11. Brown, *Gospel according to John*, 667–68, observes a detailed chiastic structure that focuses on this verse.

12. Note as well that John is alone among the Gospels in locating Jesus' betrayal in a "garden" (John 18:1, 26). The only other mention of a garden in the New Testament is in Luke's version of the mustard seed parable (Luke 13: 19).

13. For a broader survey of potential allusions, see M. Cambre, "L'influence du Cantique des Cantiques sur le Nouveau Testament," *Revue Thomist* 62 (1962): 5–26. Other texts, however, do not have the same level of specific connections to Song of Songs texts.

14. Brown, *Gospel according to John*, 2: 940.

15. An early interpretation that observed these parallels is Cambre, "L'influence du Cantique des Cantiques," 17–19. The most thorough treatment is Ann Roberts Winsor, *A King Is Bound in the Tresses: Allusions to the Song of Songs in the Fourth Gospel* (New York: Lang, 1999), 35–48. She also mentions the prominence of words for "turning" in both the Song of Songs and John 20. See also Adele Reinhartz, "To Love the Lord: An Intertextual Reading of John 20," in *The Labour of Reading*, 62–67, who observes some possible connections between John 20 and the Eden garden as well (63), and the more homiletical observations in a similar direction by Jack R. Lundbom, "Song of Songs 3:1–4," *Interpretation* 49 (1995): 172–75.

16. In Matthew, the women do grasp Jesus (Matt. 28:9).

17. Mary Rose d'Angelo, "A Critical Note: John 20:17 and Apocalypse of Moses 21," *Journal of Theological Studies* 41 (1990): 529–36.

18. For a helpful discussion, see Colleen Conway, *Men and Women in the Fourth Gospel: Gender and Johannine Characterization* (Atlanta, Ga.: Scholars, 1999), 195–98. As she points out (196), far too much has been made of the idea that Jesus might be criticizing Mary for holding him. Moreover, there may be other antecedents to this phrase in addition to the Song of Songs (197). These allusive connections are not necessarily mutually exclusive. For a balanced perspective, see also Reinhartz, "To Love the Lord," 64–66.

19. I am indebted to Colleen Conway's analysis of Mary Magdalene at this point in particular.

20. Brown, *The Gospel according to John*, 1: 452.

21. Note also Rev. 19:7–8; 22:17.

22. Rita Nakashima Brock, *Journeys by Heart: A Christology of Erotic Power* (New York: Crossroad, 1988).

23. These possible connections to the Song of Songs were highlighted by Cambre, "L'influence du Cantique des Cantiques," 12–13, as part of a broader

discussion of other connections between the Song of Songs and Revelation (5–13).

24. For some stimulating reflections on sacramentality and sexuality, see Maaike de Haardt, "Bodiliness and Sacramentality," in *Embracing Sexuality: Authority and Experience in the Catholic Church*, ed. Joseph A. Selling (Aldershot, England: Ashgate, 2001), 42–55.

CHAPTER 12

1. For parallels, see David Carr, "Passion for God as a Center in Biblical Theology," *Horizons in Biblical Theology* 23 (2001): 5–12.

2. Carey Ellen Walsh, *Exquisite Desire: Religion, the Erotic and the Song of Songs* (Minneapolis, Minn.: Fortress, 2000), 93–94, notes homologies between the Song's discourse of desire and the Exodus narrative.

3. Quoted in Carter Heyward, *Touching Our Strength: The Erotic as Power and the Love of God* (San Francisco: Harper & Row, 1989), 120.

4. The final line follows the rendering of Robert Bly, *Selected Poems of Rainer Maria Rilke* (New York: HarperCollins, 1981), 37.

5. Poem by the author.

Index of Scriptural Citations

Index